RUNNING A BIOGAS PRO

RUNNING A BIOGAS PROGRAMME

A handbook

DAVID FULFORD

INTERMEDIATE TECHNOLOGY PUBLICATIONS 1988

Intermediate Technology Publications,
103–105 Southampton Row, London WC1B 4HH, UK.

ISBN 0 946688 49 4

Typeset by J&L Composition Ltd, Filey, North Yorkshire
Printed in Great Britain by A. Wheaton & Co Exeter.

Contents

viii

Acknowledgements

This book is dedicated to the memory of Sanfred Ruohoniemi, who was the first Executive Director of the Gobar Gas Company in Nepal and who died suddenly while in office.

Acknowledgements are made to the rest of the DCS Biogas Research Team: Andrew Bulmer, John Finlay and Mamie Wong, who put Biogas Research in Nepal on an effective scientific footing. Thanks are offered to the Mennonite Central Committee (MCC) who, with funds from the Canadian Internationa Development Administration (CIDA), financed the setting up of the DCS biogas programme, and to the United States Agency for International Development (USAID) who funded the continuation of this work.

Acknowledgements are also made to Dan Jantzen, who was Director of DCS when the biogas programme was first started, as well as S.K.P. Upadhaya, the General Manager of ADB/N and the Chairman of the Board of Directors of the Gobar Gas Company. Mention must also be made of the support of Odd Hoftun and Al Schlorholtz, who were successive Economic Development Secretaries of UMN during the project period.

The contribution of the staff of the Gobar Gas Company in Nepal must also be recognised, especially that of Govinda Devkota, the Company Research Scientist and West-Central Regional Manager, as well as Narayan B. Pradhan, who was West-Central Regional Manager before he left.

Key people who helped in the writing of this book were Rani Chowdhury, whose M.Phil. thesis provided a lot of the detailed material on laboratory research in biogas technology, and Joy Clancy, whose course notes on the mechanisms of biogas digestion provided a clear model for that chapter. Also my wife, Jane, helped in the checking of the manuscript.

Finally, the author and the publishers would like to thank Mr John McKechnie whose generosity made the publication of this book possible.

Notation used in Drawings

The notation used in the drawings and equations in the book follows international engineering practice as far as possible.

Almost all dimensions are in millimetres, so 1000 is 1 metre.

A few dimensions (such as GI pipe) are also shown in inches.

Tolerances are not usually shown on drawings. In general, masonry dimensions are rounded to the nearest 10 mm implying a tolerance of ± 10 mm. Machined parts (such as in gas stoves) are shown to the nearest 1 mm.

When a drawing is of the outside of an object, in elevation, only the outline is drawn. When an object is shown in section, cut across to show internal details, the sectioned parts are shaded or patterned to indicate the material from which they are made. A key to these patterns is given below.

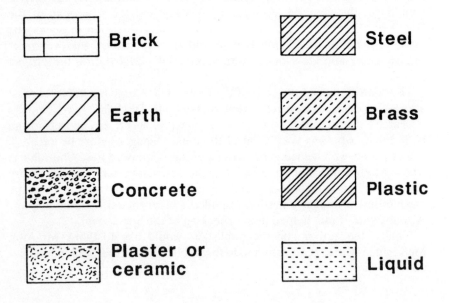

Brick	Steel
Earth	Brass
Concrete	Plastic
Plaster or ceramic	Liquid

The equations given in this book are designed to be used with a simple electronic calculator. A scientific calculator, with trigonometric functions, is most useful.

Logarithmic functions are used in some of the equations. Logarithms to base 10 are denoted by: 'log', while logarithms to base: e (2.71828) are denoted by: 'ln'. Most scientific calculators have both functions, but conversion from one to the other is given by: $\log(x) = \ln(x)/\ln(10)$.

CHAPTER 1
An Overview of Biogas

1.1 A world view of biogas

There are many advantages to biogas technology for people living in the rural areas of a developing country. A biogas plant can digest materials that are readily available on small farms, such as animal dung and crop wastes. Biogas digestion not only produces a clean, high-grade fuel gas, it also gives a residue that is a good fertilizer. The quality of this fertilizer is often higher than if the same materials were composted by more traditional methods.

Biogas is much more convenient to use than traditional fuels, such as firewood, dried dung and even kerosene. It gives a hot, clean flame that does not dirty pots or irritate the eyes, as does the smoke from other fuels. The compost from the plant does not smell or attract flies. Once it has been dried, it is easy to apply to the crops in the fields.

Biogas can be used in engines to drive machinery and water pumps. Groups of farmers can come together to buy and run a biogas plant with an engine and they will all benefit from the income earned from a cottage industry, such as a grain mill, or from the increased crop production resulting from pumped irrigation.

The concept of replacing wood fuel and petroleum oils by alternative fuels, such as biogas, has encouraged governments in various countries to set up biogas programmes. In India, for example, over 200,000 biogas plants were reported to have been completed by 1984, in a programme that started in the 1950s. In 1985 the government set a target for another 1,500,000 plants to be built in the five years to 1990. In China, the total claim for biogas plants built by 1985 was over 10,000,000 (including both Moulik's[1] and Cui's[2] totals for plants built before and after 1979).

Biogas programmes in other Asian countries have had erratic histories. Korea had 30,000 plants in 1979,[3] but problems with poor gas production in Korea's cold winters seem to have reduced the impetus.[4,5] Thailand has had a small biogas study programme for many years, but an adequate supply of other fuels has meant a slow growth in the extension to rural areas. The high cost of imported fuels and a high national debt have encouraged Brazil, along with other South American nations, to start biogas programmes. Between 1980 and 1985 Brazil built 7,530 plants.[6]

However, biogas technology does not always seem to have lived up to expectations. Despite government subsidies (25 per cent to 50 per cent for

1

family plants, 75 per cent to 100 per cent for community plants) and high-pressure salesmanship by extension agents the uptake of biogas technology in India is much slower than government targets (between 1975 and 1980, 5,000 to 6,000 plants were built per year, compared to the annual target of 20,000 plants.[7]) Biogas technology has only really reached one stratum in Indian society, the richer land-owners in the rural areas, because of the way the programme is approached. There are attempts to reach poorer people through the use of community biogas plants, but there are many problems.[8]

After the initial enthusiasm for biogas in China inspired by Chairman Mao, the image of biogas technology has weakened, partly due to reports of a 40 per cent to 50 per cent failure rate.[9] Many of the plants built in the 1970s had short lives (less than five years).[2] The actual failure rate can be assessed from the claim in 1979 that China had 7,000,000 biogas units.[1] The 3,300,000 units built since 1980 are of much improved quality.[2] However, the total number of working plants in China in 1985 was claimed to be 4,480,000,[2] suggesting that few plants built before 1980 have survived, despite a reported government-sponsored repair programme.[1]

Western nations and development agencies have been much less enthusiastic about biogas technology. Being labour intensive, it does not fit well into mechanised Western farming techniques and automating a biogas plant appears expensive. Plants in Europe and in the more northerly states of America suffer from low winter temperatures, so must be well insulated and heated if they are to produce year-round gas.

In Britain and the USA especially, biogas also has an unfortunate political flavour. The early advocates of alternative energies included people from counter-cultures that rejected philosophies of fast growth and energy from nuclear fuel. The enthusiasm of these radicals for biogas technology was based on the work of a very few pioneers, such as L.J. Fry (South Africa and USA)[10] and Harold Bates (UK).[11] When the oil price rises of the 1970s made people take alternative fuels more seriously, the lack of adequate experience with biogas technology became apparent. Several attempts to commercialise biogas failed because of poor design work and weak economic analysis.[12]

During the 1980s biogas has developed a more acceptable, if more mundane, image. Much research has been done, in both Europe and USA, and many different designs and types of plant are now available.[13] The commercial application of biogas in the West is still very limited;[14] less than 100 farm-scale plants are reported in USA, although some of these are of a very large scale (up to 10,000 cu.m working volume).[15]

The atmosphere in Europe is also slowly changing. Agencies in places such as Sweden and Germany (such as the Beier Institute and BORDA) are keen to advocate biogas, especially in their programmes of aid to the Third World. In other countries, such as Belgium and France, concern

2

over pollution from farms has led to an improved economic climate for building biogas plants as a means of reducing the oxygen demand of animal wastes.[16]

In general, biogas technology faces the future from a weak base, but with increasing opportunities for its use. If planners are not to repeat the mistakes of the past as they attempt to fit biogas into development and aid programmes, they need to understand the limitations of biogas technology as well as its benefits. The economic, technical and organisational difficulties of setting up a biogas programme need to be faced and plans made to overcome them.

1.2   Biogas in Nepal

The biogas programme in Nepal is small, as befits a small developing country. Between 1974 and 1984, 1,400 plants were built and the extension programme moved from being a local test programme into one that sold plants over the whole country. The programme was launched by the Agricultural Department of His Majesty's Government of Nepal (HMG/N), but the responsibility of continuing it lies with Gobar Gas tatha Krishi Yantra Bikash (Pvt) Ltd. This private company was set up as a joint venture by the United Mission to Nepal (UMN) and the Agricultural Development Bank of Nepal (ADB/N), with the help of the Fuel Corporation of Nepal.[17]

The particular position of the Nepal programme, small enough to analyse easily, but national in scope, makes it a valuable base from which to consider biogas programmes in general. Our experience in this programme, with our understanding of some of the reasons behind both its successes and its failures, allows us to suggest guidelines that would help biogas programmes in other places.

1.3   Challenges of biogas

The challenges that face attempts to popularise biogas are not so much difficult as unexpected and complex. Biogas is very difficult to define as an academic subject, as it includes many different disciplines.

The process by which biogas is made is microbiological. The biochemistry of anaerobic fermentation is very complex. While the details are becoming clearer as a result of an effective research effort in many countries, such as USA and China,[18,19,20,21] the next step, to design microbiological systems that are more effective and efficient at biogas digestion, appears to be still in the future.[22,23]

The practical problem of making cheap but effective biogas plants is one of civil and mechanical engineering. Again, research effort has produced many different designs of plant.[15] The selection of the right plant for

3

the job requires well-informed and accurate technical judgement. Once biogas is produced, suitable, cheap biogas appliances must be designed and manufactured.

The economics of biogas are important; people will not use a new technology, however good, if it costs more than the alternatives. There are also sociological implications: biogas is called 'gobar gas' in Nepal and India, as 'gobar' is the word for cow dung. The cow is a holy animal to a Hindu, so gobar is an acceptable source of cooking fuel. Pig dung and human faeces are not acceptable feedstocks for a biogas plant for many Hindus, even though the gases produced from them are almost the same.

Since biogas technology uses animal dung and agricultural residues as feedstocks and produces a fertilizer as well as a fuel gas, it should belong to the subject of agriculture. The main users of the technology are farmers. The use of the effluent from a biogas plant brings in the subjects of soil science and horticulture. In China, where composting of all agricultural residues, including human faeces (night soil) is held in high esteem,[24,25] the use of biogas plants for producing good compost is often more important than the fuel gas.

The organisation of biogas programmes has proved difficult, particularly as there may be political dimensions. In India, the government gives large subsidies for the construction of biogas plants and annual construction targets are defined. In China, while biogas technology was given an initial impetus by Chairman Mao's Great Leap Forward, the ongoing incentive lay in biogas plants and pigs being owned privately, in the midst of a state-run economy.[9] In Nepal, the organisation was further complicated by making the extension work the responsibility of a commercial concern. This company was supposed to make a profit on the sale and construction of biogas plants. The Agricultural Development Bank was also involved in giving loans so that farmers could pay for their plants.

When a government department or an aid agency plan to start a biogas programme, they are faced with this set of closely related challenges that demand a very wide range of skills and experience. A biogas team cannot usually employ experts in every field, so people involved in biogas technology must be 'generalists' with skills in different fields.

1.4 Economic challenges

While the economics of biogas have received much attention,[26,27,28,29] the conclusions are not hopeful. The running costs of a biogas plant are low, but the capital costs per unit of energy produced are fairly high. This is a factor common to most alternative energy technologies, because the energy density in biomass, or wind or sunlight, is much lower than in coal, oil, nuclear energy or even hydro-power. The physical dimensions of a

4

plant to extract that energy must be larger per unit of energy produced than for conventional plants.

Conventional energy plants also rely on economies of scale to extract large amounts of energy in centralised units. Alternative energy technologies tend to be diffuse; plants are small and scattered, and this also increases the capital cost per unit of power produced.

Many analyses of the economics of biogas consider only its use as a domestic fuel, such as for cooking and lighting. The benefit: cost ratio is then very sensitive to the cost of alternative cooking fuels, usually firewood (see Chapter 9). If the cash cost of wood fuel is low, the savings made by replacing it with biogas appear to be financially unattractive. The original investment made on the purchase of a biogas plant may not be recovered from these savings for seven to ten years (based on figures from Nepal). The actual cash cost to many farmers of wood fuel is often zero, as they go to collect their own supplies from the forest, although this is illegal in many countries.

The environmental cost of wood fuel is often very high, as deforestation can result in land erosion, landslides and floods. Some governments try to prevent this by giving subsidies to people building biogas plants. Even with the 25 per cent to 50 per cent subsidies given by the government of India, it has been estimated that only 10 per cent of the population can afford domestic biogas units.[9]

Approximately 0.33 litres of oil are used to produce 1 kW.hr of electricity, either in a diesel generator or in an oil fired power station. The same energy requires 667 litres of biogas, produced from 60 kg of cattle dung (i.e. 120 litres of slurry when mixed with water). The biomass occupies 360 times the volume of oil for the same energy.

The cost of an oil-fired power station in 1982 was about £1,450 per kW for medium-scale units (around 5MW). A biogas unit, producing 2 m^3 of gas a day, cost around £530. If this amount of biogas were to be used to drive a generator set, it would produce about 3kW.hr per day. This gives a capital cost of £4,270 per kW, about three times higher. However, the cost of feedstock for a biogas plant is negligible, while the cost of oil (even at $18 per barrel in 1988), is of major concern for many governments.

Also, this example does not include the cost of distribution of power. Biogas plants can be built in villages, from which the supply of feedstock comes. The cost of power transmission to remote villages becomes very expensive, making the economics of biogas more attractive.[28,29]

Example 1.1 Economic considerations

Biogas can also be used to fuel engines, which can then earn an income for the owner. However this requires a larger plant, which uses feed from more than 20 cattle (if cattle dung is the main feed). Either dung must be bought in from outside suppliers or several farmers must co-operate to run such a plant. The economics of a group-owned plant running a grain mill look reasonable in Nepal (see Chapter 9). The group of farmers could recover the original investment within the period of the loan (seven years). Government subsidies help to increase the economic attractiveness of this approach.

In general, biogas technology is expensive. Further technical development work may reduce the capital cost, but the present economic viability of biogas programmes seems to depend mainly on the political commitment of national governments.

1.5 Technical challenges

Economics put a severe constraint on the technologies. It is relatively easy to make a biogas plant that will produce gas and fertilizer; there are many designs available.[30,31] The more difficult task is to design a biogas plant that is both effective and cheap enough for people to afford. It may be possible to make a few low-cost plants by using scrap materials, but the technology used in a national biogas programme must be reproduced for thousands of plants by workmen with suitable training.

Biogas plants designed in the developed world, especially in USA, Japan and Europe, tend to be fairly complex, with slurry pumps and temperature control systems and they use specialist materials, especially plastics. While some of these designs are specifically for research plants, in which different parameters need to be monitored, this whole design philosophy is clearly inappropriate to rural areas in developing countries.

Low cost, simplicity and the use of local materials are the priorities when designing biogas plants for rural farmers. These requirements pose special problems. In Nepal the materials available, such as cement and steel, are of undefined and variable quality, so can not be used in designs that demand accurate specifications. An over-emphasis on low cost, as in the late 1970s in China, can also cause problems. The plants did use local materials: lime and locally made cement, but they had short life-times and quickly failed.

Design data and principles learned in a developed country are often misleading. Techniques and design approaches need to be adapted to the local situation. Simple, appropriate technology often demands scientists and engineers with more skills and wider know ledge than does the sophisticated, but routine, technology of the developed world.

1.6 Organisational challenges

The advocates of appropriate technology tend to be engineers, so the technical side of a programme is often emphasised to the neglect of other areas, especially those of organisation and management. In the enthusiasm to develop a technology, management can be left to chance.

The result is 'crisis management', a series of decisions made to meet problems only as they arise. Since these problem-solving decisions are seldom well-planned, they give rise to further problems that need solutions. These crises become more difficult and frequent as the programme gets bigger and more complex. The neglect of well-planned decision-making in the early stages of a biogas programme can give rise to administrative problems that can slow, or even destroy, its progress.

A biogas programme must be well-planned from the beginning. The managers and senior technicians who are to be involved in the running of the programme should be appointed and trained early enough for them to be involved in the planning process. Technical and extension staff should be trained in administration, book-keeping and personnel management, so they can run their sections of the programme effectively.

CHAPTER 2
National Biogas Programmes

Biogas programmes in many countries have followed a similar pattern. Interest in biogas technology is first encouraged by a few entrepreneurs and enthusiasts. After some time (a decade or longer), the government, or a key figure in the country, takes up the idea and launches a biogas programme. A feature common to most government programmes in any country seems to be poor organisation, as government planners set high achievement targets without the skills, experience or resources to back them up. In time, the programme finds its own level, its progress relating more to political and socio-economic factors than planners' aims.

2.1 Biogas in China

Biogas technology was introduced into China by an entrepreneur, Lo Guorui, who set up a private company for the building of biogas plants in the 1930s. He developed the Chinese displacement digester principle, in which slurry is displaced from the digester pit into a reservoir as gas collects under the roof of the pit (see Chapter 5). Several hundred units were built, mainly for rich land-owners, of which about fifty survive and still work well.[1] Most of these plants had rectangular digester pits, although a few cylindrical designs were also made. Their sizes ranged from 6 to 108m^3 internal volume and they were made of brick or stone, with concrete roofs. While the quality of construction was very good, the cost of the plants was very high.

After the communist take-over, Chairman Mao introduced biogas as part of the Great Leap Forward in the 1950s.[2] Government cadres in the Communes mobilised local people to build their own biogas units. The Communes were set up as the basic administrative structure in rural China and would contain 4,400 to 5,800 households. Supplies of cement, bricks and reinforcement steel were obtained from new local factories set up under the same programme. People from a Production Team (30 to 80 households in size) would exchange 'work points' as a means of paying for each others' labour in building biogas plants, animal sheds and other projects.

A large number of plants were built, but their reliability was not good and many did not function for long. The basic design was poor, as it used a flat-roofed digester pit,[3] which was difficult to make gas-tight. The local supplies of cement, brick and steel were of variable quality and there was a lack of trained masons who could guide the local people in their construction work.

The biogas programme was revived in the 1970s, apparently spontaneously, by local people's groups in Sichuan Province.[1] New designs appeared, such as plants with domed roofs, apparently as a result of peasant farmers' attempts to improve the technology. Its initial success attracted government attention, and the widespread use of biogas plants was again encouraged. As in the 1950s, the mistake was made of trying to expand the programme too fast, with inadequate resources and skills. Records suggest that about 1,600,000 plants were built each year at a very low cost (40 yuan, about £13, each), but after only a year or two problems began to appear.[4]

The Cultural Revolution created a further problem as it caused many people with technical expertise to be removed from universities and research institutions. Is is possible, of course, that technically trained academics, who were forced to work in the communes alongside peasant farmers, were able to suggest design improvements to biogas plants being built in their villages.

As the programme developed in the 1970s, support was required from higher political levels, such as provincial and national governments. Supplies of cement, bricks and lime (or coal with which to make them) had to be traded between communes. Many leading figures in China, including Chairman Mao, were keen supporters of the programme, so political pressure encouraged its continuation.

A national biogas organisation eventually grew out of the needs of the popular programme. As the demand for information and training increased, provincial governments had to set up their own biogas bureaux. As academic institutions were re-established after the effects of the Cultural Revolution had faded, they became interested in doing research on biogas, so became involved in the dissemination of information. By 1978 the Chinese national Ministry of Agriculture had set up a biogas office at Beijing in Sichuan. After several national biogas conferences to discuss the problems of the programme, especially the short life-times of the 'popular' design (less than five years,[4]) the Chinese government recognised that a nationally coordinated approach was required.

A 'Leading Group' was established to coordinate the biogas programme on a national level, with members from the Planning, Economic and Scientific Commissions.[5] At the time of writing their decisions are implemented by the National Biogas Extension Office (NBEO), coordinating the activities of 25 provincial extension centres. The Chinese Academy of Sciences was encouraged to become involved in research and development (R & D) work in fields related to biogas technology at some of its research institutes, such as the Chengdu Institute of Biology, the

Guangzhou Institute of Energy Conservation and the Beijing Energy Research Institute. Staff from these places work with the NBEO, helping solve some of the more difficult problems that arise from the extension work. Some provincial extension offices have also set up their own experimental stations.

Since 1979 standards have been issued for the construction of better quality biogas designs.[6] Only trained, certificated technicians are allowed to build plants and they are encouraged to join digester building teams (of which there were 7,000 in 1985). The teams are themselves being formed into biogas service companies (716 in 1985). These companies undertake contracts for digester building and management, are self-managed and funded and are as close to being private limited companies as present attitudes in China allow.[1]

The plants built by these teams cost much more than those that people built themselves (200 yuan, about £63, for a family unit), but they are expected to have much longer lifetimes.[4] The rate of construction has decreased, being around 20,000 per year during 1982/83, for the whole country.[5] An emphasis on the use of good designs, the employment of skilled workmen and effective quality control have ensured that the plants that people use are much more reliable than previously.

There is a growing interest in extending the scope of biogas technology; for example using the gas from sewage digesters and from plants using food processing waste to fuel power stations. In some places, central biogas plants supply gas to homes in the surrounding area, using wastes such as distillery dregs as the main feedstock. This is related to a growing concern to restrict pollution from the new industries that are being established in many parts of China.

2.2 Biogas in India

The Indian biogas programme was inspired by research carried out by the Indian Agricultural Research Institute at Delhi,[7] in connection with a sewage plant in Bombay. The idea was taken up by J.J. Patel of the Khadi and Village Industries Commission (KVIC) in 1951 and the commission set up its own national biogas programme. The KVIC was originally set up to encourage village industries, especially 'khadi'—hand-spun and woven cotton goods—along the lines inspired by Mahatma Gandhi. It has an effective team of extension agents, with good technical training, although there are not enough of these people to fulfil all the demands made upon them. KVIC is also involved in the extension of other technologies, such as soap-making and carpentry (up to 20 different rural industries).[8]

Various biogas plant designs were tested at the KVIC Biogas Centre near Bombay, but the choice of design for the extension work was unfortunate. Due to a misunderstanding of the results of the initial research work done in Delhi (see Chapter 11), a design using a counter-balanced floating steel gas drum was used. This caused many problems for customers.[9] KVIC continued the research and development work, coming up with a better design which was called the 'Gramalaxmi III'. This still used a steel gas drum, but it was allowed to float on the surface of the slurry and was held upright by a central guide pipe (see Chapter 5).

Other groups became interested, such as the one led by Ram Bux Singh of the Planning, Research and Action Division of the State Planning Institute of Uttah Pradesh in Lucknow.[10] He set up a biogas research centre in the village of Ajitmal near Etawah. Some of his early plants were more successful and are still working, including some larger-scale ones (up to 100m³ working volume). By 1974 over 6,000 plants had been built in India, mainly in the Western states of Gujarat and Punjab and in Uttah Pradesh. Mr Patel started a private company himself, Patel Gas Crafters, to make biogas stoves and lights for the programme.

In 1975 the Department of Science and Technology of the Indian government decided that the biogas programme needed a broader scientific and organisational base.[11] Many more agencies became involved, including those in the local voluntary sector as well as academic institutions.[12] The All India Committee on Biogas (AICB) was set up in Delhi, with the aim of coordinating all the agencies involved in the programme and, especially, to encourage research institutions to consider problems relating to biogas technology. In all, 192 different organisations became involved, including government institutions such as the National Energy Board, the Indian Institute of Technology and the State Bank of India. As well as semi-government corporations, such as the Agro-industries Corporation, many state run groups are also involved, as are 30 private enterprises, including that Tata Energy Research Institute. The most effective sector for biogas extension seems to be the non-governmental organisations (NGOs), although they often lack technical skills and knowledge.

The committee put emphasis on the extension of the 'Janata' (people's) plant—a version of the Chinese fixed-dome design developed at PRAD. This design was supposed to be much cheaper than the floating drum design, as it did not require a steel gas holder. One voluntary organisation in particular, Action for Food Production (AFPRO), based in Delhi, has built over 1,000 plants to this design,[13] and has also trained many masons to be proficient in its construction.

The Structural Engineering Research Institute (SERI) at Roorkee developed a design of floating gas holder made of ferro-cement, where a thin layer of cement mortar is reinforced by wire mesh.[14] KVIC have been using this design in their extension work in some areas, such as Andra Pradesh and Madhya Pradesh in the south-eastern part of India.[15] By 1980, 80,000 plants had been built in India, although the reported failure rate was about 30 per cent.[16] Between 1980 and 1985 the Indian government

11

established a National Project on Biogas Development to build 400,000 family-sized biogas units at a cost of Rs.50 crores (about £33 million).[12] For the Seventh Development Plan (1985 to 1990), government planners have defined that another 1,500,000 plants should be built.[11]

The high cost of the National Project on Biogas is a result of the Indian government's policy of giving subsidies for biogas plants in many areas of the country. These range from about 30 per cent of the construction costs for most applicants to up to 55 per cent for scheduled tribes and for people in hilly areas where deforestation is becoming a problem.[12] Incentives are also paid to the agencies involved in constructing biogas plants as well as to extension agents whose job it is to persuade farmers to buy plants. The rest of the cost of a biogas plant can be borrowed from commercial banks.

Emphasis in both the Sixth and Seventh Development Plans has been laid on building biogas digesters for communities of farmers and for institutions, such as dairy schemes and agricultural colleges. Subsidies of up to 100 per cent are being made available for these projects. Ten such plants were to be built between 1980 and 1985, but this part of the programme has not been very successful. In 1986 about 25 community/institutional plants were being used in the whole of India, but many only survive through subsidies from groups such as KVIC and PRAD (see also Chapter 12).[11]

The Indian biogas programme is a massive one, involving many different organisations, including national and local government ministries and corporations as well as national and state banks and research institutions. It appears very successful on the surface, achieving its targets for the number of biogas plants sold and built. However the programme does have its weaknesses, especially at the local level, where lack of cooperation between the different agencies appears to be a major problem.[8]

Competition between different workshops to build biogas drums has led to state-run enterprises trying to put smaller private concerns out of business. Poor management and an over-emphasis on red tape has often led to long delays in obtaining finance and materials to allow plants to be built. A customer may have agreed to take a loan to buy a plant and his name entered into the statistics a year or more before his plant is actually built. In many cases these 'pending' plants may appear as 'plants sold' in more than one year's figures.[8]

Despite a high emphasis on research and development, the results of this work seem to take a long time to reach the extension workers. There is a lack of communication between research centres and the field that prevents an effective flow of experience and ideas between the two. Ideas that prove successful in one area of India are seldom used in another.

2.3 The biogas programme in Nepal

The pioneer of biogas in Nepal was B.R. Saubolle S.J., a Belgian teacher at St Xaviers school. He built a demonstration plant in 1955.[17] Two other plants built in Kathmandu are still running. In 1968 KVIC built a plant for an exhibition in Kathmandu. In 1974, the Energy Research and Development Forum at Tribhuvan University recommended that biogas be considered as an alternative energy resource for Nepal.[18]

The Department of Agriculture planned a programme of biogas extension. The aim was to build 250 biogas plants during the 'Agricultural Year' of 1975/76. Several contractors were asked to make steel gas drums to the KVIC design, while the Department's local extension agents (Junior Technical Assistants, (JTAs)) were to sell plants and find local builders to make the brick-lined pits. The Agricultural Development Bank of Nepal (ABD/N) were to offer zero-interest loans for biogas plants during this first year.

In 1974, the Development and Consulting Services (DCS) (part of UMN) built four biogas plants to the KVIC design. The Butwal Engineering Works (BEW), then part of Butwal Technical Institute (BTI), made the welded steel drums. A small demonstration plant, built by BTI, was shown at an exhibition held at the coronation of King Birendra in 1974. BTI was asked to make steel gas drums for the agricultural-year programme, while DCS set up a programme to install the biogas plants.[19]

According to the records, 196 plants were built during this year. DCS built 95 of these and helped with the installation of 14 more. Four US Peace Corps volunteers also helped with the building of plants under a two year programme. However, the Agricultural Year was not as successful as the records imply. The JTAs had received little training on biogas and many plants had technical problems.[20] In some cases, loans were used for purposes other than building biogas plants.

The next year proved disappointing. DCS managed to build only half as many plants, while the rest of the national programme seemed to evaporate. The JTAs were required to put emphasis on other agricultural extension projects and the Peace Corps volunteers finished their contracts and went home.

The two groups still involved in biogas extension—DCS and ADB/N— decided to pool resources by setting up a commercial concern to sell biogas plants. The Gobar Gas Company was formed in 1978, with capital finance from UMN, ADB/N and the Fuel Corporation of Nepal, based on the DCS biogas extension organisation. UMN has a policy of setting up its development programmes as private limited companies; a model that allows more control to pass to local managers as they gain experience. Most of the staff of the new company were Nepali citizens, apart from an expatriate Executive Director. DCS retained the research and development side of the programme, offering technical back-up to the staff of the company. Responsibility for research and development passed to the Company in 1984.

The company set up branch offices in about nine strategic places in

13

Nepal, mainly on the Terai (the plains area). Transport was far more difficult in the hills and the higher ambient temperatures below 300 metres altitude allowed better year-round gas production. By the middle of 1987 the Company had built over 2,300 biogas plants in Nepal, including those built under DCS. The work of follow-up, started by DCS, has continued, ensuring that at least 95 per cent of these plants continue to work. For each plant built a seven-year guarantee is offered against design or construction faults; yearly visits are made by company staff to the owners for the period of the guarantee.[21] This approach was encouraged by ADB/N, mainly to safe-guard the repayment of loans.

Even after eight years of trading, however, the Gobar Gas Company had not made a profit. It was under-financed for the sudden expansion from a local extension programme to a national organisation, and this also put severe strains on staff and resources.[22] The follow-up programme means very high overheads, which cannot be fully financed from plant sales.

Sudden expansion resulted in technicians, who had only been trained to supervise the building of biogas plants, being promoted to area managers, with little management training. They were expected to look after their office accounts and stores inventories, act as salesmen to farmers, liaise between farmers and bank officials for loans, supervise the construction of plants and follow-up all their customers, all with no transport in a country that has few roads. Most were given motorbikes in 1983. These men have gained experience over time and received on-the-job training, so their weaknesses are being overcome.

Nepal is a difficult country in which to do business. It is landlocked and dependent on India for supplies of most materials. Shortages of basic commodities such as steel and cement in India mean that a quota and licence system operates. Very careful planning and management is required to ensure the correct quantities of materials are available at the right time, together with enough money to pay for them. Political disturbances, especially during the first five years of the Gobar Gas Company's trading, have caused problems for all commercial concerns in the country.

While there are biogas programmes in other countries,[23] they are less well documented than those in India, China and Nepal. Thailand had about 3,000 family-sized digesters in 1984[12] and a government programme for 25,000 more to be built by 1990. They had problems with the floating drum design and changed to the fixed dome design. The government of Taiwan is promoting the use of bag digesters using red mud plastic. In 1982, 1,200 of these plants had been built, but there is a lack of information on how successful they have been or how the programme is progressing.[12]

2.4 Lessons to be learned

While the Chinese and Indian programmes started very differently, the practicalities of building biogas plants for large numbers of customers has

14

meant that the organisational structures are becoming similar. The Chinese programme started as a 'people's movement'. In some ways the programme followed the 'ideal' model for the extension of an appropriate technology, with people discovering the benefits for themselves and making their own decisions. The economics of these plants looked very good, as people had to pay the production team for fuel, either firewood or crop stalks, but were paid for the composted fertilizer from the plant. Despite all these advantages, the Chinese programme up to 1979 was considered officially as a failure, mainly because of the short lifetime of the plants.[1] The Chinese government recognised the need for central coordination and planning, especially in the development of effective technologies and in providing standards for quality control.

The Indian programme started as a centrally planned operation, first by KVIC as a national organisation, then by the AICB. The main weakness of the programme appears to be at the local level, where the cooperation encouraged at national level does not seem to have penetrated.[8] The difficulties faced by a farmer attempting to set up a biogas plant include the paperwork required to obtain a loan and the subsidy, and the need to arrange for supplies of materials to be available at the correct time. Extension agencies, such as KVIC, are now employing 'supervisors' or 'motivators' to contact farmers and oversee all aspects of the project, assisting them through the bureaucracy involved.[13] The time required to get a plant built can be reduced from a couple of years to a few months.

So, while the emphasis in the Chinese programme has shifted away from a decentralised approach to one which has greater central control, the Indian programme has had to become less centralised.[2] The Nepal programme is directed fairly firmly from a single head office, although the control passed from a government agency to the Gobar Gas Company early in its history. The programme would probably be more effective if the managers of the local company offices had more autonomy in planning and decision-making.

2.5 Aspects of a biogas programme

A biogas programme is a complex operation, involving many components, such as extension, construction, publicity, finance and research and development. All these must work effectively, both individually and with each other, if the programme, as a whole, is to be successful. Each aspect of the programme usually involves a different organisation, each with its differing attitudes and approach, so careful coordination is required to ensure good cooperation.

The core of the biogas programme is the extension work. Salesmen must go to potential customers to persuade them to buy biogas plants. Once a customer has agreed to purchase a plant and loan finance (if necessary) has

15

been arranged through a bank, building materials must be supplied and masons and other technicians called in to build the plant. The building work must be supervised and the quality of work inspected. The farmer must be taught how to run his new technology. He should know to whom to go if something goes wrong. Technicians also need to be available to help the customer in follow-up and routine maintenance.

In India and Nepal it is the job of supervisors to do most of these tasks, from selling the plant through supervising the construction to follow-up. In India, the supervisors are paid by KVIC and other implementing agencies, funded by national or state governments. Only the wages of the construction workers form part of the cost of the plant paid by the customer. In Nepal the salaries of the supervisors are part of the overheads of the Gobar Gas Company, which is supposed to be self-supporting from its sales. In China in the 1970s 'selling' was done by Communist Party cadres, working in the communes, while customers were responsible for obtaining materials and doing most of the construction work themselves. Both selling and construction work are being taken over by the biogas construction teams, which are self-supporting at the local level. The provincial biogas offices are funded by central or provincial governments.

A key factor in reducing the rate of plant failure is that of follow-up. The Gobar Gas Company took over the guarantee and follow-up programme started by DCS and records indicate that 95 per cent of all plants built by the Company continue to work.[21] If plants fail because of poor workmanship, they are repaired by the Company free of cost. The biogas extension programme started in Brazil in 1980 uses a similar approach and can claim similar success rates (a failure rate of 7.5 per cent in the 7,530 units built between 1980 and 1985).[24] Follow-up is best carried out by construction staff and field staff from a national or regional office. Since the companies will be local, they will have close contact with their customers, who can come to a local office if they have problems. Follow-up by agents from a central biogas office provides quality control and the compilation of national (regional) statistics for on-going evaluation of the programme.

An effective extension programme is dependent on well tested and proven technology. The early biogas programmes in both India and China lost impetus when the technology they were using proved unreliable. On-going research and development is an essential part of such a programme from the early stages. The value of this research and development is only demonstrated when it is used by customers in the field. Close links between the research and extension staff are essential in a biogas programme. The research staff must have personal experience of work in the field, so they can relate their research to the problems there. They can assist in follow-up surveys, looking at wider questions than those usually considered by the extension staff, such as the socio-economic environment of the programme in different areas of a country. It is helpful for extension staff to make

16

regular visits to research centres to see new ideas and to receive training in new techniques, so that the results of research and development may be quickly applied in practice. Research and development originally inspired the Indian biogas programme and KVIC has continued the tradition with a research department attached to its Bombay office. However, the research work done at the centre does not seem to be very closely related to the needs of Indian villagers. The emphasis appears to be more on technical problems.[13]

The opposite extreme obtained in China, where the farmers themselves experimented with new ideas and designs. Many of these designs were imaginative and did work, the best ideas being shared with others through the Chinese propaganda machine. As academic research became acceptable again after the disruptions of the Cultural Revolution in the early 1970s, the Chinese government recognised the lack of scientific method in the peasants' work and set up biogas research centres. There were over 50 biogas research projects in different institutions in 1985.[1]

DCS in Nepal attempted to link the extension and research and development sides of their project from the start. The follow-up programme started as part of the research programme, as a series of surveys of how well the first 95 steel-drum biogas plants built by DCS were working. Several problems were identified during this survey, allowing the original KVIC design to be adapted to meet the needs of the people who were using the plants in the field. The research and development work continues in the Gobar Gas Company, the staff acting as trouble-shooters if extension staff discover problems with the plants they are building. They are also continuing more basic research projects, such as the use of alternative feed stocks in biogas plants.[21]

Another aspect needing early organisation is that of finance. Capital is required to set up the programme infrastructure, such as manufacturing facilities and research laboratories, and to obtain adequate stocks of materials. Few rural farmers can find enough cash to purchase a biogas plant outright, so loan finance is also required. Arranging loans and collection of repayments and interest is a specialised job, best done by banks or an agricultural credit scheme. If national subsidies are provided, government departments become involved, although money can be disbursed through the bank that provides the loans.

The banks are very involved in the Indian biogas programme, with the National Bank of Agricultural and Rural Development (NABARD) providing reserve financing to commercial banks to allow them to lend to farmers.[12] Commercial banks ask an interest rate of 11 per cent for a loan period of five to seven years, depending on the size of the plant. Bank officials have problems with loan security, as a biogas plant is a permanent installation and cannot be moved. Banks prefer the steel drum design, as at least the gas holder can be repossessed in case of non-payment of debts. In

Nepal, the Agricultural Development Bank (ADB/N) is deeply involved in the programme, both as the main source of loan finance and as a shareholder in the Gobar Gas Company. Loans are offered for 7 years at an interest rate of 11 per cent. The ADB/N, itself, is financed by soft loans from the Asian Development Bank as well as grants from groups such as UNDP.

Finance was not a key concern in the Chinese programme until recently. The early plants were considered to be so cheap that families could pay for them directly from their earnings, either in the form of cash or work credits. As the cost of biogas digesters has risen the provincial offices are having to make arrangements for loan finance and for subsidies.[6] The cost of loans from the Agricultural Bank of China is low (2.1 per cent interest).

If the idea of biogas is to be presented to potential customers publicity is required, through national newspapers and radio. The idea of biogas only became well-known in rural India after 1970, when the government of India made the subject newsworthy enough for the national media to take an interest.[8] While a national publicity campaign as such has not been organised in Nepal, certain civil servants and journalists have become interested enough in biogas technology for the subject to appear regularly in newspapers and on the radio. In communist China, a massive publicity campaign formed an important part of the 1970s biogas programme. The use of demonstration plants in strategic places formed the basis of this popularisation campaign which proved very successful.[2]

CHAPTER 3
Organisation and Management

One of the most important factors in ensuring that a biogas programme continues effectively is the way it is organised and managed. However good the ideas and technology may be, poor management can cause a programme to fail and lose credibility with the public.

A major mistake made at the start of the Nepal biogas programme was to try to set up a whole national programme in one go. With inexperienced staff and a lack of coherent infrastructure, the programme almost failed before it was properly started. The Gobar Gas Company was set up as an organisation that was able to rescue the programme and keep it going. In India KVIC already had an infrastructure of area offices and extension staff into which the biogas programme could fit. Even so, its programme has suffered from poor management, with too many decisions made at central offices.

This chapter is meant only as an introduction to the particular problems faced in the management of a biogas programme. Full information on the management of development projects can be found in other books.[1]

3.1 Starting a biogas programme

The initial priority of a new biogas programme, in either a country or a region which does not already have a programme, is good, well-proven technology. Staff who understand the technology and can test it are required. The second priority is staff training. People can only learn how to build a biogas plant, or to supervise the building or to manage the different aspects of the programme, by actually doing it.

These priorities can be covered by a pilot extension programme. A limited number of plants are built for customers in a defined geographical area. While the customers must pay the market price for the plants (less any subsidies that may be planned for the programme), adequate guarantees and compensation must be available in case of failures due to poor design or lack of skill in the builders. Any failures must be put right quickly, without argument, to ensure continued confidence in the programme. Funds must be set aside to allow for a 100 per cent guarantee for all the plants built under the scheme. Therefore this pilot programme will be relatively expensive, but it will provide much-needed data for the planning of the main programme, as well as giving staff on-the-job training.

19

The 95 floating drum biogas plants built by DCS for the Agricultural Year in Nepal acted as a pilot programme for the national programme under the Gobar Gas Company. Ninety-five proved too large a number for the limited resources of DCS, as finance was insufficient to cover the cost of the failures against which guarantees had been given.

As staff skills develop and technology becomes reliable, the pilot scheme will merge into an on-going extension programme. The temptation to expand too fast must be resisted. The rapid expansion of the 1970s' programme in China led to a high plant-failure rate. Similarly, when the Gobar Gas Company was formed from the local DCS programme, staff were not prepared for the sudden increase in work and responsibility.

Staff training must continue as the programme expands. In the early stages of expansion the programme will be overstaffed, with two people being trained for each job. This approach allows for drop-out of staff as well as for expansion. Some of the more able personnel will discover they can use their training in other areas which may pay more money than the biogas programme. Management staff are particularly important. DCS trained technical staff very effectively, but management skills were given a lower priority. The Gobar Gas Company therefore built good-quality plants, but was poorly administered.

An important factor at the start of a programme is research and development, so a research centre should be included early in the programme plans. Scientific and technical staff are required who can learn the basics of the technology and teach the extension staff. They are also required to monitor the progress of the pilot programme and to identify design and construction faults so they can be corrected quickly.

3.2 Coordination of the programme

The governments of India and China recognised in the 1970s that the way to make their programmes really effective was to set up a coordination committee composed of senior people from all the organisations involved in biogas technology. In Nepal one of the first moves of the government planners when setting up their biogas programme, was to appoint a Biogas Committee to supervise it. Such committees include representatives from government ministries, such as Agriculture, Energy, Industry and Finance, so that appropriate political decisions affecting the programme can be made. A weakness on the Nepal committee was lack of representation from the Ministry of Finance, which meant that decisions about subsidies and problems that the Gobar Gas Company had with tax payments took a long time to sort out.

This type of coordinating committee should be set up either before the programme starts or soon after. As well as civil servants, it needs to include senior managers of the banks involved in loan finance and the senior people in the programme concerned with extension, manufacturing and research and development. The formation of a committee should mean that problems can be sorted out quickly at a high level.

It is also helpful to set up similar committees at the local programme level, to ensure local organisations are also working together effectively. Again, all those involved with the programme (at regional, state or provincial level) should be represented, together with bank managers, local government officials and politicians.

3.3 Programme structure

Under the coordinating committee, and responsible to it, the programme will have an Executive Director or General Manager and a full-time staff. In China this central administration is based in the National Biogas Extension Office, while in Nepal it consists of the management of the Gobar Gas Company. In India responsibility for the implementation of the biogas programme is divided between KVIC, government departments and corporations and many other organisations,[2] so the programme lacks full-time staff directly responsible to the coordinating committee.

The recent Chinese approach appears to be the most effective, with a central biogas office directly responsible for the planning and organisation of the national programme. The main job of such an office is to make yearly plans for the progress and expansion of the programme under the direction of the coordinating committee. It will also assign personnel and resources to meet these plans and evaluate the performance of the different aspects of the programme against the plans, making regular reports to the committee.

In a typical national or regional biogas programme, different functional managers in the central office would be responsible for the various aspects of the programme, such as finance, manufacturing, extension, research and development and publicity. Some of these activities may be carried out by groups directly employed by the central office. The Gobar Gas Company in Nepal, for example, relies on its own in-house manufacturing, extension and research facilities. Other activities may be done by outside organisations under contract to the central office, so it retains some control over what is done. In India there is very little effective direct central control over the different organisations involved in the different aspects of the programme, as they have independent management structures.

One of the major decisions to be made by the coordinating committee is the nature of the funding for the programme. The cost of a large extension programme is fairly high, particularly at the start, so budgets and sources of finance need to be carefully worked out before the programme begins. The process is straightforward if the programme is funded by a national or regional government, as the ministries involved would already have their

21

own budgeting systems. If a programme is being set up by a non-governmental organisation and finance is required from an outside funding group, such as an aid organisation, then programme plans must be made very carefully for several years in advance. In Nepal the central office is funded by the extension programme, adding high overheads on to the cost of biogas plants. This approach is not recommended: the central office should be funded from a source not dependent on plant sales; such as government funds or the profits of a bank. In practice in Nepal the biogas programme is being subsidised by the ADB/N.

An effective extension programme needs to be decentralised, with area offices running their own programmes under the direction of the central office. With communications being poor in China, India and Nepal, all these programmes have to have offices in different places within the country. An area office is set up in a similar way to the central office, with an area manager and staff under him responsible for the various aspects of the work. The main function of area offices will be extension work, with the area manager looking after teams of extension agents and construction workers. Some area managers may have additional responsibility for liaising with local manufacturing workshops or material suppliers in their area, on behalf of the central office. Others may have research laboratories or test sites in their area.

Responsibilities need to be carefully defined in written job descriptions, with lines being carefully drawn between the different geographical and functional areas for which different offices have oversight. Also clear lines of authority need to be defined by the central office, to ensure that every member of staff knows to whom they report. Such careful planning while the organisation is being set up saves a great deal of upset, worry and trouble later on.[3]

3.4 Programme planning and evaluation

One of the main functions of a biogas coordinating committee is that of planning the programme and evaluating its progress. The Indian programme is centrally planned with government planners defining how many plants should be built each year (300,000 between 1985 and 1990). This number is divided between the agricultural departments, Khadi Boards and NGOs in the different states of India. State government officials then assign construction targets for the different districts and blocks within the state, often in an arbitrary manner. Such an approach allows target allocation decisions to be based on relationships between officials rather than on the needs and resources of different areas. The result is that the actual number of plants built each year seldom comes close to the target (often being less than half). Such an approach to planning often hinders rather than helps a programme.

22

The approach in Nepal was similar, with senior staff in the Department of Agriculture and (later) in ADB/N making decisions about how many plants should be built in any year, with little reference to local conditions. The governing parameter seemed to be the amount of money available for loans for biogas plants.

When USAID gave a grant to the programme in 1979, they insisted on the proper use of planning procedures. With a better understanding of the process of planning, the Gobar Gas Company began to involve local supervisors in preparing targets for their own areas. They had become habituated to over-planning, so the yearly national target at the time of writing (1987) remains much higher than the Company is capable of achieving (typically, a target of 400 to 500 and an achievement of 200 to 250). This has the advantage that, while orders are based on the target figures, supplies of materials (such as cement and steel) tend to arrive late and in inadequate quantities, thus balancing out the over-ordering. However, income budgets based on the targets are never met, so the Company always makes a loss. More realistic and carefully designed plans and targets, taking into account the variability of supplies, would ensure a more effective and economic programme.

Effective planning takes place before the programme starts. A pre-planning stage is required when senior technical and management staff are hired and trained to allow them to be involved in planning the programme they are to administer. Plans must be based on accurate and up-to-date data, so this stage also involves market surveys and economic analyses. The lines of responsibility between the managers of the different aspects of the programme should be clearly defined at this point. Initial budgets should adequately cover every aspect of the programme, as funding agencies are more prepared to give money at the start of a programme than while it is running.

The plans should also include set times for programme evaluation. Several assumptions have to be made in order to design the plans and these assumptions should be identified, so they can be tested during the evaluation. If assumptions prove to be invalid, the approach to programme implementation may have to be changed to achieve the set goals of the programme. Evaluation also allows weaknesses in the programme to be highlighted, so that financial or staff resources can be diverted to strengthen these areas. Certain people may need further training or may need to be moved to jobs more appropriate to their skills.

Information from each geographical area and functional sector is required for a complete evaluation of the progress of the programme, identification of problem areas and for the drawing up of accurate plans for the following year. Good plans should include a list of measurable indicators of the progress of different parts of the programme, such as the number of plants built per month in a geographical area. Under-managers can simplify their reports if they are given a list of definite questions related to these indicators to answer. Further detailed information is only required if any indicator deviates markedly from its planned value.

Planning and evaluation are effective tools that assist in the smooth running of a programme. However, the skills required are not well understood and many administrators feel threatened by the process. Further information on planning and evaluation is available in books on the subject.[4]

3.5 Extension work

While the central and area managers are responsible for coordinating the work of the programme, it is the extension agents who actually get the job done. They are the ones who visit a farmer to persuade him to have a biogas plant, make links with a bank for the farmer to receive a loan to pay for it, and arrange for the right materials to be delivered to the site. They also arrange for construction workers to be there at the same time to build the plant, check that the plant has been built to the correct standard and finally make follow-up visits at appropriate intervals to ensure the plant continues to work well. In Nepal these people had the additional task of supervising the building work to ensure it was done according to the plans supplied by the technical advisers. In many programmes all this work has to be done in remote rural areas where roads and communication facilities are minimal.

The training of extension agents in management as well as in the technical aspects of biogas is therefore crucial to the progress of a biogas programme. They need to know how to look for potential customers and how to persuade them to buy a biogas plant. Western approaches to hard-selling are unlikely to be effective in developing countries. Sales techniques need to be culturally appropriate to the people with whom the extension agents are working. They need to develop good relationships with bank staff and with the construction staff in their sales areas, as they will be working closely with both groups. Finally, the extension agents need a basic understanding of how biogas works and how a biogas plant is made, so they can explain the technology clearly to customers and be effective in quality control and follow-up work.

Travel in remote areas can add greatly to the cost of a programme. If extension agents are expected to use public transport and bicycles the travel cost per journey is reduced, but they can achieve far less work in a given time, because so much time is taken up in moving from place to place. They can be provided with motorbikes, which are expensive to run and maintain, but they achieve much more work each week. Jeeps or Landrovers are not usually economic for extension workers in remote areas. In the mountainous areas of Nepal, where roads were not built and even motorcycles were unable to go, it was found that there was no alternative to walking. Horses and mules were too expensive to feed and look after.

The progress of each plant sale should be monitored at area office level, with periodic checks being carried out with bank offices that loan applications are being processed and with construction groups that sufficient staff are available for their side of the work. Area offices need to carry sufficient stocks of materials locally to ensure that all current orders can be supplied in good time. In Nepal customers are normally expected to collect their own materials from the area offices, as they often have a tractor and trailer or a bullock cart that can be used. Customers often arrange their own supplies of bricks directly from suppliers. Sand and aggregate can often be obtained from local riverbeds by farmers supplying their own transport and labour. As far as possible, customers are also asked to provide local labourers to dig the holes for the digester pits and to assist the skilled masons in mixing concrete and carrying materials on the site. The price paid by the customer for his biogas plant reflects the amount of work he is able to contribute towards the building of the plant.

An area office may employ several construction teams to build their plants. Each team would consist of a master mason with one or two assistants and labourers. A team may also include a specialist pipe fitter to connect up the gas pipe lines. These teams may be employed directly by the area office, as in Nepal. Alternatively, they may be employed by independent construction firms who build biogas plants under contract to the area office, as in India and China.

The use of small independent contractors has several advantages. Being local people, they are available to customers for repair work and maintenance of the plants they have built. They also have a motivation to sell biogas plants that is separate from that of the main programme and geared to the local situation. Their efforts to advertise biogas plants can reinforce those of the extension agents from the biogas programme.[5]

The use of larger national building firms as contractors may be less effective, as they do not have the local facilities and knowledge that smaller firms possess. National firms also have their own motivations and priorities that may conflict with those of the biogas programme. If the company is a large one, or has political influence, as with some Indian government corporations, it can influence the direction of the whole programme.[6]

Quality control is important, as contractors may try to cut corners to increase their profits. Contracts with construction firms should include provision for training their staff in the building of biogas plants, both at the beginning of the contract period and at regular intervals during the contract. Masons can be taught good building procedures and their skills can be assessed during these courses. Mechanisms to encourage good workmanship can also be devised. Extension agents need to check the plant for construction faults before it is filled with slurry, to approve it for payment.

A small percentage (e.g. 10 per cent) of the fee for the work can be withheld for a year, when it can be paid after the plant has been inspected to ensure it is still working. Further checks can be made during subsequent follow-up visits. Building contracts can be cancelled if there are too many faults in certain contractors' work.

3.6 Resource management

The biogas programme needs a yearly budget as well as a plan to which everyone can work. The allocation of personnel and finance, the effective use of technical services and the ordering of materials all depend on a projection of what the programme will require in the following year. In some countries, such as India and Nepal, the purchase of strategic materials, especially steel and cement, requires government licences and quotas which must be obtained in advance for a year, so careful planning is even more important.

The programme plan should be realistic. It needs to be based on the figures of previous years, as well as detailed projections made by each of the field staff as to what they consider is possible in their own areas. The projected growth rate of the programme, especially, needs to be based on feasible assumptions. The number of potential customers able to afford family biogas plants usually forms too small a proportion of the population to allow for an annual expansion rate for this section of the programme of more than about 10 per cent. The complexities of setting up group-owned biogas plants and the time they take mean that there is unlikely to be fast growth in this part of the programme either.

Large organisations, such as biogas programmes, tend to centralise the making of financial decisions. Money is controlled fairly strictly by account-ants at the head office and area managers are very limited in the decisions they are allowed to make. This approach can stifle growth in the pro-gramme and can lead to the failure of area offices to perform well. The centralisation of financial decision-making can have a ruinous effect on special projects, such as community biogas and research and development.[7]

A much better approach involves the area and sector managers taking responsibility for their own financial planning and operation. Each area office should have its own detailed budget, devised by the area manager with the help of his extension agents and approved by the head office. The area budget would be closely based on the plan for that area and can be compared with previous years' budgets and performance and the budgets of all the other area offices. A cash-flow chart can be mapped out for each area office, indicating how much money is needed each month for salaries, purchase of materials, contract payments for construction work, etc. It would also include the money earned from plant sales, if this is regarded as an income for the programme and paid directly to the area offices. The central office then provides finance (from grants and other income) to the area offices according to the cash-flow plans and the area managers are expected to keep their spending as close to their plans as possible.

The overall funding for the programme should come from government or aid agencies, as grants. If the programme is made self-financing, with all overheads paid out from the money earned by selling biogas plants, the cost of the plants to customers is artificially inflated. A customer should only pay the direct cost for his plant: materials, skilled labour and transport.

The question of subsidies for a biogas programme is a difficult one. In principle, subsidies do little to overcome the basic economic problems associated with biogas extension; they do little to make a bad programme better. However, most biogas programmes are giving subsidies for plant construction or are considering doing so. The argument for subsidies is based on the idea that a government benefits from the programme in reduced deforestation and lower import bills for oil-based fuels. These benefits are not seen by the consumer as lower prices for the fuel from their biogas plant, as wood fuel has a low market price and kerosene and diesel are usually subsidised by the government, anyway. Therefore, the best way to pass the national benefits of biogas technology to people who are prepared to buy a plant is to give government subsidies on the capital cost of the plant itself.

3.7 Communication

Personnel management depends on good communication between people belonging to the different sectors and levels of the administrative structure. Information should flow freely from the extension agents and construction staff to the head office, as well as the other way round. Central managers should know of the concerns and needs of the field staff and be able to respond quickly to them. This type of communication requires that head office staff spend time visiting the area managers. The area managers themselves should visit extension staff working in the field at regular intervals.

Extension staff are motivated by such visits, as they feel their work is being appreciated. This policy proved effective in Nepal, where regional and central managers made a point of visiting as many field staff as possible each year, despite the difficulties of travel. Lack of interest by the central office can quickly lead to reduced morale among the field staff and a high turnover of personnel (a problem faced by the PRAD programme in Uttah Pradesh in North India).[6]

Groups of staff, especially field staff, should meet together at intervals (perhaps once or twice a year) for training weeks. There are often times in the year when field visits are difficult (such as in the monsoon in South Asia), or when potential customers are very busy with agricultural work, so training sessions need not adversely affect the progress of the programme. These times are also opportunities for administrative staff to discuss any changes in the procedures used by the programme and to listen to problems discovered by the field staff. They are also times when R & D and technical staff can present new ideas and train field staff in the use of new technology and equipment that is being made and sold. The main value of such meetings, though, is the exchange of ideas between field staff from different areas. They will all encounter similar problems, so they will be able to share their different ways of overcoming them. Much of this communication will take place over meals and during leisure activities, so the training weeks should not be too intensive.

These training weeks have been an important part of the Nepal biogas programme and they have enabled area managers to gain the management skills they lacked when first appointed. These meetings also proved a good time for writing area plans, as the process of planning could be taught to the managers in the context of their work. The different approaches adopted by the managers in their separate geographical areas could be compared and suggestions shared between them.

3.8 Management of technical projects

Most of the field and area staff will be expected to understand the basics of biogas technology, how it works and how to teach customers to use it. However, as the programme expands, especially in the use of community plants to run engines and cottage industries, more specialised technical staff will also be required. For example, if group-owned plants are to be used for grain milling and rice hulling, people with experience in setting up engines and milling equipment will be required. Help can be obtained from the company agents supplying the equipment, but the programme should also employ staff who can assist extension agents in this work, both in the setting-up and the follow-up. Another area where expert help is required is in irrigation projects.

Depending on the number of technical projects in the programme, specialist staff may need to travel from a base in the head office, or several such staff may be stationed at different area offices. If the biogas programme is linked up with other rural development programmes, then some of this technical help may be available from the area offices of these other programmes. For example, in Nepal help is available from the Small Farmers' Development Programme, which is also linked with ADB/N.

3.9 Management training

Management is a complex subject and there are many books about it. There are also many courses available to train managers, ranging from short evening classes in colleges of further education to university B.Com. and M.Com. degrees. Many of the organisations involved in a biogas programme, such as banks and government departments, will already have schemes for training their own managers, often an arrangement with a local college. These schemes can be used by the biogas programme to train its managers, if allowance has been made in the budget. Experienced managers can be seconded from some of the organisations involved in the programme to run the central office, at least until people from within the programme have gained sufficient training and experience to do so. In Nepal, senior management for the Gobar Gas Company was provided first by DCS and later by ADB/N.

CHAPTER 4
How Biogas Works

Everybody involved in a biogas programme, especially the administrative and technical staff, should have a simple understanding of the biogas process. The details of anaerobic digestion are complex and require an understanding of biochemistry (see Gunnerson for a good introduction),[1] but a simplified account is useful.

Biogas is produced by certain types of bacteria: microscopic organisms that break down the complex molecules contained in the feedstock into simpler molecules in a way that releases energy and the chemicals they need for growth. The bacteria that are used in a biogas digester are the same or similar to those that live in the gut of ruminant animals, such as cattle. Cow dung is a good source of suitable bacteria. These bacteria are adapted to the conditions found inside a cow, so a biogas digester must have a similar environment. The key factors are the exclusion of air and light and a temperature close to blood heat (between 20°C and 40°C for the mesophylic bacteria used in rural plants).

These conditions can be met in a hole in the ground, lined with brick or cement to keep the mixture of bacteria, water and feedstock (called a 'slurry') from leaking out, with a suitable cover which excludes air and light and also collects the gas. In tropical and sub-tropical areas the ambient temperature is usually about right for biogas digestion during most of the year. In cooler climates, some method of insulating and heating the slurry is required.

4.1 The anaerobic process

Several different types of bacteria live in a biogas digester and do different jobs.[2,3] Bacteria are single-celled organisms surrounded by a membrane. They secrete chemicals, called *enzymes*, through the membrane into the food around them, to break it down into simpler substances. These substances will dissolve in water, so they can be absorbed and used by the bacteria.

There are several ways of classifying bacteria. Here it is useful to consider their response to oxygen. *Aerobic* bacteria require oxygen to survive, while anaerobic bacteria cannot function at all in the presence of oxygen (they do not die, they stop working until the oxygen is removed). *Facultative* bacteria are able to use oxygen if it is present, but can use alternative digestion processes if it is absent.

30

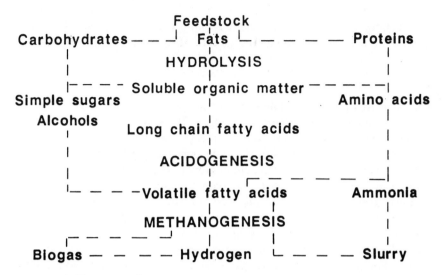

Figure 4.1 *The anaerobic process.*

When a feedstock is placed in an anaerobic digester the facultative bacteria begin to break down the complex molecules (Fig. 4.1), using up the oxygen in the feed. They will also use the oxygen in the air trapped inside the digester, thus lowering the gas pressure. These bacteria continue breaking down foodstuffs using oxygen from water once the free oxygen is finished, so this process is called *hydrolysis.*

The second stage (or the second half of the first stage, the *liquifaction* stage) is the formation of *volatile fatty acids* as well as carbon dioxide and some hydrogen. These acids are of low molecular weights and have low boiling points. Acetic acid (CH_3COOH), which is the major constituent of vinegar, is the commonest acid formed. If there is some air present the digestion process stops at this point, and the digester gives off the distinctive smell of these acids, usually associated with decaying food.

In an anaerobic digester (with no oxygen), the third stage, the *methanogenic* stage is continued by methanogenic bacteria which break down these fatty acids into even simpler molecules: water, carbon dioxide and methane (H_2O, CO_2 and CH_4), removing the smell and producing biogas. Methanogenic bacteria are *obligate anaerobes*; they cannot function if oxygen is present. Different methanogens are able to use a range of fatty acids as well as simple alcohols and even hydrogen and carbon dioxide to form methane. However, about 70 per cent of the methane in biogas is estimated to come from acetic acid ($CH_3COOH \rightarrow CH_4 + CO_2$).

The many different types of bacteria work together in a symbiotic relationship. The hydrolytic bacteria produce waste products that the acid formers can use. The acid formers, in turn, produce acids that the methanogens use, giving biogas as their waste product. If all the bacteria are working in balance the acid level remains constant, the rate of production by the acid formers equalling the rate of use by the methanogens.

4.2 Effect of pH

The measure of acidity is called *pH* (the negative logarithm, base 10, of the concentration of hydrogen ions; see Fig. 4.2). A normal value for pH in a working biogas plant is between 7 and 8 (about neutral). When a biogas plant is newly started, the acid formers become active first, reducing the pH to below 7 (increasing the acid content). The methanogens then start using these acids, increasing the pH back to neutral.

A working biogas plant is *buffered*, in other words, the acid level is controlled by the process itself. Some of the carbon dioxide (CO_2) produced by the bacteria dissolves in the water to form bicarbonate ions (HCO_3^-) which cause the solution to become mildly alkaline. The amount of bicarbonate in solution depends on the concentration of carbon dioxide and the amount of acids in the slurry. The effect of this carbon dioxide passing in and out of solution acts as a buffer to balance out small variations in the acidity of the slurry.

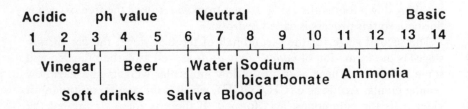

Figure 4.2 *The pH scale*

The pH of the slurry is easily measured using a pH meter or with suitable indicator papers. However, it is an insensitive measure of the way the digester is working, because of the buffering effect. If the pH of a digester drops it indicates the buffering mechanism has already failed and too much acid is being produced, usually because the methanogenic bacteria have stopped working for some reason.

A better measure of the stability of a digester is its *alkalinity*. The amount of bicarbonate in a sample of the slurry can be measured by titrating it against a known acid (see Appendix III).

32

4.3 Effects of temperature

Another way of classifying bacteria is according to their preferred temperature. *Cryophylic* bacteria work best at between 10°C and 20°C, *mesophylic* bacteria between 30°C and 40°C and *thermophylic* bacteria between 45°C and 60°C. While anaerobic digestion is very efficient in the thermophylic region, rural digestors use mesophylic bacteria because higher temperatures are difficult to maintain.

The gas production rate roughly doubles for every 10°C rise in temperature between 15°C and 35°C. The gas-production efficiency (the gas produced per kilogram of feedstock) also increases with temperature. A mesophylic digester works best at 35°C.

Methanogenic bacteria are sensitive to temperature changes. A sudden change of more than 5°C in a day can cause them to stop working temporarily, resulting in a build-up of undigested volatile acids: the plant goes 'sour'. This is less of a problem in large-volume digesters, where the high heat capacity of the slurry ensures that its temperature changes slowly.

4.4 Effect of toxins

The main cause of a biogas plant going sour is the presence of toxic substances. Antibiotics, disinfectants and pesticides are designed to kill bacteria and will stop a digester functioning, as will detergents. Chlorinated hydrocarbons, such as chloroform and other organic solvents, are particularly toxic to biogas digestion.

Care must be taken that the feedstock used in a biogas plant has not been affected by these chemicals and that the water used to mix the slurry is not polluted. The dung of any animals being given antibiotics should be kept separate and not added to the plant. If an animal shed is cleaned with detergents or disinfectants the washings must be directed away from the biogas plant. The chemicals used to clean the shed must then be washed away with plenty of water before the animals are allowed to return.

Methanogenic bacteria are not killed by toxins, but switch themselves into a non-working state.[4] Once this happens volatile acids build up and the plant begins to give off a bad smell. In principle, it is possible for a biogas plant to recover from this sour state if the pH is corrected using lime or chalk (calcium hydroxide or calcium carbonate) and the source of the problem is removed.[5] However, if the plant has been badly poisoned it may be difficult to remove the toxins without removing most of the bacteria. In this case, the digester must be emptied, cleaned with plenty of water and refilled with fresh slurry.

4.5 Properties of feedstocks

Any material containing food substances, such as fats, carbohydrates or proteins, can be digested in a biogas plant. However, the rate and efficiency of digestion of the feedstock depends on its physical and chemical form. Raw plant material is bound up in plant cells, usually strengthened with cellulose and lignin, which are difficult to digest. In order to let the bacteria reach the more digestible foods the plant material must be broken down.

Cattle dung is the easiest feedstock to use for a biogas plant: it already contains the right bacteria and it has been ground up by the animal's teeth and broken down chemically by acids and enzymes in the animal's gut. Human, pig and chicken manure are also good, but need a 'starter', such as slurry from a working plant, if they are used to start a biogas plant, because these animals do not have all the right bacteria in their gut. Some animals, such as horses and elephants, are less good at breaking down fibrous material, so their dung contains more indigestible matter. This can be screened out or chopped mechanically. Goat and sheep dungs are rich in nutrients,[6] but they are in the form of pellets that must be broken up mechanically. These pellets are difficult to collect, so there are few reports of their use in the literature.[7]

Raw vegetable matter usually needs to be treated before it can be used. It can be physically chopped up or minced, or it can be treated chemically.[8] Some plants, such as water hyacinth, have little lignin, so are easier to use. One good method seems to be to compost vegetable matter for five days before adding it to the plant, as aerobic bacteria are better at breaking down cellulose.

There are several measurements that can be made to define the properties of the feedstock or the slurry (Appendix III):

1 Total solids (TS) is a measure of the dry matter (DM) left after the moisture has been removed (by heating to 105°C).
2 Volatile solids (VS) is a measure of the organic solids lost when the dry matter is burnt (at 500°C or 600°C).
3 Chemical oxygen demand (COD) is a measure of the degree of pollution of the slurry. It is determined by chemically oxidizing a sample.
4 Biological oxygen demand (BOD) is an attempt to measure the pollution more realistically. Aerobic bacteria are used to digest the sample and the oxygen required is measured.
5 Carbon to nitrogen ratio (C:N) is an important parameter as anaerobic bacteria need nitrogen compounds to grow and multiply. Too much nitrogen, however, can inhibit methanogenic activity.

Typical values for some of these parameters are given in Table 4.1. These results depend very much on the size of the animal, what it is eating, the weather, etc. Hot dry weather will cause water to evaporate from the dung before it is collected, giving an apparent increase in TS, while humid weather will have the opposite effect. Measurements should be made of the properties of locally available feedstocks that could be used in a biogas

Table 4.1 Properties of dung from typical animals[9,10,11]

Animal	Wet Dung (kg/day)	Biogas (lit/day)	Total Solid (%)	Volatile Solid (%TS)
Buffalo	14	450–480	16–20	77
Cow	10	280–340	16–20	77
Pig	5	280–340	25	80
100 hens	7.5	420–510	48	77
Human	0.2	11– 14	15–20	90

programme and these values considered when suitable biogas plants are designed.

The total solid content of animal dung varies between 15 per cent and 30 per cent (Table 4.1), while the recommended value for slurry is between 8 per cent and 12 per cent. This means that dung must be diluted with water before it is used in a biogas plant. A low solids concentration mean that the digester volume is used inefficiently. It can also lead to separation of the slurry, the heavier solids sinking to the bottom to form a sludge layer and the lighter solids floating to form a scum layer on top of the liquid (supernatant). The scum layer can dry out to form a solid mat, preventing gas release from the liquid and blocking pipes. This should not happen if the TS of the slurry is kept above about 6 per cent.

A slurry with a high solids concentration (greater than 12 per cent) does not easily flow through inlet pipes. If toxins are present, such as a high nitrogen concentration, bacteria are more likely to be affected in a thick slurry. However slurries of up to 30 per cent total solids can be digested in a dry fermenter.[12,13]

The volatile solid content of dung is usually around 80 per cent of the total solids (Table 4.1). The remaining ash (fixed solids) is composed of soil particles, inert portions of vegetable matter (some grasses, e.g. rice, concentrate silica in their stalks) and some solid carbon left from the decomposition of foodstuffs. VS is not an ideal measure of the digestibility of a feedstock. Lignin and other indigestible solids will burn at 500°C, while some digestible solids, such as sugars, leave a carbon deposit when heated. It is an easy measurement to make (Appendix III).

COD and BOD are also not ideal ways to predict when proportion of the feedstock will be digested in an anaerobic digester, as they were designed as measures of the aerobic digestibility of materials. While they may give a more valid answer than VS, these measurements are much more difficult to make (Appendix III). The best way to determine the anaerobic digestibility of a feedstock is to digest it in small laboratory digesters (2 litres) in controlled temperature baths (see Appendix III).

35

COD is useful in that it is possible to define a value for methane. Using this figure, a digester should produce 350 litres of methane for each kg of COD digested.

The ideal C:N ratio is reported to be 25:1. The measurement of total carbon and nitrogen requires a well-equipped laboratory, but values of C:N are quoted in the literature for many feedstocks (Table 4.2) and the ratios for mixtures can easily be estimated from these values.[14] However, the values of total carbon can be misleading, as some of the carbon is bound up in indigestible lignin. The nitrogen content of plant materials varies with the age of the plant (e.g. barley straw contains 39 per cent protein at 21 days of growth, but only 4 per cent after 86 days).

Table 4.2   Carbon and nitrogen content of feedstocks

Material	C:N	% N	% C	% Water	Comments
Cattle dung	20–30	3–4	35–40	72–85	Grass/Grain fed
	25–35	1–2			Straw fed
Horse dung	25	2	58	70–75	
Sheep dung	20	3.8	75	68	
Pig dung	14	3–4	53	82	
Poultry dung	8	3.7	30–35	65	
Human faeces	6–10	4–6	40	75–80	
Human urine[15]	0.8	15–18	13	95	
Water hyacinth[16]	15–23	1–9	24–35	93–95	Dried
Rice straw[17]	47.2	0.6	40	5–10	

Notes: Data for fresh dung. All dung will lose water and nitrogen on keeping, especially if air humidity is low.

In general, the C:N ratio of dung from cattle fed with poor feeds, such as straw and dry grass, tends to be too high (up to 35 per cent). The values quoted in Western literature (20 per cent or less) are measured using dung from cattle that eat more protein-rich foods. If the C:N is high, then gas production can be enhanced by adding nitrogen in the form of cattle urine or urea, or by fitting a latrine to the plant. If the C:N ratio is low, for example if chicken manure is used as a feedstock, the addition of carbon, such as chopped grass or water hyacinth, can reduce the possibility of toxicity from too much nitrogen affecting the bacteria.

4.6   Types of digester

A biogas digester can be operated as a batch process or a continuous one. In a batch digester the waste is put into the plant, usually with a starter

(5 per cent to 30 per cent by volume), and the gas collected as it is given off. There is a lag time of between one and 14 days before the first gas is given off (depending on the slurry temperature and the amount of starter).[9] For the first day or two the gas will be mainly carbon dioxide. The gas production rate will rise to a peak and then fall off (Fig. 4.3). There may be subsidiary peaks in the gas-production rate as less digestible material becomes available to the methanogens.

The advantage of a batch reactor is that the feed can contain lignin and other indigestible matter, as it does not have to be fed through inlet and outlet pipes. A batch digester can be run at a high solids content (as a dry reactor), reducing the volume of water required. Since the gas production varies with time, several batch reactors are usually run together, started at different times, so that some are always producing gas.

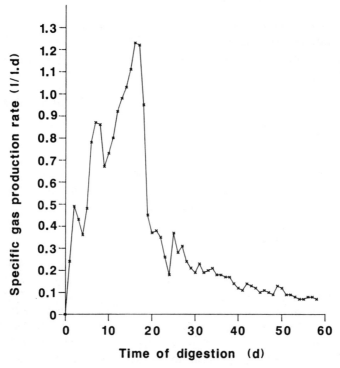

Figure 4.3 *Rate of gas production with time*

A continuous digester is fed regularly once it has been started. The feed is mixed with water outside the digester and fed through an inlet pipe. The outlet is arranged so that spent slurry either overflows into a collecting pond as new slurry is added, or it can be removed with a bucket. Once the digestion process has stabilised, the gas production rate is fairly constant (with constant feed rate and temperature). Care must be taken that the inlet and outlet pipes are not blocked by indigestible matter.

Many digesters in China are run in a semi-batch mode. They are started as batch digesters and filled with vegetable matter, such as straw and garden wastes, and animal dung and a starter. However these digesters are also fed daily, with dung (usually from pigs and an attached latrine) and vegetable wastes. The gas production remains fairly constant, as the daily feed is digested, but it is enhanced by the slow degradation of the less digestible matter. The Chinese empty these plants once or twice a year, removing the undigested materials and using the slurry as fertiliser on their fields. The disadvantage of this approach is the break in gas production during the time the plant is being emptied and restarted.

4.7 Digester design parameters

When a biogas digester is designed the main variable to be defined is its internal volume. The amount of gas produced depends on the volume of slurry in the pit. The digester volume is related to two other parameters: the retention time (R, measured in days) and the feed rate. For a batch digester, the retention time is simply the time the slurry has been left in the pit. For a continuous digester, it is given by the volume of the digester pit (V, m^3), divided by the volume of the daily feed (V, m^3/day):

$$R = \frac{V}{v} \text{ days.} \tag{3.1}$$

The volume feed rate (v) is given by the mass of total solids (m, kg) fed daily, divided by the proportion of total solids in the mixed slurry (assuming the density of feed is 1000 kg/m^3):

$$v = \frac{m}{TS \times 1000} \text{ or } v = \frac{m}{TS\% \times 10} \text{ m}^3/\text{day} \tag{3.2}$$

The retention time is always a compromise between gas production rate and efficiency. If the supply of feed is limited and the temperature low (less than 20°C), the retention time should be as long as possible (up to 100 days) to get the maximum gas from the feed. Long retention times also allow less digestible materials in the feed to be broken down. The volume of the plant will be large, though, making the cost high. If the feed is in plentiful supply and the temperature can be kept high (30°C), a retention time of 10 days is possible, giving a high rate of gas production. Special high-rate thermophylic reactors can have retention times down to one or two days, but these are very expensive to build and operate.

At low temperatures it is important to keep the retention time long, as the bacteria grow more slowly. If the bacteria are removed with the spent slurry faster than they can replace themselves in the digester pit, 'wash-out' occurs and the plant will fail. As the methanogens multiply more slowly than acid-forming bacteria, the main symtom of wash-out is the plant becoming sour. The plant may recover if feeding is stopped for a time.

The loading rate (r, kg.VS/m^3/day) of a digester is defined as the mass of volatile solids added each day per unit volume of digester. It is related to the mass feed rate:

$$r = \frac{m \times VS}{v} \text{ or } r = \frac{m \times VS\%}{v \times 100} \text{kg. VS/m}^3\text{/day} \tag{3.3}$$

Typical values for the loading rate are between 0.2 kg.VS/m^3/day and 2.0 kg.VS/m^3/day.

4.8 Effluent slurry

Anaerobic digestion not only breaks down plant materials into biogas, it also releases plant nutrients, such as nitrogen, potassium and phosphorous and converts them into a form that can be easily absorbed by plants.[18] These fertiliser chemicals are not removed or created in a biogas plant, although the removal of carbon, oxygen and hydrogen as methane and carbon dioxide means that the concentration of these other chemicals is increased (Table 4.3). For example, protein and amino-acids in the feed-stock are converted into ammonia, which forms soluble ammonium compounds with the fatty acids.[19]

While the value of biogas effluent as a fertiliser is well-known to biogas workers, most biogas programmes have given it too little emphasis. Farmers tend to assume that the removal of one benefit (biogas) from the feed must reduce its effectiveness in other directions (as a fertiliser). This attitude prevails even in China, where the people have a long tradition of composting wastes (especially night-soil)—despite intensive propaganda on the benefits of biogas.[21,22] Few Indian and Nepalese farmers, are convinced of the fertiliser value of the effluent, except those who have tried it and have become impressed with the results. One such farmer claims to be saving 80 per cent of the urea he used to put on his crops. A few institutions in India run biogas plants purely for the fertiliser they produce.

Table 4.3 Plant nutrients in air dried manure and effluent measured in Nepal[20]

Material	Nitrogen %	Phosphorous %	Potassium %	Indigestible ash %
Buffalo dung	1.01	1.11	0.92	26.43
Biogas effluent	1.41	1.18	1.48	28.64

Biogas slurry must be used correctly for its full value to be realised. Preliminary trials of slurry in Kathmandu, at the Department of Soil Science and Agricultural Chemistry, suggested that the concentration of nitrogen in the slurry was too high for transplanted rice seedlings, which grew too fast and weakened. The presence of hydrogen sulphide may be toxic to some plants,[9] especially when pig dung is used as a feedstock. However, frogs were able to live happily in the slurry pits of Nepalese biogas plants using cow dung as feed, so this may not be a major problem.

If biogas slurry is used carefully it does make an excellent fertiliser and soil conditioner. It is free from odour and does not attract flies. Most of the harmful bacteria and parasites in the original feed are either killed or considerably reduced in number.[23,24] The benefits of slurry use build up over several years. Tests in China show a productivity increase in rice production of 11 per cent to 14 per cent after biogas slurry had been applied to the fields regularly for four years.[19,25]

The major problem with effluent slurry is transporting it to the fields as it is in liquid form. Chinese plant owners often collect the slurry daily in buckets and carry them to nearby vegetable plots. Slurry has a total solids content of about 8 per cent, so 92 per cent is water, which is bulky and heavy to carry over long distances. A large volume is required to get an adequate quantity of fertiliser.

The usual practice in India and Nepal is to collect the effluent in shallow ponds and allow it to dry in the sun. This reduces its weight and volume considerably. Any toxic substances, such as hydrogen sulphide, evaporate and any remaining harmful bacteria are killed. However, ammonia is also lost by evaporation into the air and by leeching, as water drains into the soil. The loss of nitrogen from dried slurry (7 per cent to 15 per cent)[26] appears to be less than from drying raw cattle dung (20 per cent to 45 per cent).[6] However, sun drying takes up a lot of space and is difficult in the rainy season.

Digested slurry can be introduced into irrigation canals, so the water washes it to the fields. This approach was used in a biogas irrigation scheme in Parwanipur, Nepal.[27] Unfortunately, more slurry was deposited near the sluices from the canal than reached the far ends of the fields. Slurry can be put in tanker trailers and pulled by animals or tractors. In some communes in China, the slurry is then sprayed onto the fields, using a small biogas-powered pump.[25] This approach requires machinery and is expensive.

Slurry can be added to dry plant material, such as straw or leaves.[26,28] The dry material absorbs the plant nutrients and water and conserves them. The slurry contains facultative bacteria that composts the plant material, increasing its fertiliser value.

4.9 Research on microbiology and slurry use

Since the anaerobic process is complex, a biogas extension programme needs to have available the skills of a qualified microbiologist or biochemist as well as the services of well-equipped laboratories and trained personnel to run them. The digestibility of different local feedstocks needs to be tested and the causes of any plant failures discovered. A large programme might have its own laboratory and staff, but most biogas programmes employ university or government research laboratories on a consulting basis, paying for research and test work as required. In India and China, as well as other countries such as Thailand, the Philippines and Brazil, there are many research institutions involved in biogas-related research projects. In less-developed countries, special research programmes may need to be funded to ensure that specialist help is available when needed by the extension programme.

Much more work needs to be done on the use of slurry as a fertiliser. For example, a low-cost appropriate technology is required that can separate the solid from the liquid fractions of effluent slurry. The liquid can be used on nearby vegetable plots, leaving the less bulky solids to be collected and used on crops in more remote fields.[29]

A biogas extension programme should also have land available, either its own or loaned by agricultural research stations, on which the use of biogas slurry on local crops can be tested. These plots would also serve as demonstration and training areas to teach local farmers to make the best use of the fertiliser from their plants.

CHAPTER 5
Biogas Plant Designs

A biogas extension programme must have at least one design of biogas plant that can be sold to customers and built by its staff. It must be possible to make it in a range of sizes, suitable for different applications. Both the Indian and Chinese programmes started badly because they used unreliable and unproven designs. A large number of failures at the start of a new programme can bring bad publicity and loss of public confidence. So the choice of the right design of plant with which to start a biogas programme is one of the most important decisions to be made during planning.

5.1 Digester design criteria

There are many different designs of biogas plant available.[1,2,3] Some have been made only as prototypes, to test an idea; others have been made in thousands in extension programmes. A biogas plant must perform a basic set of functions: it must contain the slurry for a suitable length of time; it must keep out air and light; it must keep the slurry at a reasonable temperature and it must collect and store the biogas until it is required.

There are several criteria against which different designs may be considered, when choosing one to act as the basis of an extension programme. A biogas plant should be:

1 Strong
2 Leak-tight
3 Built of local materials
4 Cheap to build
5 Easy to use
6 Easy to maintain
7 Easy to insulate and heat
8 Reliable

A large volume of slurry ($5m^3$ to $1000m^3$) exerts high pressure on the walls of its container, depending on the depth. The easiest way to support the container walls is to place them in a pit in the ground. The space between the walls and the undug earth must be filled with hard-packed earth for strength.

Some of the above criteria are linked; a plant built of local materials, such as those used to build local houses, will be much cheaper than one made from imported materials. Some are in conflict: a biogas plant built of welded steel sheet will be strong and leak-tight, but will be expensive. The cheapest building materials: mud, wood, bamboo etc. are not suitable, as slurry and biogas will leak through them. Mud can be used to add weight to support a lighter material. Concrete and brick seem to be the best materials for building a digester, although care must be taken in the construction to ensure that it does not leak slurry or gas.

Rubber and plastic materials have also been used in biogas plants, as they are leak-proof. However, sheets of rubber and plastic are not strong and can be damaged by rodents and by sunlight. Great care must be taken during transport and construction that they are not damaged by sharp objects. In Nepal, where these materials are mostly imported, they can be as expensive as the steel required to do a similar job.

A farmer will not buy a biogas plant that is difficult to use. If a man has to carry buckets of slurry up a tall ladder each day to feed the plant, he will soon stop using it. The same is true if the plant fails frequently and is difficult or expensive to repair. Farmers are willing to do simple, regular maintenance work, as long as they understand what they must do and the work does not require expensive supplies. A biogas plant must be designed with maintenance in mind. For example, taps in a gas line must be fitted so they can be easily removed for repair if they become stuck or break.

In the tropics the slurry temperature in a plant should remain above 20°C for most of the year. In colder regions of the world, a biogas plant must be designed so it can be easily insulated and heated if biogas is required in winter.

The most successful biogas plant designs are shaped as a cylinder or as part of a sphere, as these shapes are stronger and easier to make leak-tight. Corners are very difficult to seal against slurry or gas leaks. If components, such as gas storage drums, are to be made in a workshop, the transportation of these components to a plant site must be considered.

5.2 Basic plant designs

While there is a wide range of plant designs available, only three will be considered for use in extension programmes: the floating drum, the fixed dome and the flexible bag digesters. These are the most used designs and many other plants are only variations of them. Both the floating drum and the fixed dome designs are built in Nepal and they are versions of the original designs adapted to local conditions. The Nepalese versions also incorporate improvements to the original designs that make them cheaper to build and easier and more reliable to use.

5.3 Floating drum design

The floating steel drum design has formed the basis of the Khadi and Village Industries Commission programme in India since the 1950s. It was originally developed in Bombay by Mr J.J. Patel, who called it the *Gramalaxmi III* design.[4] It is now more commonly called the *Indian* design.

43

The slurry is kept in a cylindrical pit in the ground. The pit is usually lined with brick masonry, similar to a dug water well. The soil around the pit supports the brick walls and allows them to take the hydraulic pressure. If the brickwork is made carefully, the walls should not leak. Small holes are filled by the slurry seeping through and drying out within them.

The gas is collected in a cylindrical steel gas drum that floats mouth downwards in the slurry. As gas collects in the drum, it floats higher in the liquid. As gas is used, the drum sinks back down. If the drum becomes full, the gas bubbles out around its sides and is lost into the air. The drum usually has a steel bar framework fixed inside it, so that when the drum is rotated by hand it stirs up the surface of the slurry and breaks up any scum formation. It often has handles fixed to the top with which it can be rotated and also carried, when it is being transported to or removed from a plant. The drum is usually made from mild steel sheet, welded around a light frame made of welded steel angle bars.

The gas drum is held in the right place by a central guide pipe running vertically through a second pipe at its centre. This system allows the drum to move up and down and to rotate about its central axis. It stops the drum moving sideways or toppling over and jamming on the walls of the digester pit.

The standard KVIC design uses a deep, straight-sided cylindrical digester pit,[5] the depth being two to three times the diameter (Fig. 5.1). This shape is not optimum as it requires a deep hole to be dug and does not

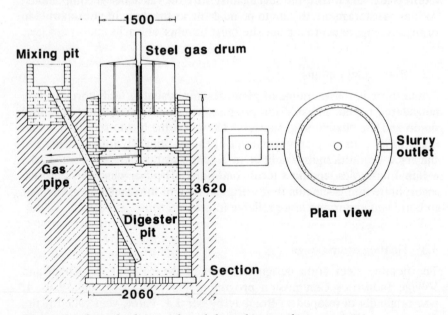

Figure 5.1 *Straight design of steel drum biogas plant*

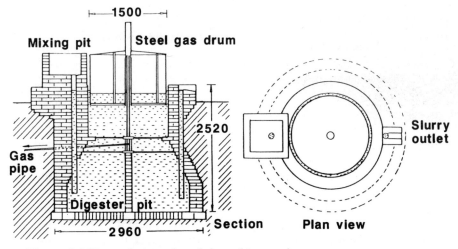

Figure 5.2 *Taper design of steel drum biogas plant*

make the best use of materials. A shallower, wider pit (the depth being about the same as the diameter) should be cheaper to build.[6] The problem of digging deep pits in the plains (Terai) of Nepal, where the underground water table is often near the surface, inspired the taper design (Fig. 5.2).[7] The internal volume of this plant is the same as the straight version of the corresponding size and both use the same number of bricks and size of gas drum (see Appendix I). The tapered version requires a much shallower hole. A central dividing wall is used to stop new feed slurry coming out of the outlet pipe before it is digested.

A second improvement made to the Nepal version by DCS is in the way the gas is removed. The KVIC design has a gas tap fitted to the top of the gas drum and a flexible plastic pipe hose links this to the permanent gas pipeline. This plastic pipe needs to be replaced regularly (once or twice a year) as it degrades in the sunlight, gets brittle and cracks. The drum used in Nepal has holes leading into the central guide-pipe, which is sealed to atmosphere. The gas is removed under the side of the drum (see Fig. 5.3). The drum can be rotated more easily and maintenance is reduced. As the central guide pipe is closed to the air, it is less likely to corrode than the KVIC version, which has a typical lifetime of only five years.[8]

Other versions of the floating drum design include rectangular digesters and drums (used in Korea and Taiwan), but these are more difficult to seal against leaks. KVIC have a shallow version of their design, which uses a rectangular slurry chamber built slightly inclined to the horizontal. The drum floats in a circular hole at the higher end of the chamber.

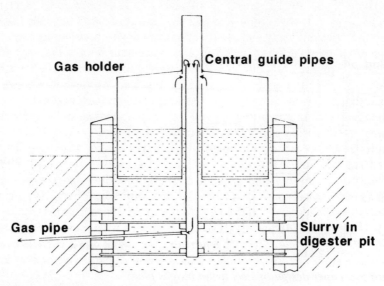

Figure 5.3 *Gas removal system for DCS drum design*

A standard digester can use floating drums built of different materials. KVIC have experimented with the use of drums made from HDPE (high density polyethylene), PVC and ferrocement.[9,10] DCS have also tested plastic and ferrocement drums, with little success. HDPE expands and contracts in the heat of the sun and quickly cracks. Ferrocement drums are very heavy and difficult to transport. Small hairline cracks easily occur and they are difficult to seal against gas leaks.

Galvanized steel (GI) sheet has been successfully used for gas drums. The seams must be sealed with solder or glue to ensure they are leak-tight. GI drums are very light, so require weights on top to give enough gas pressure. Any small scratches in the zinc coating can allow galvanic corrosion that quickly creates holes in the drum.

An early version of the KVIC design used a steel drum supported by ropes passing over pulleys and attached to counter-balance weights. The reduced gas pressure was supposed to improve gas production; but the extra 'biogas' was actually carbon dioxide coming out of solution. This design was very dangerous, as air could leak into the drum and form an explosive mixture with the biogas. Some of these plants have blown up. Other drums designs, without the counterweights, are much safer to use.

5.4 Practical aspects of the drum design

Over 800 plants to the DCS version of this design have been made in Nepal and many more have been made in India (over three-quarters of their

200,000 total). Follow-up surveys show several problems, especially that of corrosion of the steel drums.[11] Eighty-six of the first 95 built in Nepal showed signs of rust within a year of being installed. Although the chlorinated rubber paint was cleaned off and replaced with bituminous paint, 50 per cent of these drums needed total replacement within the next four years. An estimate of the life of KVIC drums is about seven years.[8] Cracks were reported in the walls of some of the digesters of these first plants in Nepal, but as masons learned their work this type of fault became rare.

Biogas slurry is corrosive to steel, so gas drums must be protected against it. Corrosion resistance is partly a matter of good design work; there must be no corners or ledges where slurry or rain water can sit and start rust formation.[12] It is also a matter of using an effective paint scheme. The finished drums must be carefully cleaned of welding slag, rust and mill scale (a blue oxide coating). Hand cleaning with wire brushes and sandpaper is hardly adequate, although it is the usual approach in many workshops in Nepal and India. Machine cleaning with rotary wire brushes and sanders is better. Sand or shot blast cleaning removes all corrosion and provides a good key for painting, but it is the most expensive and difficult approach.

The cleaned steel must quickly be primed with a metalised antisaline primer paint before rust can form again. Pressure spray painting gives the best results, but is expensive. Air spray painting is not appropriate for the thick paints that need to be used. The primer coat should be followed with a coat of bituminous paint (such as 'high-build black'). A second coat of this paint is required after the drum has been delivered to the plant site.

Steel drums should be painted each year they are in service, if they are to last. Some steel drums in India are over 30 years old, because they have been carefully looked after. The ones that failed within five years were poorly cleaned and painted at first and have been scratched and not regularly repainted while in service.

5.5 Fixed dome design

The fixed dome design is the basic design used in China. It is an underground digester pit, lined with brick or concrete, with a dome-shaped cover, also made from brick or concrete, placed over it. The cover is fixed and held in place with earth piled over the top to resist the pressure of the gas inside. A second pit, the slurry reservoir, is built above and to the side of the digester. As gas is given off by the slurry, it collects in the dome and displaces some of the slurry into the reservoir. As gas is used, the slurry flows back into the digester to replace it (Fig. 5.4). This system of gas storage is called the displacement principle.

The Chinese use a range of different shapes for their digesters ranging from a fully spherical container to a flat-roofed rectangular one.[13,14] The

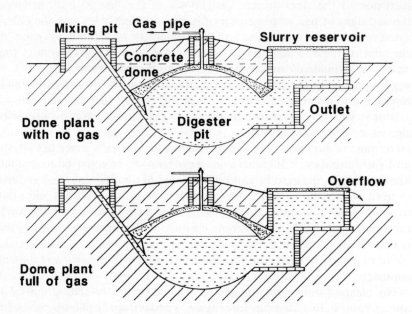

Figure 5.4 *Displacement principle for fixed dome plants*

rectangular shape was used early in the Chinese programme, but proved unreliable, as the corners were difficult to make leak-tight. The most commonly used shape has a roof and a floor made as segments of a sphere, joined by a cylindrical or conical section (Fig. 5.5). If the included angle at the centre of the spherical segment is less than 110° the material of the

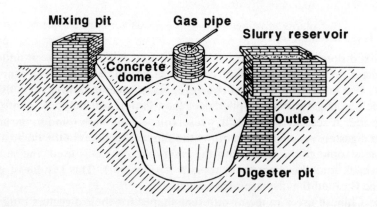

Figure 5.5 *Fixed dome design of biogas plant*

48

dome is always in compression and a minimum of steel reinforcement is required.

A version of this design is used in Nepal. It is made by first pouring a concrete dome over a mould shaped in mud in the ground. Once the concrete has set the digester pit is excavated from under the dome and lined with cement plaster applied directly to the mud walls. If the soil is weak or crumbly, the plaster can be reinforced with wire mesh, making ferrocement. The weight of the dome is taken by a thick collar formed around its perimeter that rests directly on the undisturbed soil around the edge of the digester.

The reservoir pit is made from brick or stone masonry. The gas is taken out from the centre of the dome, via a pipe which is supported by a small masonry turret. Access to the digester pit during building, and also if the pit needs cleaning, is through the slurry reservoir and outlet. (*Note*: For safety, no-one should enter a digester pit until every trace of biogas and slurry have been removed and flushed out, as it is possible to be suffocated by any biogas left in the pit.)

The gas pressure inside a dome plant can be as high as 1200mm of water and can exert a force of several tonnes upwards from under the dome. A mass of soil, about one metre deep, is placed over the dome to hold it down. Some of the Chinese versions have a man-hole in the centre of the dome, to allow the digester to be emptied easily: a concrete plug is sealed in the man-hole with thick clay which is kept moist with a pool of water. The plug must be held in place against the gas pressure with heavy rocks. If the plug leaks gas, bubbles can be seen in the pool above it.

PRAD in India also have a version of the 'Chinese design', called the *Janata* (people's) plant.[15] They claim it is much cheaper than the drum design, but gas leakage through the dome seems to be a problem.

5.6 Practical aspects of the dome design

At least 10,000 plants have been built to various versions of this design in China, but most have been of poor quality. The average lifetime has been less than five years. While the cost of the plant can be covered in less than this time, through the saving of other fuels and the sale of fertiliser,[16] a failed plant in the back garden brings loss of face and embarrassment to the owners. A biogas plant is not a throw-away item of consumer technology. The present approach in China puts emphasis on high quality, despite higher costs. The oldest Chinese plants have lasted 50 years, so long-lasting plants do have potential in China.

Over 1,100 plants have been made to the Nepal version of this design and surveys have shown few problems. However, masons need more careful training to make this design than the drum plants, especially in the shaping of the mud mould for the dome and in making a gas-tight plaster seal inside it. The few plants that did fail in Nepal had faults caused by poor workmanship, such as the use of stale cement. Minor design changes made the shape of the plant easier to measure and check. The owner of one plant put slurry in the digester before the dome had been covered with soil. The dome rose out of the ground with the pressure of gas inside it. Once the slurry had been removed, the dome was put back in place, the cracks plastered over and the plant worked as well as any other.

The main problem with the dome design is that concrete and brick masonry are porous to biogas unless they are very carefully sealed. The Chinese biogas manufacturers mainly use a cement and lime plaster inside the dome,[13] although polymer-based paints such as vinyl emulsion are also recommended.[17,18] Coatings that are dissolved in a volatile solvent, such as chlor-rubber, epoxy and polyurethane paints, cannot be used in the enclosed space inside a digester, as the fumes are toxic, both to the painters and the methanogenic bacteria. Many paints cannot be applied until the inside of the dome is completely free of moisture.

In Nepal, the best coating was found to be an acrylic plastic emulsion mixed into a thin cement plaster applied to the inside of the dome. The cement provides strength, while the polymer paint fills in the pores in the plaster. The emulsion is water based, so there is no toxicity problem and the plaster layer can (and should) be applied over damp concrete. Acrylic emulsion is the most stable of the polymer paints (more so than vinyl), so this coating should have a long lifetime. The first plant built in Nepal using this technique is seven years old and is still working well.

5.7   Extended dome design

An adaptation of the basic dome design was developed by DCS in Nepal for larger plants.[19] The extended dome design looks like a tunnel closed at either end with half a dome (Fig. 5.6). The reservoir pit is usually dug first and lined with brick or stone masonry. The roof of the plant is then cast over steel moulds to give the correct shape. Excavation of large volumes of soil ($50m^3$ or more) through the slurry outlet was considered too time-consuming. If steel moulds are not available the digester pit can be covered with wooden boards and a mud mould made on top for the roof. The same system is used to make a roof over the slurry reservoir (Appendix I).

More than 18 plants to this design have been made in Nepal (most of $50m^3$ volume) and they work well. The manufacture and transport of the steel moulds is expensive, but the cost can be spread over several plants if they are made in the same area. Consideration has been given to the use of 'permanent formwork' sections made from lightweight, fibre-reinforced cement. These act as forms for the casting of the dome and are left in place. The insides of these sections are plastered with cement mortar mixed with acrylic emulsion as usual.

50

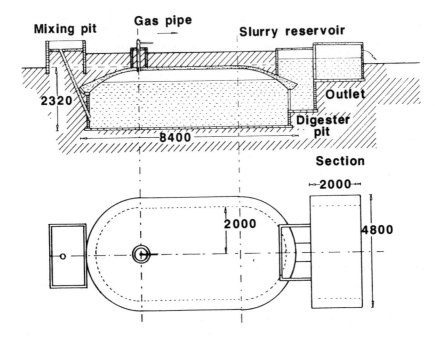

Figure 5.6 *Extended dome design of biogas plant*

5.8 Flexible bag digesters

The flexible bag digester was developed in Taiwan in the 1960s and is now creating interest in mainland China.[20,21] The original design uses a long cylindrical bag (shaped like a sausage) made of plastic, supported in a trench lined with masonry, concrete or compacted sand or mud. The slurry fills the lower two-thirds portion of the bag and the gas collects above it. As the biogas is used the bag collapses, like a balloon being emptied of air (Fig. 5.7.).

A variant uses a masonry or concrete-lined trench to contain the slurry, with a flexible tent-like roof. The edges of the roof are held down to the edges of the trench with clips or poles passing through loops in the plastic. This tent design has been exhaustively tested at Cornell University in USA.[22] It has been built for farmers in the Ivory Coast and is becoming more popular in Taiwan.[23]

The tunnel plant, which has been made and tested by DCS in Nepal, could be considered a version of the bag digester. It has a roof made of concrete arch pieces, lined with plastic sheeting. The gas storage system uses the displacement principle so the plastic lining is kept inflated against the concrete roof.

51

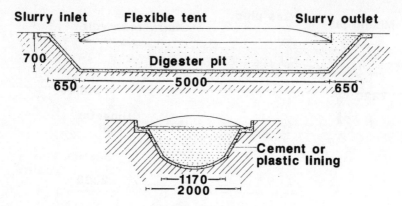

Figure 5.7 *Flexible tent design of biogas plant*

5.9 Practical aspects of the bag design

Over 2,000 bag digesters have been made in Taiwan, where manufacturers are selling bags and tents ready-made for installation in a trench. The original material used for this design was a nylon-reinforced neoprene rubber, but this proved expensive and did not last. The present success of the design depends on a new material: red mud plastic (RMP), a polyvinyl chloride (PVC) plastic which uses a byproduct from aluminium refining as a filler. It is a very strong and flexible material which is resistant to sunlight. The manufacturers claim a ten-year life-time.

Only six tunnel digesters have been made in Nepal for customers. They all work well, but the builders reported difficulties with the PVC lining. The black PVC lining used is stiff and brittle and the workers were afraid of cracking or puncturing it as it was put into the digester and fastened to the roof.

PVC, especially the RMP version, can be welded using a high-frequency, electronic plastic-welding machine. This is easy to use, once the operator has learnt the basic procedures. Manufacture of the bags or tents is similar to making fabric tents and other goods. Transport of the made-up parts is easy, as they are light and can be rolled to take up little space. If the bag is punctured a patch can be glued on, using PVC glue.

The main problem with bag digesters seems to be the removal of gas. A flexible PVC pipe coupling can be welded into the top of the bag or tent, but it must be capable of moving with the bag as it inflates and deflates. DCS had problems with sealing the connection between the gas pipe and the plastic lining of the tunnel plants, even though the plastic did not move. A fixed pipe can be fitted that passes through the bag underneath the surface of the slurry, where a seal is easier to make. However, this introduces extra problems: the bag or tent can rub on this pipe when it deflates. In addition, slurry can easily enter this pipe and block it.[22]

5.10 Choice of plant design

The choice of design for a biogas programme depends on the cost of making the different designs in the locality. While an RMP bag or tent digester may be the cheapest design available in Taiwan, where they are made, transport costs may increase their price in other places (such as Thailand) to the point where other designs are cheaper.[23]

In Nepal the drum design was the most expensive, with the equivalent dome design costing about 25 per cent less. The price of a tunnel plant was even lower (about 64 per cent of the equivalent drum plant). A similar calculation for Thailand makes the tunnel plant more expensive than an equivalent dome plant;[23] illustrating the need to calculate the costs of different designs in the place where they are to be made. The cost of a bag digester in Nepal made from RMP would be relatively high, even if DCS were able to import one from Taiwan. Indian and Nepali import restrictions cause problems with the purchase of many materials from other countries.

A second consideration is the lifetime of the different plants. It is better for a farmer to spend more on a design that is longer-lasting, as a biogas plant is a substantial structure, than one which is cheaper, but has a shorter life. Loan schemes should reflect this emphasis, offering larger loans with longer pay-back periods (five to ten years). Unless a steel drum is regularly cleaned and painted, its life-time can be short (about eight years in India).[8] A steel drum can easily be replaced without affecting the rest of the plant, but it is a major extra expense (about one-third of the cost of a new plant).

The life-time of bag digesters has not been carefully studied. If they are well looked after and protected from damage, the manufacturer's claim of ten years is probably justified. On a typical village site, where there are small boys with sticks, goats with sharp hooves, pigeons that peck and other sources of damage, it is doubtful that an unprotected bag would last long. In Nepal, an experiment with a polythene tent over a gas plant lasted less than a week. In Brazil, bag digesters quickly fell from favour with customers because of the risk of damage.[24]

The life-time of a well designed, properly-made dome digester should be over twenty years, although the acrylic/plaster seal might need renewal after ten years. Some of the early Chinese biogas plants have lasted fifty years.

The gas pressures from the three designs of digester are different. The displacement principle means that a dome digester produces gas pressures up to 1000mm water gauge (the height of water in a pipe the pressure will support) or more, although it varies (down to about 200mm water) as gas is used. This high gas pressure did not seem to cause owners in Nepal any problems when using biogas with conventional stoves, lights or engines. Many people prefer the higher pressures as they have a greater degree of control over the gas flow. Higher pressures also allow smaller pipes to be used in gas supply lines.

Drum digesters produce a fixed pressure, calculated by dividing the drum weight by its surface area ($1kg/m^2=1mm$ water pressure). A drum is usually designed to give a pressure of 100mm water, although the pressure can be increased by placing weights on the drum. No problems were encountered in Nepal with running biogas appliances with these pressures, apart from one gas light brought from China. It had been designed for use with displacement digesters, so did not work with biogas at lower pressures.

The pressures from bag and tent digesters are inherently low, unless weights are placed on the bags. The weights must be placed on a smooth plank in a way that does not allow the plastic sheet to be punctured. Care must be taken when designing the slurry inlet and outlet pipes for these digesters, to ensure that they are long enough, otherwise, slurry may come out of them when the gas pressure is increased. These plants can be used to supply biogas engines without the use of weights, as gas is drawn into the carburettor by suction.

Biogas plants do have to be cleaned, especially if woody material, such as straw, is added to them. Plants that are fed with vegetable wastes may need to be cleaned once or twice a year. If only dung is used and care is taken to remove most pieces of straw and other indigestible matter, a plant could be run for five years without cleaning. A floating drum can easily be removed from its digester to allow cleaning (unless it is made of ferro-cement). Tent digesters are also very easy to clean, as the plastic cover can be removed. Bag digesters can be more difficult, although solid matter can be washed out and dried deposits can be broken up by flexing the outside of the plastic film. Dome digesters are the most difficult to clean, as access is through a small opening in the slurry outlet or in the roof of the dome (in most of the Chinese dome designs).

The issue of stirring the slurry in rural digesters has concerned many designers. High-rate digesters do work better if they are stirred, but the gains in gas production from using a stirrer in rural digesters do not justify the extra cost. Steel drums usually contain stirrer bars, although only the surface of the slurry can be stirred in this way. Their main job is to break up any scum that may form on the surface.

Displacement digesters seem to suffer less from scum. The constant movement of the slurry surface in and out of the dome reduces the tendency for scum to form. Many of the early DCS dome digesters had scum breakers fitted, but owners did not find much benefit from their use. The motion of the slurry also ensures it is well mixed. Scum formation can be a problem in bag and tent digesters, as they have a larger surface area to the slurry, which is fairly stagnant. One design of digester, which used a concrete 'bag' but which worked on a similar principle, suffered very badly from scum.[25]

In cold climates the insulation and heating of biogas digesters has to be considered. Drum digesters are very difficult to insulate, as the steel drum allows heat to escape. Some community plants in India have been enclosed in a plastic 'greenhouse' that improves solar heating and reduces heat loss;[26] but this is an expensive approach. Dome digesters can easily be insulated by placing a thick layer of straw on top. Storing straw or haystack over the roof of the digester during the winter should be recommended to owners. Bag and tent digesters could be covered with straw in a similar way, although the straw would tend to move as the plastic inflated and deflated.

5.11 Plant sizes

All these biogas plant designs are available in a range of sizes, chosen to supply gas for different purposes. The smallest units have a working volume of between $5m^3$ and $10m^3$ and supply between $1m^3$ and $2m^3$ of biogas each day from 8kg to 12kg of dry feed (40kg to 60 kg of wet cattle or pig dung). If dung is the main feed, this amount can be obtained from four to eight animals. $2m^3$ of gas is considered to be the amount required by a family of four to eight people each day for cooking.

In Nepal, the smallest drum plant (SD100) had a working volume of $7.1m^3$ (Table 5.1). For a drum plant, the working volume is the capacity of the digester pit. The plant produced enough gas in the summer (ambient temperatures between 30°C and 40°C) to run two cooking burners and two lights for a family (five to eight people). This plant had a retention time of 59 days. In the winter when gas production was reduced (temperatures down to 18°C), some owners complained of a lack of gas.

The working volume of a dome plant is more difficult to determine, as some of the slurry moves in and out of the digester. One definition is the volume of the 'permanent' slurry plus half the volume of the gas storage dome. A simple mathematical simulation of the average amount of slurry that is producing gas over a whole day confirms this assumption. DCS took account of the fact that owners need to have sufficient gas during the winter and made the smallest dome plant with a total volume of $10m^3$ (giving a working volume of $9m^3$ and a retention time of 75 days).

The working volume of a bag or tent digester is the amount of slurry that it will hold. This is normally about two-thirds of the total internal volume of a bag; or the total volume of the trench of a tent digester. The mechanism for gas production is slightly different for 'plug-flow' reactors, which are not stirred. The populations of bacteria in the slurry vary along the length of the trench. The facultative bacteria are most active near the inlet end, while the methanogens predominate in a section from around the centre towards the outlet. The plug-flow principle is somewhat more efficient than a stirred reactor and should produce 15 per cent to 20 per cent more gas from the same input of feed with the same retention time.[27]

The tunnel digester is not a plug-flow reactor as the displacement principle for gas storage produces horizontal mixing in the slurry. Experiments in Nepal suggest that the gas production from drum, dome and tunnel digesters is very close, within the limits that can be accurately measured.

Table 5.1   Characteristics of plant designs used in Nepal

Plant Type	Digester vol. m^3	Storage vol. m^3	Work vol. m^3	Dry feed kg/day	Retention time day	Gas Production m^3/day		
						20°C	25°C	30°C
SD100	7.1	1.7	7.1	12	59	1.3	1.7	2.9
SD200	13.0	3.4	13.0	24	54	2.5	3.4	5.7
SD350	24.0	6.0	24.0	42	58	4.5	6.0	10.2
SD500	34.0	8.5	34.0	60	57	6.4	8.5	14.5
CP10	7.3	3.3	9.0	12	75	1.4	1.9	3.1
CP15	9.7	5.6	12.5	18	69	2.1	2.7	4.5
CP20	14.1	5.6	16.9	24	70	2.8	3.7	6.1
EP50	39.9	14.6	47.2	60	78	7.4	9.4	15.5
EP65	51.1	19.3	60.7	80	76	9.7	12.5	20.6
EP95	73.5	28.5	87.7	120	73	14.3	18.5	30.6

Notes: The feed is assumed to have a TS of 10 per cent.
The gas production is calculated using a model (Appendix IV)

Larger sized plants ($30m^3$ working volume and upwards) are required to provide enough fuel for engines. A SD500 plant, or its equivalent, should run a 3kW engine (5HP) for seven hours a day on 40kg to 60kg dry feed (250kg to 300kg wet dung from twenty to thirty animals), at summer temperatures (above 30°C).

While the largest drum plant made in Nepal was the SD500 (working volume $34m^3$), much larger plants have been made in India, up to the equivalent of SD1500 (working volume $100m^3$). A major problem with these larger plants is the transport and installation of the drums. Such a drum can be carried to the site in pieces and welded with a portable welding machine, but it would still need a crane or a large gang of labourers to lift it up and lower it on to the digester pit.

56

The largest dome plant that can easily be made has an internal volume of $20m^3$ (CP20 with a working volume of $17m^3$). The extended dome design can be built with a working volume of $80m^3$, or even larger. The transport problem is much reduced, as there are no large components. Bag and tent digesters can be made to any size. A typical large-volume bag plant has a total volume of $100m^3$, but tent plants have been made with a working volume of $540m^3$.[22]

5.12   Site selection for biogas plants

Biogas salesmen and technicians who are responsible for installing plants need to be trained to select the right sites. The soil must be of good quality; if it is loose and sandy or water-logged, the digester pit may collapse while it is being dug. However, the Chinese do have a special spherical design that can be used in these conditions. If the ground is hard and rocky excavation will be time consuming and expensive.

There are several other factors that affect the choice of site, such as the length of the gas pipeline as gas pipe is expensive; and the distance dung and other feedstocks have to be carried. There must be room not only for the plant, but also for the mixing pit and slurry storage pits to be dug. If trees are too near the digester roots may grow into it and crack the walls. The digester must be at least 15m away from any drinking water source, in case of contamination.

The plant should be in a warm place, if possible. A location that is sheltered from the wind and heated by the sun is ideal. Finally, the site must be away from places that can be flooded, as flood water can dilute the slurry and damage the plant. A typical site plan is shown in Fig. 5.8.[27]

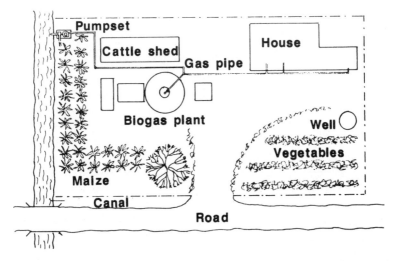

Figure 5.8 *Typical site plan for a biogas plant*

In China farmers are encouraged to link latrines to biogas plants.[14] Human night-soil has a high nitrogen content, so it improves the fertiliser value of the effluent. In many cases, where the C:N ratio of the feed is high, the extra nitrogen from night-soil will improve gas production.

The latrine can be connected to the digester using a second feed pipe between the pan and the pit. This approach has several disadvantages. The latrine floor must be at least 0.3 metres above the slurry outlet to avoid flooding, which usually means that access to the latrine is up a flight of steps. The night-soil is not broken up and mixed in the digester pit, so its digestion is poor. There is a risk of excess water entering the pit when the latrine is flushed or cleaned. An alternative approach is to connect the outlet of the pan to a settling pit. The solids can be pumped out of the pit with a slurry screw pump and the excess liquids allowed to drain into a gravel-filled soaking pit. However, this approach has not yet been tested in practice.

CHAPTER 6
Ancillary Equipment

Although the plant is the major part of a biogas system, it cannot exist by itself. A biogas plant must be fed, usually daily, with suitable feed, spent slurry must be removed and the biogas taken to where it is required. Suitable equipment must be provided to allow customers to use the gas, either in domestic appliances, such as stoves and lights, or in engines that drive useful machinery.

In Nepal and India a biogas plant is usually supplied as a 'package', which includes the appropriate ancillary equipment to fulfill the task for which it was purchased. When Chinese peasants were responsible for setting up their own plants, they usually had to make their own stoves and lights, often of poor quality and low efficiency. The present emphasis on higher standards means that designs for more efficient and reliable stoves are becoming available.[1]

6.1 Slurry handling

The feedstock must be mixed with water into a smooth slurry before it is put into the digester. The bacteria cannot easily reach foodstuffs at the centre of lumps of animal dung or vegetable matter. A masonry pit is usually provided at the entrance of the slurry inlet pipe, where this mixing can be done. A plug, made of wood or concrete, is used to close the pipe until the feed is ready.

In Nepal and India cattle dung is usually mixed with water by hand. This is a culturally acceptable practice, as a cow is a holy animal to a Hindu, but it is not recommended on health grounds. Animal dung often contains intestinal parasites, such as amoeba and giadia. A simple hand-mixing tool, shaped like a hoe with a blade made of wire mesh, was designed by DCS (Fig. 6.1) for use in Nepal.[2] It worked well, but was not for some reason popular with customers.

Larger biogas plants in Nepal and India use a mixing machine (Fig. 6.2), designed by KVIC, based on a machine used to break up pulp for paper making. It consists of an elliptical masonry trough with a paddle-wheel beater set in it. A coarse sieve removes straw and other fibrous material. The machine works fairly well and is popular, despite its tendency to splash slurry over the operator.[2]

59

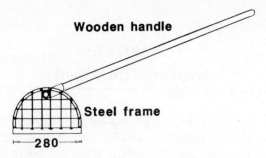

Figure 6.1 *Hand tool for mixing slurry in inlet pit*

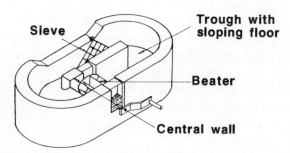

Figure 6.2 *Machine for mixing feed slurry*

Vegetable matter needs to be chopped up before being compressed into a biogas plant. It is best fed to the surface of the slurry, rather than to a position close to the floor of the digester, as is common with plants fed mainly on dung. A plunger can be used to push vegetable matter down the inlet pipe.[3] One suggestion, not yet tried, is to use a screw pump, similar to a large-scale domestic food mincer, both to chop fibres and to push them into a digester.

The effluent slurry is usually stored in shallow pits until it can be removed, usually for use on the fields as a fertiliser. The pits are usually left unlined, unless the soil is of poor quality, when walls can be made from masonry. The size of the pits depends on the daily output from the plant and the number of days for which slurry is to be stored. Deep pits are not recommended, as slurry then cannot dry effectively. They are also a danger to animals and children.

6.2 Gas piping

Pipes must be used to convey the biogas produced in the plant to where it is used. These pipes are often laid underground to be out of the way and also for protection. Biogas contains moisture which condenses in the gas pipes and must be removed, or it blocks the gas flow. The pipes should be laid so they slope towards one or more drain points (Fig. 6.3). The slope should be at least 1:100.

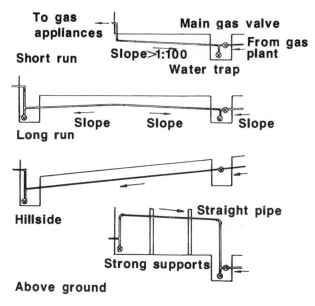

Figure 6.3 *Location of drain points in typical gas lines*

Galvanised steel gas pipe (GI pipe) is often used, as it is resistent to the corrosive effects of biogas, but it is expensive. It comes in straight lengths (2 metres) that are joined by screwing the threaded ends into sockets. Different types of fittings are available. The screwed joints must be sealed

Table 6.1 Pipe lengths used with drum plants

	Flow rate (litre/min)				
Maximum pipe length (m)	10	20	30	40	50
Gas pipe sizes					
16mm ID (½in. GI)	73	31	12	–	–
21mm ID (¾in. GI)	215	107	71	26	16
27mm ID (1in. GI)	589	294	196	100	59
35mm ID (1½in. GI)	1665	832	555	416	237

Note: Pressure drop is 10mm WG (water guage) in 60mm WG.

with paint or putty, with the help of a filler, such as string. Special tools are required to thread the pipes and to bend them.

Plastic pipe, made from HDPE (high density polyethylene) or PVC (polyvinyl chloride) can also be used. Low-quality plastic piping is not suitable as it can crack and leak gas. Plastic pipe is usually available in long rolls and joints can be made by heat welding. Pipe fittings are also available, which are pushed into the ends of the pipe after it has been softened by heating. Plastic pipe is more easily damaged than GI, but is often cheaper. It should be protected from sunlight if used above ground, and from sharp stones and heavy weights if used underground. A layer of sand around the pipe (about 300mm round) will protect it from damage by rodents (mice, rats, porcupines) which may gnaw it. Tools for heating and welding the pipe are required.

The size of pipe required in any installation depends on the length of the pipeline, the volume flow rate of the gas and the permissible pressure drop along the pipe. The pressure drop is caused by the friction of the gas flowing along the pipe and can easily be calculated (Appendix II). The gas pressure from a drum plant is low (40mm to 80mm water gauge) so only a small pressure drop is acceptable (10mm WG; Table 6.1). The higher pressure from a displacement digester (100mm to 1200mm WG) means a larger pressure drop can be allowed (50mm WG; Table 6.2), so longer lengths of smaller, cheaper pipe can be used.

Table 6.2   Pipe lengths used with dome plants

	Gas/flow rate (litre/min)				
Maximum pipe length (m)	10	20	30	40	50
Gas pipe sizes					
16mm ID (½in. GI)	361	54	60	33	22
21mm ID (¾in. GI)	1073	536	254	130	81
27mm ID (1in. GI)	2932	1466	977	497	295

Note: Pressure drop is 50mm WG in 100mm WG.

The maximum gas flow can be found by adding the gas consumption from all the appliances served by the pipe (Table 6.3). The pipe length is measured from the gas plant to the point the pipe divides to the different places where gas is used. In a simple system allowance can be made for pressure lost in gas fittings by adding 5 per cent extra to the length. The correct gas pipe size to use can be read from these tables or by using Appendix II.

Different water traps can be used to catch the water that condenses in the pipe. The simplest is a short length of pipe in a 'T' fitting at the lowest point of the line. A simple tap can be used to release water when required. Deeper pipe lines must be fitted with a 'U' tube and bucket arrangement to catch the water condensed in the pipe (see Appendix II).

Table 6.3 Gas consumption of various appliances at 75mm WG.

Biogas appliance	Biogas consumption (75mm WG)		
	litre/min	m³/hour	ft³/hour
Gas lamp (per mantle)	2.4	0.14	5
Refrigerator burner	2.4	0.14	5
Domestic burners (stoves)	4 to 15	0.2 to 0.9	8 to 32
Commercial burners	20 to 50	1 to 3	40 to 100
Dual fuel engines (per kW)	9	0.56	20
Spark engines (per kW)	11.5	0.7	26

6.3 Gas valves

Valves are used to turn the gas supply on and off. A main gas valve is needed near the plant, as well as gas taps for each appliance. Water taps (globe valves) are not suitable, as they require fluid pressure to lift the washer. Gate valves can be used, with a metal 'gate' that is pushed into a slot by a rotating spindle (Figure 6.4), but they are not reliable. Users can over-tighten and break them and the gate wears out and leaks.

Plug cocks, or quarter-turn gas taps (Figure 6.4), work well at low pressures. The tapered plug has a slot in it that can be aligned with the pipe. The plug can wear and become loose in the body, but a spring can be used to keep the fit tight. This design tends to leak when used with the higher pressures from displacement digester.[2]

The best design of tap is the ball valve (Fig. 6.4). This uses a ball with a hole in it, which can be aligned with the pipe. Round seals press against the ball and prevent gas leaks. This type of valve tends to be more expensive, as the ball is usually made from stainless steel.

Accessories for biogas systems, such as valves, need to be made from materials that are resistant to corrosion. Unprotected steel quickly rusts if it is used with biogas. Galvanised steel can be used, if the zinc coating is not rubbed off. Stainless steel is good, but expensive and difficult to machine. Brass is a suitable material, as long as the lead content is low (1 per cent). Plastic and aluminium are resistant to biogas, but are not usually strong enough to stand hard usage.

Casting is a quick and cheap way of making large numbers of small items, but it must be of good quality. A poor casting can be porous to biogas. Metal-to-metal seals are unreliable at higher pressures. Rubber or plastic seals such as 'O' rings are more reliable, as long as the metal parts are accurately made.

There are many other designs of gas taps available. Several designs were made and tested by DCS.[2] A biogas programme needs to find good valve

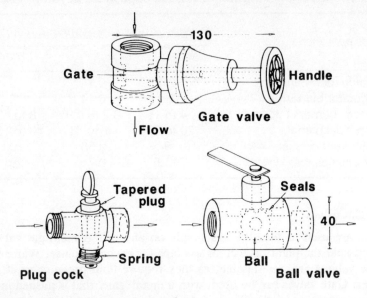

Figure 6.4 *Different types of gas valve.*

designs, as well as suitable manufacturers to ensure sufficient numbers are available.

6.4 Biogas stoves

There are many different designs of biogas stove available. Several manufacturers in India, such as Patel Gas Crafters (Pvt) in Bombay, are supplying stoves to the KVIC and other biogas programmes. The Chinese government has issued a set of standards for stoves made in China to ensure better quality ones are available for their programme.[1] A biogas stove was designed in DCS, which is now manufactured and sold by the

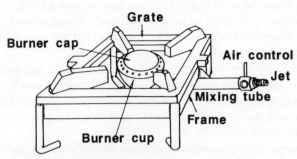

Figure 6.5 *Biogas stove designed in DCS.*

64

Gobar Gas Company for the Nepal biogas programme.[2] It works well and is about 55 per cent efficient, similar to the best of the Indian designs.

The DCS stove (Fig. 6.5) illustrates the different aspects of a stove that have to be considered when it is being designed (Appendix II) or when different stove designs are compared. A burner mixes gas and air in the correct proportions and feeds the mixture to a burner head, which supports the flame under the vessel to be heated. The flow of gas into the burner is controlled by the size of the main jet, as well as the gas pressure. Most stoves are designed for a standard pressure of 75mm WG, the pressure from a drum plant. The most popular size of domestic burners uses about 450l of gas per hour, at this pressure, giving a heat output of 9680kJ per hour. This would heat 1 litre of water from 20°C to boiling point in about four minutes, assuming a 55 per cent efficiency.

The 'primary' air supply that is drawn in by the jet is controlled by an air control. This can be opened or closed down, to adjust the efficiency of the burner. A 'lazy' flame, with reduced air supply, is easier to light and the flame can then be adjusted by opening the air supply to give maximum heat, once a pot has been placed on the stove. The mixing is done in the pipe that leads to the burner ports; the length of the pipe should be about ten times its diameter.

The burner ports are usually arranged in a circle, so that the underside of a pot is evenly heated. Free circulation must be allowed for the 'secondary' air that the flame requires and for combustion products to flow away from the flame. The cap containing the burner ports must be easy to clean, in case food and grease are spilled on it.

The distance between the burner ports and the bottom of the pot is important. If the pot is too low, the flame is 'quenched' and burns inefficiently. If the pot is too high, much of the heat is lost. The frame and grate of the stove must be carefully designed to ensure this height is correct. The DCS stove has a cast-iron grate that can be inverted for use with either round-bottomed or flat-bottomed pans, as both shapes are used in Nepal. The frame must be stable, so it does not wobble or fall over when food is being stirred during cooking.

Some stoves are supplied with a gas tap attached, while others use a gas tap fixed to the supply pipe at the wall. Usually a rubber tube is used to connect the stove to the supply. A wall-mounted tap is much safer, as it can be turned off if the rubber pipe pulls away or splits.

A much larger prototype biogas was also designed and made in DCS, which uses a 450l/hr burner at the centre, with a 900l/hr burner around it.[4] The two burners have separate jets and supply pipes, so can be operated independently to give good control over cooking large amounts of food.

Over 4,000 stoves to the DCS 450l/hr design have been made and sold in Nepal. The production from Patel Gas Crafters and other manufacturers in India is much larger. These stoves are now well-established technology, although they are still fairly expensive, as they are usually made of a metal such as cast iron. Ceramic stove designs are also being made, although most are at a prototype stage, such as the one made at Reading University (Appendix II).[5]

An alternative approach adopted in China is to use a simple biogas burner in the grate of a traditional wood-burning stove. While the burner is less efficient than a well-designed biogas stove, much less heat is lost, as it is absorbed by the thick mud walls of the wood stove.

6.5   Biogas lights

Where there is no electricity, as in most parts of rural Nepal and many parts of India and China, biogas can be used to give light. While biogas lights are inefficient, expensive and need regular servicing, they give as good a light as a kerosene pressure lamp and are easier to use. A gas lamp gives the same illumination as a 40 to 60W electric light bulb and uses between 90l and 180l of gas an hour.

Different designs of biogas light are also available from manufacturers in India and China. The Indian designs are usually made mainly of metal, such as cast iron, brass, aluminium and enamelled steel, and are fairly expensive. The designs available from China are often made mainly of ceramic and are much cheaper. These designs are less reliable, however, and can be difficult to use.

An example of an Indian-made lamp (Fig. 6.6) can be used to illustrate how a biogas-powered lamp works. It uses incandescent mantles which glow brightly when heated. The gas supply is controlled by the size of the main jet and by the control valve. The Indian jet is of brass (it is made of glass in the Chinese lamp), with a steel needle partially closing it to adjust the gas flow. The primary air is drawn into a 'venturi', a tapered tube in which the gas and air mix. The air supply can be controlled by means of an

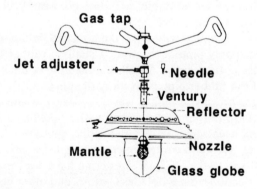

Figure 6.6 *Biogas light (made in India)*

air control or by moving the gas jet to the best position within the venturi (as in lamps made in China). The flame is supported on a 'nozzle', usually made of ceramic. This nozzle is usually composed of one main flame port, surrounded with a ring of much smaller ports, which give the flame stability (Appendix II).

The mantle is held around the nozzle in the hottest part of the flame. The mantle is made of a silk mesh soaked in a solution of rare earth salts (thorium and cerium).[6] When the mantle is first lit the silk burns away leaving a fragile matrix of these salts, which glow brightly in the flame. The flame must be carefully adjusted to give the best light. A 'reflector' above the mantle deflects the heat and burnt gases away from the air inlet and controls.

A glass shield (or globe) is usually supplied with many Indian-made lamps, to protect the mantle from draughts and insects. The mantle is very fragile and breaks if the lamp is knocked or if an insect flies into it. New mantles are fairly cheap. The most common problem with biogas lights is a blocked venturi. Insects make webs in the pipe, which collect dirt. The webs are easy to clean out, although the mantle is usually broken while it is being done.

6.6 Supply of ancillary equipment

Suppliers of these items of ancillary equipment must be found for a biogas programme. Suitable prototype designs must be purchased from manufacturers already making them or made by the programme technicians if suitable manufacturers are not already available. These prototypes should then be thoroughly tested. Manufacturers and suppliers must be found for the best designs, so that sufficient numbers will be available as required.

KVIC licenses manufacturers and suppliers of mixing machines, valves, stove and lights to supply the biogas programme in India. The Gobar Gas Company in Nepal either purchases these items from suitable suppliers in India or manufactures them in its own workshops. As the demand for higher standards for biogas equipment grew in China, entrepreneurs in several production brigades started making improved versions of the simple items that villagers had been making for themselves. The supply and use of these better designs of ancillary equipment (such as the Beijing-4 stove) is now being encouraged by biogas agencies in China.[1]

Using of local workshops to make biogas equipment encourages the growth of local businesses, although mechanics and fitters from the workshops may need to be properly trained to ensure good-quality workmanship. Careful inspection and quality control of these items is important to ensure that the biogas systems built by the extension programme continue to work well.

CHAPTER 7
Biogas in Engines

Biogas is a 'high-grade' fuel, because it burns at a fairly high temperature. Biogas can therefore be used for purposes other than just cooking and lighting, such as a fuel for running internal combustion engines for small-scale cottage industries.

Development depends partly on energy; people who want a more advanced life-style than is available in a village tend to move to places where energy is available. These are usually areas such as main towns and cities, as energy is produced by large power stations, based on central supplies of coal, oil or natural gas. Electric lines and gas pipes are easy to install in factories and houses that are close together. It is much more expensive to supply the same sort of energy to villages that are widely scattered and distant from population centres.

Biogas offers a decentralised power supply. The energy is created in the villages, where the animals are kept and crops grown and harvested. Biogas can be used to supply energy for cottage industries in the villages themselves, so catalysing development away from the towns. Village people can begin to consider a slightly more advanced standard of living, as they become able to earn money in the place where they are already living. Biogas technology offers the rural areas of developing countries the possibility of increased self-sufficiency and reduced dependence upon supplies from the towns.

7.1 Running engines on biogas

Biogas is commonly used in dual-fuel engines; converted diesel engines in which biogas is introduced into the cylinder with the air supply. A small amount of diesel (about 20 per cent) is still required to ignite the mixture. Lubrication oil is also required, but the running costs of the engine are lower and the amount of diesel fuel that needs to be transported out to the village is reduced, compared to an engine that runs on diesel alone.

There are two types of internal combustion engine: the 'Otto' (the petrol or gasoline) engine and the 'diesel' engine. The Otto engine uses a spark to ignite the fuel, while the diesel cycle relies on the fuel being ignited by the high pressure and temperature in the engine, as the air is compressed (Fig. 7.1.). Biogas can only be used in four-stroke engines, as two-stroke engines rely on oil mixed with a liquid fuel for lubrication.

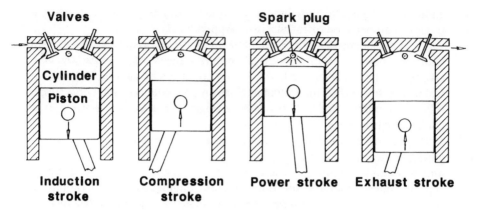

Figure 7.1 *4-stroke cycle for diesel (Otto) engine*

Biogas can be used directly in Otto engines, but it is not commonly done. Biogas is used inefficiently in such an engine, because of the low compression ratio (7:1 to 9:1) and it produces only 60 per cent of the power available when the engine is run on petrol (gasoline).[1,2] Hydrogen sulphide is burnt to sulphur dioxide in the engine and this tends to corrode the exhaust valves and manifold.

When biogas is used in a dual-fuel engine, based on the diesel cycle, the much higher compression ratio (14:1 to 21:1) means that the fuel is used more efficiently. The power loss is just 20 per cent of diesel-only operation, at full power. At other power levels there is little difference.[3] There seems to be much less corrosion in a dual-fuel engine, probably due to its far heavier construction. An advantage of the dual-fuel approach is that the engine can run on diesel alone if supplies of biogas are inadequate.

A third alternative is to adapt a diesel engine to work on an Otto cycle, by replacing the diesel injector by a spark plug.[4] This type of engine has the advantages of the high compression ratio, good efficiency and heavy construction associated with a dual-fuel engine, but no supplies of diesel are necessary. Such a conversion requires good engineering skills. As well as a mounting for the spark plug, the engine must be fitted with a small generator, a spark-timing and distributor system and a storage battery. This type of engine cannot be run on other fuels if the biogas supply is limited.

7.2 Practical aspects of biogas in engines

There are many dual-fuel systems running in China, India and Nepal. The Kirloskar Oil Engine Company in Pune, India, manufactures a series of dual-fuel engines (2kW upwards) that are designed for village use.[5] They have a relatively low compression ratio (17:1) and run at 1500rpm at normal load. The Gobar Gas Company has installed over 40 of these engines in Nepal and they have proved fairly reliable. They use a simple mixing chamber type of carburettor (Appendix II).

Other diesel engines can be adapted for dual-fuel operation. A Japanese Yanmar engine was fitted with a venturi type of carburettor by DCS (Appendix II). This engine had a higher compression ratio (23:1) and ran faster (2000rpm) than the Indian engines and it would not run with a simple mixing chamber. The key to adapting engines in this way is the correct choice of carburettor.[6]

Maya farms in the Philippines use Japanese spark-ignition car engines to generate electricity and to supply the power needs of their food-growing and processing complex.[1] Their system appears to work well, although reports suggest that the life-time of these engines is limited (about six months of continuous running). The system is only economic because the farm is able to obtain second-hand engines very cheaply from Japan.

Dual-fuel and spark-adapted diesel engines appear to have much longer lifetime when used with biogas (over five years). A dual-fuel engine is started on diesel and the gas valve is opened once the engine is running smoothly. The engine governor automatically closes the diesel control valve until the engine runs at the set speed, keeping the diesel:gas ratio to about 1:5. If too much gas is supplied the engine will begin to misfire.

Dual-fuel and spark-adapted engines run at a higher temperature when

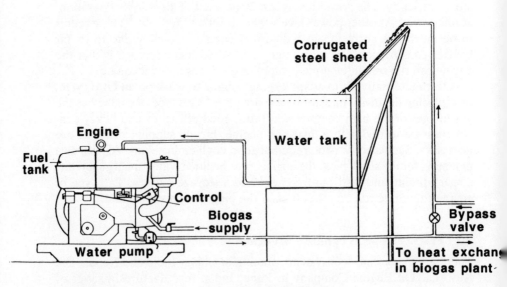

Figure 7.2 *Cooling system for a dual-fuel engine*

70

used with biogas, so the cooling system must be more effective. A circulation system is needed for cooling, such as the use of a water bleed from the outlet of an irrigation pump. If other machinery is being used a thermosyphon system may be used, with a water reservoir above and to the side of the engine, or a small water pump may be needed to circulate water through a radiator.

The hot cooling water from an engine can be pumped around a heat exchanger in the slurry pit, to warm the slurry to improve gas production. A by-pass valve and a water cooler must also be provided, to allow both the engine and biogas plant temperatures to be set correctly (Fig. 7.2).

If the use of engines is to be made part of a biogas programme then villagers must be trained to operate and maintain the engines that they buy. There must be trained mechanics available to visit the villages to service the engines and to make repairs. Most failures of engines in rural situations have simple causes. Operators forget to top-up or change the engine oil; bolts shake loose, allowing parts to crack or gaskets to blow; filters are not changed in time or are left out. If villagers are trained to recognise these simple faults and to put them right, engines should last much longer.

7.3 Use of engines in villages

The most popular use of a biogas-fuelled engine in Nepal is for food processing. People are usually willing to pay to have rice hulled, or maize, wheat and millet ground into flour: owners of rural mills can make a good living. The most profitable activity is the expelling of oil from mustard, sesame and other oil seeds. Hand milling is a very labour-intensive and time-consuming activity and machine milling is much more efficient. Up to 50 per cent more oil can be pressed from mustard seed with a good machine than is possible with simple hand tools.

A typical small mill, designed for these tasks, can use a 5kW dual-fuel engine using gas from an SD500 or ED50 biogas plant for five hours a day. The different milling tasks tend to be seasonal, so the engine would run one machine at a time, depending on the main task to be done. If cattle dung is used to run such a mill, the dung from thirty animals is required. Such a system could hull 750kg of paddy per day or process 450kg of flour or 150kg of oil seed. Several such systems have been installed in Nepal and India both for individual entrepreneurs and for groups of farmers.

The engine and milling machinery must be properly installed. It should be mounted on strong concrete foundations with wood or rubber mountings to absorb vibrations. Traditional mills in many countries use flat belt drives, which are inefficient and dangerous. 'V' belts are to be recommended. Again, operators must be trained to look after and maintain

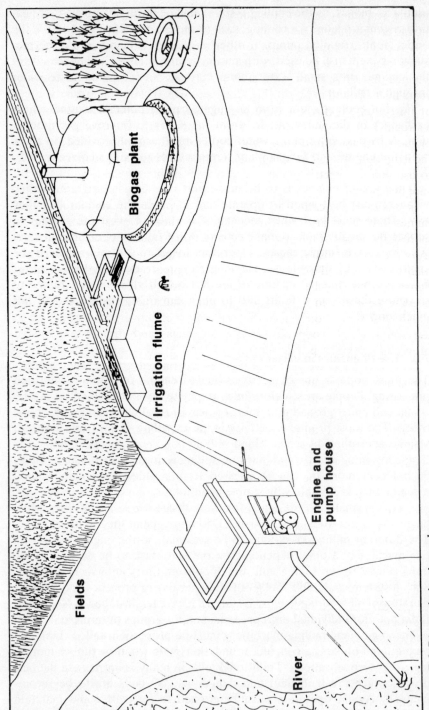

Figure 7.3 Biogas irrigation scheme

milling machinery and well-trained technicians must be available in the biogas programme to follow up systems that have been installed.

A second use for engines is to drive irrigation pumps. Kirloskar sells a series of dual-fuel pump-sets, using centrifugal pumps matched to the engines that drive them. One such system has been running for over six years near Birgunj in Nepal (Fig. 7.3). An SD500 plant, fed from the dung of thirty buffalo, fuels a 4kW engine that pumps $700m^3$ of water from a stream 3.3m below, when used seven hours a day. The effluent from the biogas plant is fed into the irrigation flume and is washed to the fields by the irrigation water. The owner claims it is much cheaper and more reliable to use than an electric pump that is also available, as the local electricity supply is poor.

In this case, the cattle sheds, biogas plant, pump, stream and irrigation flumes have been arranged to be close together. In other places, one or more components of a biogas-fuelled irrigation system may be some distance from the rest. Feedstocks may need to be carried some distance to feed the plant; gas may need to be piped along a long pipe; a new canal or irrigation flume may need to be built. In many situations wells or bore holes may need to be made to exploit underground water tables. Advice must be sought from irrigation specialists on the most effective ways to obtain and use water. Close cooperation between biogas and irrigation extension programmes should prove fruitful.

Biogas engines have also been used to generate electricity. Many production teams in China have set up their own small (3kW to 15kW) biogas-fuelled generators to provide power for lights, radios, cassette players and even televisions.[7] It is much more efficient to use electricity for lighting than gas. 700 litres of biogas can generate 1kW.h of electricity to run sixteen 60Watt light bulbs; the same gas can only run five biogas lights for an hour.

Electricity generation must be regarded as a luxury, though, as it is uneconomic unless the power can be sold to hotels or government offices which are willing to pay for it. Apart from lighting and supplying power for electronic equipment, biogas can be used much more efficiently to give direct heat or mechanical power via a suitable engine, than if it were used to generate electricity to do the same job.

7.4 Biogas used in cottage industries

Biogas can also be used in cottage industries that require heat. Several such industries have been considered, such as making soap from vegetable oils and caustic soda, extracting medicinal oils such as menthol, making jam and other preserves and roasting coffee beans, but few have been set up. In Nepal a cheese plant was built by the Swiss Association for Technical Assistance (SATA), that was to be powered by a mixture of solar energy and biogas.[8]

The Pauwa cheese plant was at an altitude of 1800 metres in the Himalayas. Solar heaters preheated the water which was then made into steam in a biogas boiler. The biogas plants, also heated with solar energy, were fed with dung from pigs that were fed on the whey from the cheese plant. Local farmers supplied the milk and also owned the pigs. This approach proved very expensive. Ill-health among the pigs has been a recurring problem and the antibiotics used to cure them has resulted in poor biogas production.

Ideally, the cattle that provide the milk to process into cheese would also provide enough dung to give biogas to process the milk. However, the Dairy Development Corporation in Nepal tend to build centralised cheese plants that can process 1000*l* of milk a day. If such a plant were run on biogas the dung from 150 cattle would be required. While farmers are willing to carry milk to the cheese plant each day (often an hour's walk) they would not carry dung that far.

If biogas is to be used in this type of village industry a different approach must be used. Several very small processing units (such as cheese plants processing 100 or 200*l* of milk together with a biogas plant) should be sold or rented to farmers, who do the processing themselves. A central office would supervise the farmers and offer quality control, marketing and maintenance facilities. This approach, of using a service centre to help village-based industries and workshops, has proved successful in other contexts.[9]

The potential of biogas in a range of cottage industrial activities is immense. To realise this potential biogas programmes need to be linked to other rural development programmes in order to share expertise. The experience and skills to develop biogas-based rural industries already exist in organisations such as KVIC in India, ADB/N in Nepal and in many communes in China, as they are involved in a range of other rural development programmes alongside their work with biogas. All that is needed is a willingness on the part of specialists in the different programmes to discuss ideas together and to discover how biogas can be used as a rural energy resource within these other programmes.

7.5 Industrial uses of biogas

One of the earliest uses of anaerobic digestion was in the reduction of the pollution load of municipal wastes such as sewage. The scale of municipal plants is usually much larger than most rural digesters and the technology is well established. The Indian biogas programme was inspired by the building of such a plant in Bombay in the 1930s. Most builders of municipal waste digesters rely on specialists in the subject, but scientists from biogas extension programmes may be asked for advice. DCS was asked to build a nightsoil digester to cope with waste from latrines in a local jail in Nepal. The biogas programme in China, especially, has been involved in building small urban digesters.

Many industries, too, are concerned to reduce the pollutants produced by the waste products of their processes. Agro-industrial and other food-processing concerns are potential users of anaerobic digesters. The Maya farm complex in the Philippines[1] is run as an agro-industry using biogas as the main source of fuel for all its processes. A brewery in the Sichuan province of China digests all its waste products and uses the biogas produced to generate 340kW of electricity and to supply heating fuel.[7]. It also runs a small fleet of lorries on biogas, although the costs of the compressor and the storage cylinders required proved fairly high. If gas is to be stored under pressure the hydrogen sulphide and carbon dioxide needs to be removed by scrubbing, which also adds to the cost. Normally, biogas is used in engines without being scrubbed.

If some of the staff of a biogas extension programme are to become involved in municipal or industrial waste digesters, then they will need to study designs for medium- and high-rate digesters. Several new technologies have been developed for these types of waste, which are often more dilute than rural biogas feedstocks (less than 4 per cent total solids). Details of these technologies, for example the anaerobic filter and sludge blanket digesters, are available.[10] The application of these technologies to the needs of different industries offers many challenges to researchers in the biogas field.

CHAPTER 8
Operating a Biogas System

Once individual farmers or groups of farmers have had a biogas plant built, they need to be taught how to use both the plant and the equipment that was purchased with it. The technicians from the biogas programme need to visit new owners to train them in the use of their technology. Further follow-up visits in the first year of operation give the owner confidence in his equipment and allow the technicians an opportunity to put right any fault.[1]

8.1 Starting a digester

Most new owners will need advice on and help with starting their continuous digester, once it is complete. The digester pit (of a drum, dome or bag design) should be filled with digestible feedstock within as short a time as possible (usually within a week). Feedstuff can be collected before and while the digester is being built, but it must not be allowed to dry out. If cattle dung is used as the main feed the digestion process should start by itself within a few weeks (depending on temperature). If other feedstocks are used, such as pig or other animal dung, or vegetable matter, a starter is required. Between 5 per cent and 30 per cent by volume of effluent slurry from a working biogas plant should be mixed with the new feed. The more the starter, the faster the digestion process will start.[2] A starter can also be used to speed up the initial operation of cattle-dung digesters, especially if the temperature is low.

The feedstuffs should be mixed with water to give a total solids content of between 8 per cent and 12 per cent. The TS can be measured (see Appendix III) or it can be estimated from the slurry consistency. It should be as thick as possible, like a thick lentil soup, while allowing it to flow down the inlet pipe. Vegetable matter should be chopped as small as possible and any fibrous material, such as stalks, should be removed. Sawdust, rice husk, moss and pond weed tend to float on the surface of the slurry and cause scum, so they should be avoided.

The new feed can be put in a drum plant before the drum is placed on top. If this type of plant has a central wall, both sides of the wall must be filled equally, otherwise the wall might collapse. The gas outlet valves on dome and bag plants should be left open to allow air and initial gases to escape. They should not be overfilled; the reservoir pit of a dome plant should only just have its floor covered.

Once a plant is full of slurry it should be left until gas formation starts. The gas valves can be closed and the gas storage volume allowed to fill up. A floating drum will rise up out of the slurry until gas escapes under its sides. A full dome plant or bag is indicated by bubbles coming from the slurry outlet. The first two or three plant-fulls of gas must be allowed to escape into the air. While it is probably mainly composed of carbon dioxide, which will not burn, it also contains the air that was present in the plant while it was being filled. If enough methane were present it could form an explosive mixture with this air. For the same reason, all pipework must be flushed with gas before any light is applied to gas appliances. The gas can be detected by its 'bad eggs' smell.

The main tasks required to keep the digester running, after it has successfully started, are to feed it with the correct amount of mixed slurry each day (see Table 8.1) and to remove the water from the gas-line traps each week. It is important to be consistent in feeding a biogas plant. Sudden changes in feeding practice can unsettle the bacteria and cause reductions in gas production. If a change in the amount of daily feed or in the slurry consistency is to be made it should be done slowly, a bit at a time. It does seem possible, however, to reduce the feed to a plant, when less gas is required, and to add the stored feedstock when more gas is needed, as long as the changes are made slowly.

Table 8.1 Recommended feed for different biogas plants.

Plant type	Work. vol. m^3	Retn. time day	1:1 Mix			1:½ Mix		
			Dung kg	Water lit	Gas m^3	Dung kg	Water lit	Gas m^3
SD100	7.1	59	60	60	1.7	80	40	2.3
SD200	13.0	54	120	120	3.4	160	80	4.5
SD350	24.3	58	210	210	6.0	280	140	8.0
SD500	34.0	57	300	300	8.5	400	200	11.4
CP10	9.0	75	60	60	1.9	80	40	2.5
CP15	12.5	71	120	120	2.7	120	60	3.6
CP20	16.9	73	120	120	3.7	160	80	4.9
EP50	42.5	71	300	300	9.4	400	200	12.6
EP80	74.1	74	500	500	15.5	670	330	20.7
EP95	81.1	68	600	600	18.5	800	400	24.7

Notes: The daily gas production is calculated from a theory based on data from Nepalese trials (Appendix IV)[3]

In some cases, especially in plug-flow digesters, it is helpful to add effluent slurry (10 per cent to 30 per cent) to the daily feed, in place of the equivalent volume of water. This replaces some of the bacteria removed from the plant with the effluent.

8.2 Control of temperature

Since both the rate of gas production and the gas production efficiency are reduced at lower temperatures (less than 30°C), attention should be given to methods of insulating and heating biogas plants where the ambient temperature is low. While rural biogas plants in the tropics and sub-tropical areas of the world are seldom heated, records suggest that soil temperatures can drop during winter months (to 20°C in the plains of Nepal). In colder climates soil temperatures can go below freezing point, so the heating of biogas plants is essential in these places.

Dome and bag plants can be insulated and heated by covering them with a layer of composting straw and other vegetable matter. The compost heap needs to be more than 1m thick and raw cow dung and biogas plant effluent can be added. Facultative bacteria can produce heat by hydrolising food materials in the presence of oxygen. The compost must be kept slightly damp, but not too wet, to produce the right rate of heating. In rainy weather it should be covered with a plastic sheet.

Steel drum plants are more difficult to insulate. A woven straw mat may be made to cover the drum, although it would be wetted by the slurry. The whole plant can be enclosed in a plastic tent, like a greenhouse[4], but this is expensive and unlikely to last long.

The slurry temperature can be reduced if cold water is used to mix the input. The mixing water can be left in the sun for a few hours, in a black-painted drum, or else the slurry can be solar heated after it is mixed. If the slurry is held in a shallow mixing pit (about 70mm deep), which is covered by a plastic sheet during the hottest part of the day, its temperature can rise by as much as 9°C (4.5°C on a cloudy day).

The cooling water from an engine can also be used to heat a biogas plant (Fig. 8.1). A heat exchanger for an SD500 biogas plant was made from 10 metres of 35mm OD pipe. Water at 70°C was pumped round it at 1.2l/min. The heat exchanger was placed in the bottom of the digester pit, so that convective flow in the slurry would circulate the heat. Extra heat can be obtained from the engine by making another heat exchanger to absorb heat from the exhaust gases. Tests indicated that the heat available from such a system was adequate to heat the biogas plant: in warmer weather, it was excessive and a system for cooling the water had to be devised (see Chapter 7).

If the biogas is used for purposes other than fuelling engines, a separate heating unit and pump and required if the plant is to be run in cold weather. Where electricity is available, a domestic-type water heater and

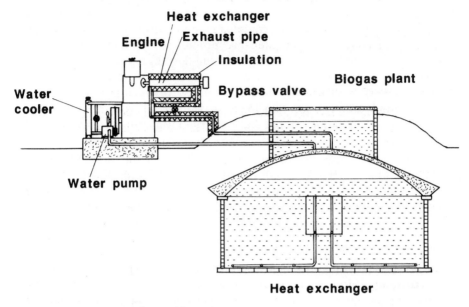

Figure 8.1 *Heating plant with engine water*

pump can be used, suitably adapted for biogas (by changing the size of the main jet and air ports). Domestic sensors and control valves can be used to regulate the water and slurry temperatures. If the plant is well insulated, about one-third of the gas production may be required to keep the slurry temperature between 30°C and 35°C at ambient temperatures below freezing.

A self-actuating steam displacement pump was developed at Leicester Polytechnic in Britain.[5] This can be used both to heat and pump water using a fuel gas such as biogas. As a pump it is not efficient, but the waste heat goes to heat the water, so the overall efficiency of the pump/heater is good. A secondary boiler, controlled by simple pressure-actuated control valves, can be used to ensure water and slurry temperatures are regulated.

If a biogas plant is being heated by any of these methods, more effective insulation than a compost or straw covering may be required. Blocks of polystyrene foam are fairly rigid and can be incorporated into the walls and roof of dome, extended dome and tent digesters. The tent plant tested at Cornell University was insulated in this way and produced plenty of gas even when covered with snow.[6]

8.3 Stirring biogas digesters

Stirring digester slurry has two functions: the breaking up of surface scum and the agitation of the bulk of the liquid to assist bacteria to reach foodstuffs. Designers of high-rate digesters put a lot of emphasis on stir-ring, as methanogenic bacteria move very slowly. The value of bulk stirring for low-rate rural digesters is questionable, especially as they are expensive to make and give extra maintenance problems. Bag and tent digesters should not be stirred at all, as they are plug-flow digesters.

Gas drums of floating drum digesters usually have scum-breaker bars fitted inside them. The drum should be rotated for about five minutes each day to break up any scum that might be forming. This rotation will also cause a mild agitation of the bulk slurry. Displacement digesters are effectively self-stirring, since the slurry moves in and out of the slurry reservoir as gas is produced and used. Any scum on the slurry surface will be broken up as it moves within the domed roof. DCS did put stirrers into the first dome digesters made in Nepal, but owners saw little value in using them. They often broke and they caused a few gas leaks.

8.4 Solving digester problems

Biogas plants should have few problems if they are well made and run correctly. Most problems are caused by faults in construction, which should be discovered during the final inspection before a plant is filled or during the initial follow-up visit by programme technicians. Construction faults, such as cracks in digester walls, are the responsibility of the organisa-tion building the plant and must be put right at its expense.

The most common fault in biogas digesters is gas leaks, either from the gas pipeline, especially around valves, or from the gas storage volume. All the joints in a gas pipeline should be checked before it is finally buried. Gas should be put in the line, usually from the plant once it starts working. Soap solution is then brushed around the joints and gas leaks show up as bubbles. Plastic pipe can be cracked where it goes round sharp corners and it can be cut or broken by ploughs and hoes or by animals and machines passing over it, so it must be carefully checked and protected where these things are likely to happen (see Appendix II).

Steel gas drums can leak gas through porous or cracked welds or through holes caused by corrosion. Small holes can be sealed with epoxy glue, but larger holes may need to be rewelded. Large areas of corrosion mean that the whole drum must be replaced. If the fault is due to bad workmanship, then the construction organisation must put it right at its expense. Some faults can arise from the owner's neglect: welds can crack if the drum is dropped and corrosion will occur if the paint is scratched. New owners need to be warned of the dangers of mishandling their drums.

Dome plants can leak gas through the dome, if it has not been properly plastered and sealed. Cracks or rough patches of plaster may be visible during the final inspection, but plaster leaks are not always easy to see. If a dome plant appears to produce little gas, despite careful checks that the

80

pipeline is leak-tight and the slurry is producing gas, then the plant will have to be emptied and the plastering redone. The use of acrylic plastic emulsion mixed with the final plaster layer improves its sealing properties.

Bag and tent digesters can leak gas through cracks or tears in the plastic. Small holes in PVC and RMP can be repaired by gluing patches over them with PVC solution, preferably on the inside of the digester. Larger tears may need to have a patch welded over them, using a high-frequency electronic welding machine. While the removal of the plastic cover from a tent digester is not a major job, a bag digester would need to be completely emptied and cleaned out before it could be welded.

A less serious problem is the leakage of slurry through the walls and floor of the digester pit, which can occur if the lining is porous to water. Poor quality bricks or cracks in cement mortar linings can cause leaks, especially in the reservoir pits of dome plants. Small leaks are often self-sealing, as the slurry dries within them. If leakage continues the plant must be emptied and the inside replastered with a good cement mortar.

Another cause of a sudden loss of gas supply is a blockage in the gas pipeline. As biogas flows through relatively cool pipes underground, water condenses out and can stop the flow if arrangements for its removal have not been made. All gas pipelines should slope (1:100) towards one or more water traps, from where condensate can periodically be removed.

Blockages can also occur in the gas outlets from dome, bag or tent digesters, if slurry, scum or froth enters this pipe. Dome plants can be overfilled if gas production is low or gas usage is high, so the dome never gets more than half full of gas. A screw top is often provided in the gas outlet, which can be removed to allow a rod to be pushed in to clear blockages. Care must be taken when cleaning the gas outlet of a dome plant as slurry can be ejected from the pipe under the relatively high gas pressure.

8.5 Microbiological problems

If the biogas plant is free from leaks and blockages a loss of gas production may be due to a failure of the bacteria in the digester. If the causes of these faults are to be fully tested the facilities of a small laboratory are required. Measurements of the parameters of slurries will need to be made and samples of slurry tested in small-scale temperature-controlled reactors to see if they are producing the expected amount of biogas (see Appendix III).

If a new digester fails to start at all, then the correct bacterial population may not be present. If the slurry temperature is reasonable (between 20°C and 35°C), the first response is to leave the plant, without feeding it, for another week or two. If gas is still not being produced, then a starter can be added: 10 per cent to 30 per cent of slurry from a working digester. If the contents of the plant have become acidic (if the pH is below 6.5), then chalk or lime can be added as well. Tests should be done by titrating a small sample of slurry against the chalk or lime to determine the correct amount to add.

If the plant is still not producing gas a month later, then the slurry has probably been poisoned by a toxic substance. Samples of the slurry, the original feedstock and the source of mixing water should be tested in the laboratory. Attempts can be made to digest these samples in small bench reactors, while the samples can also be analysed to try to identify the poisons. The plant will probably have to be emptied and cleaned out thoroughly before being refilled with fresh feedstock, starter and water, all from sources that have been checked for freedom from contamination.

Problems with plant start-up are more likely to be encountered if unconventional feedstocks are used, such as different vegetable materials or food-process waste. Laboratory tests of the digestibility of these feedstocks should be made before they are used in full-scale plants. Some of these feedstocks may be more easily digested if a plant is started on animal dung and the new feedstock introduced with the dung in gradually increasing concentrations.

If a plant that has been working well suddenly fails the most likely reason is poisoning by toxic substances.[7] Sudden changes in temperature, feed rate or feed composition may cause a temporary reduction in gas production, but the plant should recover within a week or two, especially if the change is slowly corrected. A reduction in feed rate will help the bacterial population to stablise. A plant that is poisoned will fail and not recover. The pH will probably drop and the slurry will accumulate noxious-smelling fatty acids.

The source of the poison should be identified before the plant is restarted. Possible sources are: animals being given antibiotics, chemical sprays used on crops or in animal houses against insect pests or fungal infections, disinfectants being washed into the digester or pollutants in the water used to mix the slurry. Chlorinated hydrocarbons, found in many solvents, are particularly toxic to methanogens and could cause contamination by being spilled into rivers or irrigation canals. Heavy metal salts, such as copper, zinc, lead or nickel are toxic in high concentrations, such as may be found in wastes from some industrial processes like galvanising.

Attempts can be made to restart the plant, by adding chalk or lime to correct the pH and by adding a starter to provide the correct bacteria. However, if the poisons are still present in the plant it may not restart and the whole plant will have to be emptied, cleaned out and filled with slurry that is free from contamination.

This type of problem is not usual; it occurs less than once a year among the 2,000 plants that are being followed-up regularly in Nepal. It is more likely where the use of chemicals such as pesticides and fungicides is more

82

common, as in Europe and USA. The poisoning of a biogas plant is also more likely if a latrine is attached. People who are taking medicines may use the latrine, or even throw excess medicine into it. People may also use disinfectants to clean a latrine or throw water containing detergents or solvents into it. Plant owners should be warned of these dangers.

8.6 Servicing of biogas plants

Apart from the removal of dried effluent slurry from places where it tends to build up, there is little regular servicing necessary on most biogas plants. Gas valves should be oiled monthly to keep them from getting stiff.

Steel drums should be painted each year to prevent rust. The gas supply should be turned off for 24 hours, so the drum fills up and rises in the slurry. It should be carefully washed of dried slurry before a new coat of paint is applied. The same paint should be used as was applied during manufacture (usually a bituminous paint, such as high-build black). The paint needs to be dry before the supply valve is opened and the drum allowed to sink again.

Surface scum may build up in a digester, especially if the feeds contain straw or other vegetable matter. Animal hair and grease from dung can accumulate over several years. Mud and sand can also be introduced into the plant with the feed. They accumulate below the inlet pipe and reduce the digester volume. The interval between cleanings depends very much on the type of feed. Many Chinese plant owners use a lot of vegetable matter in their feed and clean their plants every six months to a year. Most Indian and Nepali owners do not clean out their plants for five years or longer.

Dome and bag plants will need to be emptied completely to remove both scum and dirt accumulation. The gas holders of drum and tent plants can be removed to allow access to surface scum, but they, too, will need to be emptied completely if dirt accumulation is to be removed. Great care must be taken during cleaning operations as biogas will escape. No naked flames or lighted cigarettes must be nearby, as there will be a risk of explosion.

When a biogas plant is emptied all the slurry should be removed from the digester pit before anyone attempts to enter, as it will continue to produce biogas. Removal can be done with a bucket on a rope, or a slurry pump can be used. The slurry can be stored in a pit in the ground or carried directly for use on the fields as fertiliser. Up to 30 per cent may be used as a starter to get the plant working again with a new feed, if the old slurry has not been poisoned.

Biogas is not poisonous, but it does not contain oxygen, so it can suffocate anyone trying to breath it. Biogas is heavier than air so it can remain in the digester pit even after the slurry has been removed. As biogas cannot be seen it is difficult to tell when it is safe to enter the pit. An animal (a rabbit or a chicken) can be lowered into the empty pit in a basket to see if it has difficulty in breathing. The gas can be removed by using a fan or a winnowing machine or even bailed out with a bucket. If a person goes into a digester pit a friend must always be available outside, in case of trouble. A rope can be tied around the person entering the pit, so they can quickly be pulled out if they have difficulties in breathing.

In China, some of the new biogas building teams offer a digester cleaning service.[8] They have slurry pumps and air blowers driven by small two-wheeled tractors, so the slurry and remaining biogas can be removed quickly and easily. Many farmers are prepared to pay a fee to save themselves a tedious and messy job.

8.7 Safety of biogas

Biogas will only burn if mixed with air in the right proportions (between 10:1 and 5:1, biogas: air or 9 per cent to 17 per cent biogas in air). It is safer than most other fuel gases, which have wider flammability limits. Since the pressure of the gas in the pipeline is higher than atmospheric, there is little chance of air entering the line or the gas store to form an explosive mixture. The only times that this is possible is when a biogas plant is being started or after cleaning or repair work. Extra care must be taken at these times to ensure no flames are near while the pipes are flushed with gas. Flame traps in gas lines are considered unnecessary, although they are recommended by some extension groups.

Gas leaks during operation can be detected by the smell. Owners should be taught how to recognise leaks and to take the appropriate action. If a leak occurs within a confined space, such as a building, the risk of explosion is greater. Gas taps should be closed, all fires and flames extinguished and all doors and windows opened. The leak should be found using soap solution, and repaired.

CHAPTER 9
Economics of Biogas Systems

The primary reason that biogas technology is not more widely accepted in Nepal and India is economic.[1,2] A biogas plant demands a relatively high capital investment from a small farmer and he has to be convinced that it is worth it. The economics of various different alternatives available to the farmer need to be analysed, so that the best one can be chosen.[3] Under certain conditions, a farmer might expect a higher return on his investment if he uses a different system than one using biogas, such as using a diesel mill run on diesel alone, rather than going to the extra expense of a biogas plant. Economics are not the only factors to consider when making such decisions, but they are major ones.

There are many ways to approach economic analysis, depending on the point of view from which a plant is considered and the complexities that need to be introduced. The simplest approach is to look at the cash-flow position of the owner. If a farmer, or group of farmers, has taken out a loan to buy the system, he needs to save or earn enough each year to cover the repayments and interest over each year of the loan. While this is an important calculation to do for each individual project, it is not general enough to allow a comparison of the value of a biogas project with other possibilities. A more formal approach is to use 'cost-benefit analysis'.[4] This assumes a potential owner has capital to spend (either his own or borrowed) and that he can invest that money in a biogas system or in other ways, such as putting the money in a bank to earn a commercial rate of interest.

All the costs of a project must be defined; these will include the capital costs of purchasing a plant as well as the recurring costs of running and maintaining it. The costs of a project over its lifetime are calculated by defining a cost for each year and multiplying these by discount factors, obtained using a standard formula or tables (Appendix V). The 'present worth of the costs' (PWC) is the sum of these discounted values. Discounting is an attempt to allow for inflation and other decreases in the value of project work with time. The financial benefits, from savings and/or income, also need to be defined and discounted in the same way. The 'present worth of benefit' (PWB) is the sum of the discounted figures over the project lifetime.

Three indicators are used to measure the economic results of a project. The 'benefit: cost ratio' (B:C) is the present worth of benefit divided by the present worth of costs, while the 'net present worth' (NPW) is the difference of these two values. The 'internal rate of return' (IRR) is the discount rate that must be applied to the benefits to give a PWB figure close to the PWC. It is an attempt to measure the earning power of the investment the owner made in the project. The calculation of IRR is usually done by trial and error, looking up different discount factors in the tables to multiply with the benefit figures. In order to use cost-benefit analysis, suitable values for a base discount rate and a project lifetime need to be chosen. In Nepal a discount rate of 15 per cent, spread over ten years, seemed to be reasonable.[5]

A more complex approach attempts to define the costs and benefits of a project to the society around the people who purchase biogas plants. These 'secondary' or 'social' costs and benefits must be given financial value. For example, the time employed by a family without a biogas system and by the same family with a biogas system can be estimated and costed. The value (at a suitable wage rate) of this saving on time, or the extra time required, can be included as a benefit or a cost.

Many secondary costs and benefits are very difficult to quantify.[6] For example, the use of a biogas-fuelled rice-hulling mill will save the women of a village from a very laborious job (taking perhaps an hour a day). The mechanical huller, though, may polish the rice, removing nutritious bran (with protein and vitamins), so introducing a secondary cost along with the secondary benefit of the women's time. Other secondary benefits, such as employment creation, building of community awareness, an increase in people's dignity, are very important, but very difficult to measure or to define in monetary terms.

9.1 Domestic biogas plants

There have been many economic analyses of domestic biogas plants, especially in India.[2,3,7] They all suffer from similar problems,[8] but all reach a similar conclusion: that domestic biogas is only marginally economic, especially for the owner. As in most economic analyses of rural activities, many assumptions have to be made to obtain useful figures. The accuracy of these assumptions is very difficult to test and some of the parameters, such as the cost of alternative fuels, are very variable, both with place and time of year.

If biogas is used for cooking and lighting in a rural area it replaces fuels such as firewood, crop residues and kerosene. The capital costs of building a family-sized digester can easily be defined, especially if figures are available from an on-going extension programme (see Example 9.1). The running costs are less easy to define: they include the labour required to collect and mix the dung each day and the cost of maintenance. Regular maintenance costs depend on the design of plant used: a steel drum plant needs a yearly coat of paint on the drum, while dome and bag plants have a lower yearly expense.

86

The benefits from biogas are much more difficult to define. Biogas as a fuel cannot be sold on the open market, so its value must be defined in terms of other fuels. If biogas is valued according to its replacement of commercial fuels, such as kerosene or coal, then its financial benefit is relatively high and the economics look very good.[8] However, it is usually used to replace firewood or crop residues, which have a much lower market value per kilojoule of energy produced (Appendix V).

Firewood is usually given a value related to its price on the open market (see Example 9.1). This price is very variable, as it is determined by the local pressures of supply and demand. On the plains of Nepal in the dry season, for example, the price is fairly low. There are forests within half a day's walking distance from most settlements, firewood is easy to collect (despite being illegal) and there is little other work for people to do. In the hills of Nepal, during the monsoon, the price is much higher. Deforestation has removed much of the tree cover from many hills, wood is much more difficult to collect in the rain and mud and most people are busy harvesting their maize and rice crops.

Many people who might purchase a biogas plant do not pay for fuel. They collect their firewood or crop residues themselves. The value of the fuels replaced might be calculated in terms of the labour and time required to collect them. Since most of the work of collection is done by the women and children it is difficult to place a value on their time. Some husbands may even regard the time their wives and children might save as a cost: 'You don't know what they could get up to.'[1]

The value of the fertiliser 'produced' by a biogas plant is even more difficult to define. Some analysts assume the dung would otherwise be burnt, so put a price on the total fertiliser value of the slurry.[10] Others try to assess the improvement of the fertiliser value of the slurry digested in a biogas plant and stored in pits with that of raw cattle dung stored in heaps until it is needed for the fields.[9] These assumptions depend very much on the practice of the local farmer. Some people, (especially in China) are used to composting wastes and can produce concentrations of available nitrogen close to those from anaerobic digestion.[1] Figures for the extra nitrogen available from digested slurry as compared with traditional composting techniques in China, range from 11 per cent to 100 per cent.[11] Other analysts ignore the improvement value in fertiliser completely,[5] as many farmers do not take this into account.

9.2 Milling systems

Mechanical milling of grain is becoming very popular in rural areas in most countries. The removal of the hull from grains of rice and the grinding of wheat and maize into flour using hand tools is very hard work and time consuming, so people are prepared to pay for it to be done by machine.

A CP15 biogas plant built in Butwal, Nepal in 1986 by Energy and Agro Developers (P) Ltd cost (£1 = Rs.24 Nepal Currency) as given by N.P. Pradhan, manager:

	Rs.(NC)	£
Materials (Cement, sand, bricks, gravel)	6 000	250
Fittings (Gas pipe, 2 stoves, 2 lights, mixer)	4 720	197
Labour (Skilled and unskilled)	4 050	169
Guarantee Fee	1 730	72
	16 500	688

The yearly costs for running the plant are:

Labour (1 hour a day at Rs.10 per day)	456	19
Maintenance (assumed)	100	5
	556	23

The yearly benefits are:

Saving in fuel wood (2578kg @ Rs.1)	2 578	107
Saving in kerosene (146/ @ Rs.6)	876	37
Saving in urea fertiliser (84kg @ Rs.4)	336	14
(see Appendix V)	3 790	158

Loan Repayment

Assuming 7 years' repayment and 11 per cent interest,

	Rs. (N/C)	£
Yearly cost of loan:	3 517	146
Savings each year:	3 234	135

which does not quite cover the loan repayments.

Cost: Benefit Analysis

	Rs.(NC)	£
Capital cost of CP15 plant	16 500	688
Discounted running costs (15 per cent, 10 yrs)	2 790	116
Present Worth Costs (PWC)	19 290	804
Present Worth Benefits (PWB, 15 per cent, 10 yrs)	19 021	793
Nett Present Worth (PWB − PWC)	− 269	− 11
Benefit: Cost Ratio (PWB/PWC)	0.99	
Internal Rate of Return	15%	

The economics of this biogas plant appear to be marginal.

Notes

1. 15 per cent discount rate compares with the rate of inflation in Nepal.
2. 10 years' lifetime for a dome plant is short; it should last for 20 years.
   (giving: NPW = Rs.3 743, £156, B:C = 1.19, IRR = 18%)
   The lifetime of a drum plant is less: only 5 years for the gas

holder and central guide pipes.[2] The addition of Rs.2 500 after 5 years to the costs to allow for this make the economics look much worse.
3. The results are very sensitive to the cost of firewood:[2,5]

Firewood cost Rs/kg	NPW Rs.(NC) £	B:C	IRR %
1.2	2 319 97	1.12	18
1.0	− 269 − 11	0.99	15
0.8	−2 857 − 119	0.85	11

Table 9.1 *Effect of firewood price on biogas economics.*

Example 9.1 *Economic analysis of a domestic biogas plant.*

Mechanical milling is essential if grain excess to domestic requirements is sold. Most mills are driven by diesel engines, although water power is also becoming popular in hilly areas, especially in Nepal and parts of China. A small milling system can be run on biogas, which replaces up to 80 per cent of the diesel fuel required. There are many advantages in using less diesel fuel, if a mill owner or group of farmers can find enough dung to feed a biogas plant (see Chapter 7). There is also a financial benefit, which can be analysed.

The costs and benefits from using a biogas plant for fuelling a grain mill are much easier to define than those for a domestic biogas plant. Milling is done as a service to the neighbourhood and charges are made for the work done. A biogas-fuelled milling system therefore earns a cash income for the owner. The analysis (Example 9.2) is based on data from two 5kW biogas-fuelled mills in Nepal,[5] one at Tikuligarh (see Chapter 10). These surveys were made in 1983, but the figures have been adjusted to 1986 prices (assuming 15 per cent inflation per year). The mills are owned either by a single owner or a small group of farmers who share both the work and the benefits. The income may have been understated, as mill owners are cautious of giving accurate answers, in case they may be taxed on their profits. The milling work is seasonal, but the gas produced during the times when the mill is not employed can be used for domestic purposes.

The mill is assumed to have a 5kW engine to drive two machines, a rice huller and a flour mill. The engine can only drive one machine at a time. The economics of this system look fairly good and they can also be compared with a similar mill using only diesel as fuel (Appendix V). The capital costs are much reduced for a diesel mill, only Rs.26,000 as compared with Rs.76,760 for a biogas mill, but the returns on the investment are less.

The financial returns are very sensitive to the amount of grain brought for milling, so a market survey needs to be done before such a project is set up. If there are other mills in the locality and competition brings the price for milling down, then a biogas mill may have a low return. However, if local people must take their grain some distance to get it milled they will be prepared to pay extra for the time and effort saved.

Both biogas and diesel systems look better if the volume of grain processed is increased. The mills considered in the survey were in areas where there was competition from both diesel and electric mills. Also, these mills do not use heat exchangers, so the gas production in winter is reduced, although this is the time when demand is highest. In more remote areas, without an electricity supply, and using a well-designed system (with a heat exchanger), the amount of grain processed could be higher and the financial return improved.

The conclusions of this analysis are supported by the attitude of villagers using biogas milling systems. The first one set up in Nepal (Tikuligarh) has run for seven years and the owners are still very keen on showing it off to visitors. Over forty more similar systems have been installed in Nepal (both family and group-owned),[12] despite the high capital cost, and interest seems to be growing in the idea. Greater profits can be earned from an oil-expeller, but the engine must be larger (10kW to 15kW), the mill must be sited in an area where oil-seed crops are grown and there must be a market for the oil.

9.3 Irrigation systems

In a monsoon climate, such as that of many parts of India and Nepal, crop production can be greatly increased using irrigation. During the dry season water is often available underground or in streams and rivers fed by snow melt and by springs of water from mountain aquifers. If this water can be pumped up on to villagers' fields a whole extra crop a year, such as wheat, can be grown. Also a pumped water supply allows crops grown during the monsoon season (especially early paddy and maize) to be irrigated at optimum times, especially if the rain fails to arrive as expected. Crops grown by irrigation allow food to be produced during the time of year when it is normally scarce, so it has a high market value.

A water pump can be driven by a dual-fuel engine, supplied with gas from a biogas plant, in the same way as the engines used in grain mills (see Chapter 7). The costs are similar to those for a grain mill, although the fuel use is even more seasonal, depending on when water is required for the different crops (Appendix V). The analysis (Example 9.3) is based on a survey done to study the feasibility of a community biogas irrigation system for Madhubasa village (see Chapter 10). The village is on the edge of the Terai (plains) of Nepal, near Janakpur, and underground water is available for pumping all the year round. The figures for the analysis have been adjusted to 1986 prices (assuming 15 per cent inflation per year).

An SD500 biogas plant with a 5kW engine, a rice huller and a flour mill, supplied in Butwal in 1986 would cost:

	Rs.(NC)	£
SD500 plant, with accessories	48 760	2 032
5kW dual-fuel engine (from India)	18 000	750
Rice huller (from India)	4 000	167
Flour mill (from India)	4 000	167
Heat exchanger (locally made)	2 000	82
	76 760	3 198

The yearly costs for running the mill are:

Labour to run the biogas plant	475	20
Labour to run the milling machinery	4 600	192
Maintenance for all equipment (assumed)	3 000	125
Diesel used with the biogas (20%)	2 070	86
Lubricating oil (assumed)	800	32
	10 945	456

The yearly benefits are:

Income from milling operations (App. V)	24 000	1 000
Saving from gas used domestically (App. V)	7 500	313
Saving in fertiliser (420kg @ Rs. 4)	1 120	47
	32 620	1 359

Loan Repayment

	Rs.(NC)	£

Assuming 7 years' repayment and 11 per cent interest,

Yearly cost of loan:	16 290	679
Savings each year:	21 675	903

which makes a profit of Rs.5385 (£224) per year for the owner or, alternatively, the loan could be paid off in 5 years.

Cost: Benefit Analysis

	Rs.(NC)	£
Capital cost of Project	76 760	3 198
Discounted running costs (15 per cent, 10 yrs)	54 930	2 289
Present Worth Costs (PWC)	131 690	5 487
Present Worth Benefits (PWB, 15 per cent, 10 yrs)	163 712	6 821
Nett Present Worth (PWB – PWC)	32 022	1 334
Benefit: Cost Ratio (PWB/PWC)	1.24	
Internal Rate of Return	21%	

The economics of the project look fairly good.

Notes

1. A dual-fuel engine may not last 10 years in a village depending on how it is looked after. The drum of an SD500 plant may also rust out after about 5 years, if it is not painted every year. However,

an EP50 plant should last over 20 years, offsetting the shorter lifetime of the engine.

2. The results are very sensitive to the charges made for milling.

3. The result must be compared with a diesel-only mill doing the same business (see Appendix V):
(giving: NPW = Rs.2 908, £121; B:C = 1.02; IRR = 16%)

Mill charge Rs/5kg rice	NPW Rs.(NC) £		B:C	IRR %
6.0	56 112	2 338	1.43	25.5
5.0	32 022	1 334	1.24	21
4.0	7 932	330	1.06	16.5

Table 9.2 *Effect of milling charges on biogas economics.*

Example 9.2 *Economic analysis of a biogas milling system.*

The benefits of a biogas irrigation system depend on the crops that are grown. It is assumed that without irrigation the villagers' main crop is paddy, watered by monsoon rain and limited gravity irrigation (surface water is available for several days after a good monsoon downpour). While maize, vegetables and tobacco are also grown in the village, these are ignored in the analysis, as they normally use land which is not affected by the irrigation scheme. It is assumed that the availability of irrigation water allows higher yields from the paddy crop (from 2 tonnes per hectare to 3 tonnes), as water can be supplied at optimum times. Irrigation also allows higher yielding varieties of paddy to be grown, which may be more sensitive to a lack of water at critical times. These better strains of rice usually need more fertiliser, so this is added at a cost.

The main benefit from the scheme is the extra crop of wheat, grown in the dry season (December to January). This is valued at the appropriate market rate, as it can either be sold or used to replace other food which otherwise would have to be purchased. The analysis of the system (Example 9.3) suggests that the economics should be very good, with an internal rate of return of 29 per cent. The loan could be paid back within two years. The results are sensitive to the price of grain in the local market (Table 9.3), so a market survey needs to be done to check the up-to-date prices. The economics look fairly good, even when the rainfall fails, as long as the ground-water supply remains. This analysis, too, needs to be compared with one for a diesel-only irrigation system.

The economic analysis of irrigation schemes seems to be one in which the assumptions are not always valid in practice. There have been very few studies of the effectiveness of pumped irrigation as used by peasant farmers, whether these pumps are driven by diesel, electricity or biogas. Most trials

of water use and crop productivity are done in carefully controlled agricultural centres, such as the Japanese-funded Janakpur Agricultural Development Project near Madhubasa, which provided the pump-set and gave very
valuable help and advice. Despite the apparent economic advantages of a
biogas irrigation system the villagers in Madhubasa did not appear to be
earning enough money from the sale of wheat to cover the cost of the loan
repayments. They were rescued from potential economic problems by the
decision to ask the village to set up a tree nursery. To grow well, tree
seedlings need a constant supply of small amounts of water most of the
year round. The irrigation system seems more able to supply this need, but
it does not seem capable of providing the large quantities of water required
by grain crops at critical times.

An SD500 biogas plant with a 4.5kW dual-fuel pump-set supplied in
Janakpur in 1986 would cost:

	Rs.(NC)	£
SD500 plant, with accessories	48 760	2 032
5kw dual-fuel pump-set (from Japan Project)	16 000	667
Engine shed	7 500	312
	72 260	3 011
The yearly costs for running the pump-set are:		
Labour to run the biogas plant	475	20
Labour to run the pump-set	5 000	208
Maintenance for all equipment (assumed)	3 000	125
Diesel used with the biogas (20%)	785	33
Lubricating oil (assumed)	800	33
	10 060	419
The extra costs for the extra crops are:		
Seed for new crops	2 760	115
Fertiliser for improved productivity	13 970	582
Labour for extra crops	9 230	385
	36 020	1 501
The yearly benefits are:		
Income from sale of crops (App. V)	67 700	2 822
Saving from gas used domestically (App. V)	10 265	428
Saving in fertiliser (420 kg @ Rs.4)	1 120	47
	79 085	3 296
Loan Repayment	Rs. (NC)	£
Assuming 7 years' repayment and 11% interest,		
Yearly cost of loan:	15 335	639
Savings each year:	43 065	1 794

which makes a profit of Rs.27730 (£1155) per year for the owners
or, alternatively the loan could be paid off in 2 years.

Cost: Benefit Analysis | Rs.(NC) | £

Cost: Benefit Analysis	Rs.(NC)	£
Capital cost of Project	72 260	3 011
Discounted running costs (15%, 10 yrs)	180 776	7 532
Present Worth Costs (PWC)	253 036	10 543
Present Worth Benefits (PWB, 15%, 10 yrs)	296 909	16 538
Nett Present Worth (PWB − PWC)	143 873	5 995
Benefit; Cost Ratio (PWB/PWC)	1.6	
Internal Rate of Return	29%	

The economics of the project look fairly good.

Notes
1. The remarks about lifetimes of project components in Example 9.2 also apply to this analysis.
2. The results may be compared to those for a diesel-only system irrigating the same areas of crops.
   (giving: NPW = Rs.122 120, £5088, B:C = 1.6, IRR = 29%)
3. The results are sensitive to the prices of grain in the local market (see Table 9.3)
4. The economics still look fairly good even in a drought year, where the natural rainfall is reduced (Appendix V). (where: NPW = Rs.96 190, £4008, B:C = 1.4, IRR = 25%), especially if the market price increases (eg. by 50%) (giving: NPW = Rs.239 551, £9981, B:C = 2.0, IRR = 39%

Grain price Rs/t. rice	NPW Rs.(NC)	£	B:C	IRR %
2 700	211 827	8 826	1.8	35
2 250	143 873	5 996	1.6	29
1 800	75 919	3 163	1.3	23

Table 9.3 *Effect of grain price on irrigation economics.*

Example 9.3 *Economic analysis on a biogas irrigation system*

The basic problem seems to be the amount of water supplied by the pump. The analysis assumes a 50 per cent efficiency for the pump, a fairly low figure compared to the laboratory efficiencies for typical centrifugal pumps. In practice, however, farmers often seem to use their pumps at much lower efficiencies. In Madhubasa the water flow seems to be limited to 10*l*/sec, as opposed to the theoretical flow of 46*l*/s (giving an efficiency of only 11 per cent). The flow appears to be even less in the dry season (3*l*/s).

Surveys in India suggest that many pump-sets there are also operated inefficiently (a 4.5kW engine is often used to irrigate only 2.4ha rice from a 5-metre-deep well, less than half the area suggested by this analysis).[13] Some farmers even find the use of diesel or electric pumps for irrigation results in an overall loss of income. In Nepal, despite the wide publicity for the Madhubasa community irrigation scheme (see Chapter 14), the idea has not attracted the keen interest that biogas milling has done. In contrast, one of the top businessmen in Nepal uses a biogas irrigation system on his land near Birgunj and has been impressed by its effectiveness and profitability. He can, however, afford to employ well-trained technicians and farm managers who know how to make the best use of the system.

The answer to the problem of including irrigation schemes in a biogas extension programme appears to be to link them into agricultural extension programmes, employing experienced agronomists and irrigation specialists who can advise on the best use of the water. A rotation of a wider variety of crops, ensuring a more even water demand throughout the year, allows a much more effective use of the system.[13]

9.4   Economic conclusions

Despite the many different approaches to the economics of biogas systems, a few overall conclusions can be drawn. Domestic biogas plants offer only marginal economic benefits, except where firewood prices are high. Even in this case it might be more economic for villagers to plant a firewood crop than invest in biogas.[5] The use of biogas for simple cottage industries, such as grain milling, looks much more attractive, especially in more remote areas, where there is little competition from conventional mills. There appears to be a good potential in the use of biogas to drive irrigation pumps, but very careful project design and planning is required for this potential to be realised.

A biogas programme needs to employ the services of economists, either full-time or on a consultancy basis. They would be responsible for checking the economic feasibility of particular community biogas projects, as well as monitoring the economic value of different approaches to the extension and use of biogas technology as circumstances in the programme and the country vary with time.

CHAPTER 10
Community Biogas

One of the main criticisms directed against biogas technology is that only the richer farmers can afford to use it. In Nepal and India, for example, between 10 per cent and 20 per cent of the population can afford to take a loan for a family biogas plant and to repay its cost, even with 50 per cent subsidy. The concept of community biogas is based on the idea that poorer farmers can come together and match in terms of money and lifestock what the rich can provide on their own.

This idea is based on three assumptions:

A larger biogas plant will mean that the effective cost per cubic metre of biogas is lower.

The biogas from such a plant can be used in such a way that all the people in the community will benefit from it.

The people in the community will be willing to cooperate with each other in order to share in these benefits.

These assumptions need to be tested in a real environment with real people. People tend to be self-interested and want to go their own way. They will only come together to make such a project work if they can see how each one of them can benefit from doing so.

Community plants have only been properly tested in India and Nepal. Despite the apparent attractions of the idea to a communist government, very few true community plants have been built in China.[1] In many communes there has been close cooperation in the building of individual plants: many people in a village helping each other build their own plants. There is also a growing interest in the idea of 'corporate' biogas: plants run by a specialist group on behalf of other people for a fee.[2] There appear to be no examples in China of a group of people jointly owning and successfully running a biogas plant for their mutual benefit.[1].

10.1 Community biogas in India and Nepal

The past success rate for jointly owned plants in India and Nepal has been low. Three such plants were built in 1979 by HMG, Nepal with the help of US Peace Corps volunteers. Within a year two plants had failed and the third was used by only five of the original twenty-six families for which it was built [Bulmer]. In India, between 1981 and 1983, the Indian Institute of

96

Management (IIM) cooperated with KVIC and PRAD in setting up ten community plants all over India, following a survey of two others.[3,4,5]. Not one of these plants was working as expected by early 1984. Many of the plants had over-run on cost; some were being run (at a loss) by the implementing agency as a service to the community; three were not commissioned and one had failed completely.

A careful study of the causes of failure of these different projects indicates that most of the problems lay within the implementing organisations rather than in the communities within which they worked. One major failing was in communication, both betwen the organisations and the communities and within the organisations themselves. KVIC, for example, seemed to suffer problems in communicating between its different offices and with their site supervisors.

Poor communication often led to false expectations by villagers and a rejection of the project when these expectations were not fulfilled. In PRAD, dissatisfaction within the staff resulted in changes in the management team and a lack of continuity in the projects. Poor communication within both PRAD and KVIC meant that money was not available when needed, causing long delays in obtaining materials and paying workmen. This in turn resulted in a loss of interest by both the field staff and the villagers.

Several plants had technical problems. One of the plants built in Nepal used night-soil as a feedstock, from latrines serving 300 low-caste women. The gas would not burn, because the bacterial population, without a starter, lacked methanogens and the galvanised steel gas drum rapidly corroded. The latrines proved very popular at first, so they became quickly overloaded and dirty. The two systems built by PRAD in Uttah Pradesh used several $30m^3$ dome plants. These were larger than PRAD had attempted to build previously and the plans had not been properly prepared. The site surveys had also been inadequate and the builders discovered unexpected problems: a high water table on one site and a high level of vibration from a railway line on another. These technical difficulties quickly led to disillusionment by the field staff, who felt they were poorly supported by their engineers, and rejection by the villagers.

The relationships between the implementing organisation and the village community deteriorated with time. During the planning stage, the villagers were keen to cooperate and made many promises. However, they tended to see the biogas plant as the responsibility of the aid group who were paying for it. They demanded high wages for the labouring work and high prices for supplying dung, while expecting low fees for the gas and fertiliser produced. In many cases KVIC had to bring labour and dung in from outside the village to ensure the project worked. This in turn upset the villagers, who were expecting an immediate financial benefit from the project, so they became even less cooperative.

These attitudes were the result of a wrong approach: the villagers saw the community plants as projects set up by the implementing organisations. Therefore the people felt no commitment to the projects and were not interested in their success. Their only concern was to get as much out of the project for themselves as they could.

A further root cause of these problems appeared to be a lack of will to make decisions, both within the aid groups and the villages. The promises made by villagers to the staff who came to do surveys and make plans were not based on a careful consideration of the problems involved. Instead, they tended to give the answers they thought the planners wanted to hear. Within the organisations many decisions were passed up the line to the main KVIC office in Bombay or to the main PRAD office in Lucknow. This, together with poor communication, led to the many delays.[4]

Three of the Indian plants were built for employees of institutions, who lived in housing that was supplied for them. The implementing organisations only had to deal with the representatives of the institutions (two corporate trust farms and an agricultural college), who were supplying the biogas as a service to their employees. Therefore the problems of management and organisation should have been much less than in a community, where all members were supposed to be involved in decision making. That the same delays, disagreements, false expectations and lack of decision affected these plants too,[4] confirms the impression that the main causes of failure lay within the implementing organisations.

10.2 An approach to community biogas

When DCS and ADB/N agreed jointly that the Nepal biogas programme should include community biogas they carefully considered the sociological factors involved. Several questions had to be asked.

An important question involved the motives for considering community biogas. Such programmes tend to be fashionable and often attract funding, but both fashion and money can distort otherwise well-planned programmes. The main purpose had to be to help the people with whom DCS intended to work. They had to see things from the villagers' point of view, which meant DCS staff being prepared to stay with them, sharing their language, culture and food.

A project must belong to the people for whom it is intended. This means that the villagers need to have a financial commitment to the project, as well as supplying local materials (such as sand) and labour. Poor communities do not have the capital to pay for such a project, so they must take loans. The project, therefore, must generate enough income to cover loan repayments and interest. In Nepal ADB/N made a policy decision to give a 50 per cent subsidy towards community biogas projects, but to expect the groups of farmers involved in such projects to take loans for the rest. The biogas was to be used to drive either grain mills or irrigation pumps. Careful economic analyses of such projects indicate that enough income could be earned from them to cover repayments (see Chapter 9).

The selection of the right communities with which to work is fundamental to the success of a project. The policy guidelines of the implementing and funding organisations need to be taken into account; they may direct attention to particular groups of people, such as the poor and disadvantaged. There may be geographical or environmental limitations. Implementing organisations usually require good communications which allow technical staff and visitors easy access to the project, while the poorest people are often the least accessible. In general, homogeneous communities, composed of people from the same tribe, racial group or caste, are more likely to work together than heterogeneous communities.[4]

People who have shown a cooperative spirit and who already have an interest in biogas technology are likely to have the highest motivation for such projects. When choosing an area and a community within it with which to work, advice should be sought from people already working there, such as agricultural extension agents and community health workers.

Once suitable communities have been chosen contact must be made with the people. Initial visits will be formal, but they should be low key. One person walking into a village is much less threatening than a team arriving by jeep or helicopter. Great care should be taken that the villagers are not given false expectations. They will be suspicious of a stranger asking questions and will often give misleading answers.

It is important to get to know whether a group of villagers can cooperate together before going too far with project planning with them. Questions must be asked about the village leadership, about any disputes and factions in the group and whether they have been previously involved in cooperative projects. More accurate information may be gained from neighbouring villages or local tea shops. If a village has already learnt to cooperate in building a road or a school, for example, they are more likely to be successful in a community biogas project.

The cooperative spirit of the members of a community can be tested by giving them a simple job that they must do together. They could be asked to repair a road, to allow access to the village, or to dig the first 2 metres of the digester pit. This test must be unsupervised and the group leaders should report to the implementing office when they have finished. If they do this the project can move into the next stage.

The people need to have their own decision-making mechanisms, so a management committee should be organised. This committee must have authority and be recognised by all the members of the community. It will probably include the natural leaders of the community, but representatives of the less advantaged groups, such as the women and the landless people, could also be members. While the implementors can offer advice and may have to train people in committee procedures, all the decisions about the project should be made by this committee, with the agreement of the rest of the community.

The villagers must understand all the implications of the project. Members of the committee can be taken to visit other community biogas projects; pictures and models can be used for training courses for them. This process may take several months or even years, but it should not be rushed, otherwise the villagers may not be able to cope with the project.

10.3 Small farmers' development in Nepal

DCS and ADB/N cooperated in the second community biogas programme in Nepal, starting in 1981. The Small Farmers' Development Programme (SFDP), set up by ADB/N with the guidance of the Freedom from Hunger Campaign of the Food and Agricultural Organisation (FAO), had been working in Nepal for over ten years.[6] This programme helps small farmers (with less than a fixed land holding) to organise into groups which can obtain low interest loans from ADB/N for development projects, such as the breeding of improved livestock or pumped irrigation schemes.

The SFDP had gained valuable experience in working with these small groups of farmers (four to twenty families).[7] They had experienced motivators (GO/ARFs, group organisers/action research fellows) working in several areas in Nepal. These people were often well-educated local people using this work to gain material towards a thesis for a higher degree.[8] One such motivator encouraged four families in Tikuligarh Panchayat, near Bhairahawa, to take a joint loan for a community biogas plant. The SFDP found money to offer a 50 per cent subsidy. Initially, the biogas was to be used for domestic purposes only, but they were also asked to test the use of a dual-fuel engine fuelled by biogas, driving a rice-huller.

This first project proved very successful, so several others followed. By the beginning of 1984, eight others had been built and ADB/N had found money to launch a nationwide programme. By the middle of 1986 forty of these plants were working in Nepal, most used to drive small grain mills, and they appear to be successful. Most groups contain four to twelve families, although a project encouraged by the Resource Conservation and Utilisation Project (RCUP) of USAID involved twenty-two families.[8] The main motive for starting and continuing in these projects is that the mills earn a reasonable income for the people involved.

These were 'group' biogas projects, where a 'group' is self-selecting; people only join in the project if they are interested in it. They are free to leave, once they have fulfilled their commitments to the group. DCS also decided to set up a 'village' biogas project, which would include all the people living in a small natural community. This approach is more difficult, as it may include people who are less interested in the project.

100

Also past tensions and disputes within the village are brought into the project.[5]

10.4   Case study of a group-owned biogas plant

In 1980 the SFDP manager in Manigram (on the Terai in Lumbini zone) suggested to Group Number 36 that they set up a community biogas plant. They were having problems obtaining fuel wood and they had seen a family biogas plant nearby and were interested in it. DCS was asked to make a survey of the village.[3]

Five of the houses in the village of Kusongodai, in Tikuligarh Panchayat, were very close together, so the piping of biogas to these houses would be easy. All the people in the village were Brahmins and related to each other. They traditionally worked together and had been involved in the SFDP group for several years. In 1980 they were spending about Rs1,500 per household on wood and kerosene for cooking and lighting, and expected these prices to increase. Four of the families had similar land holdings and livestock and they were keen on the project. The head of the fifth family, a respected elderly priest, disagreed. The four families had twenty-seven cattle between them, just enough to feed an SD500 biogas plant.

An SD500 biogas plant was built for the four families in 1981. SFDP provided a 50 per cent subsidy and the villagers took a loan for the rest from ADB/N. Each of the houses was supplied with two ring burners and a biogas lamp. The farmers became concerned about repaying their loan to ADB/N. Early in 1982 they were persuaded to test the use of a 4kW dual-fuel engine with a rice-huller (supplied by DCS), using biogas from their plant. After six months, when the Gobar Gas Company removed the engine, the villagers took a second loan (without subsidy) from ADB/N to buy a 5kW engine and a flour mill. They later purchased the rice huller from DCS.

The villagers have carefully organised themselves to ensure that the biogas system works fairly. Each house sends a person to bring three buckets of cattle dung each day and to help mix the slurry. The main gas valve is opened at fixed times during the day, for cooking and lighting. The mill is used whenever there is a demand for its services. In winter, when there is less gas, the villagers must use firewood for cooking the evening meal. Customers come to the village to have their grain milled towards late morning. If all the gas has been used they will run the engine on diesel alone.

The effluent slurry is collected in pits at the edge of the village. Each household has its own storage pit and fills it from the central pit. They must count the number of buckets removed to ensure each household receives the same amount.

The mill is operated by two people. The driver is hired from outside the village and is paid a fixed salary of RS.300 (£14) per month, whether he works three hours a day in the slack season or eighteen hours a day after harvest. He collects diesel from a nearby town on a bicycle (20 litres a time from 7km away). He does all the repair and maintenance work required on the mill. Staff from the Gobar Gas Company are called in if there is a problem that he cannot solve.

The cashier is one the people from the four households. He issues slips of paper to the people waiting to have their grain milled. These indicate the order in which they are to be served and how much must be paid, in money or in grain. Records are kept of these amounts. The cashier's job is taken by each household in turn. House number four holds the register of income, while house number two keeps the money and grain received. The grain is sold to people who come to buy it; a person from another house must be present during the transaction.

The villagers seem to be very satisfied with the dual role of their biogas plant. They are able to use biogas for cooking and lighting, as well as earn an income from the mill. The close cooperation between the four house-holds is motivated by the benefits they see coming from the effective operation of their biogas system. The villagers will not give exact details of their income from the mill, as they are afraid they will be taxed on it. They claim that they are earning enough income to cover the repayments on their loan. The economic analysis of a dual-fuel mill (see Chapter 9) seems to be valid.

The villagers seem to be able to compete with other mills in their area: about five diesel mills within an hour's walk of their village. Their price has been lower and local people prefer to come to a small mill, which will process small quantities, than go to a larger one, where they may have to wait. As electricity comes to the area electric mills are being set up, which charge lower prices. This may have an effect on the profitability of the Tikuligarh mill in the future.

10.5   Case study of a village-owned biogas plant

The village of Madhubasa (on the Terai in Janakpur zone) had set up their own cooperative society in 1964. The village was chosen as a place for a SFDG in 1979 (number 37). There are thirty-seven families (187 people in 1983), all of whom belong to the Magar tribe and are farmers. The Magar tribe are noted for their community spirit and in Madhubasa this is combined with a strong but open leadership (also Magar) that enables the people to join in cooperative ventures. SFDP suggested the village as a site for a community biogas project and DCS did a survey in 1980.

The village lies at the base of the foothills of the Himalayan range, between two rivers. These rivers are usually dry, but they are subject to flash flooding in the monsoons, when water runs off the hills to the north.

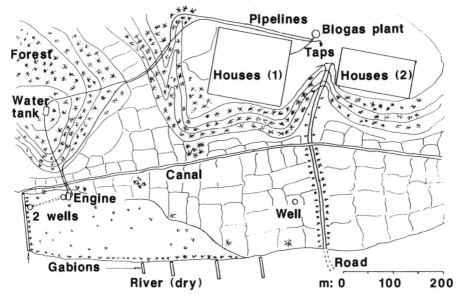

Figure 10.1 *Map of Madhubasa Project Site*

These flash floods are getting much worse, as deforestation and removal of soil cover mean that run-off is increased during rain.

The survey by DCS concentrated on the real needs of the villagers. They had little interest in domestic biogas technology: no-one in the village had seen a plant and they were close enough to the forest that fuel wood was not a problem. Their main concerns were that the flash floods were eroding their land each monsoon, and they wanted to irrigate part of their land to grow more crops. DCS decided to work in the village, with the idea of introducing a dual-fuel irrigation pump, fuelled mainly by biogas.

The land-erosion problem was urgent, so help was given to the villagers to build gabion barriers across the path of the flash floods, to deflect the water from the fields. They were taught to weave the wire baskets, using wire donated by Oxfam. Stone was brought from higher up the river with a tractor and trailer loaned by another agency. About 5.5 hectares of land were reclaimed from the riverbed. It was planted with mango and other fruit trees, to build up the soil and to provide a cash crop. This project acted as a test of the people's willingness to cooperate.

The biogas irrigation project first involved digging exploratory wells. A Japanese-funded irrigation project (JADP) became interested in the idea of biogas-fuelled irrigation pumps, so they offered much help, including expert technical advice and the loan of digging machinery. Eventually two

103

permanent wells, 80 metres apart, were constructed, connected by an underground plastic pipe.

The irrigation scheme was carefully planned. An economic feasibility study was encouraging (see Chapter 9).[9] A biogas committee was set up, the members being the office holders in the cooperative society, although no women were on this commitee. In spring 1982 six members of this committee were taken on a 'Biogas Tour'. Two of the young men of the village were sent on a course in engine operation and maintenance at JADP. The villagers were loaned a diesel engine, so they could become used to its operation.

While the biogas plant was seen as an answer to one of the villagers' felt needs, that for irrigation, other uses of the biogas were considered. The villagers wanted gas lamps, so they could hold village meetings by gas light. Two gas burners were placed in the community house, for use in making tea for meetings and for guests in the village. Irrigation is seasonal, so the gas can be used for other purposes at times of the year when water is not needed for the fields.

The Local Development Department of HMG/N had offered to pay for a drinking-water scheme, so a storage tank was built on a hill above the wells. A pump-set was chosen that could pump water up to this tank, from where it could be piped to the village. It was also able to pump irrigation water.

The site of the biogas plant was another issue. From a technical point of view the plant should have been near the pump-set, but the cattle dung would have had to be carried for 500 metres (300 or 400kg/day). The villagers wanted the biogas plant in the village, near the cattle sheds. They were also concerned about security, being as much afraid of attacks from evil spirits as of possible human interference. One of the village leaders contributed land for the plant. The gas was piped the 500 metres from the village to the pump by plastic pipe. Such a pipeline proved expensive and there were fears about the plastic being chewed by rats.

A 50 per cent subsidy for community biogas schemes is now government policy, so DCS made this available to the project. The rest of the cost had to be taken as a loan from ADB/N, and application was made in the name of SFDG number 37. Not all members of the cooperative society were members of this group; the two village leaders owned too much land to be considered as small farmers. These people would pay their contributions to the members of SFDG 37 when loan repayments had to be made.

The water was to be pumped from the wells into an existing irrigation canal that had been built to take water from the Jalad river, when it flows during the monsoon. Only twenty-two families had land in the area served by this canal. Another ten families had land in other places, while five households had no land at all. If the main benefit of the scheme came from the profit from the sale of a winter wheat crop, these fifteen families had to benefit, too.

Discussions took a year; the idea of 'gas rights', where the people using the gas paid a fee to those who did not, was rejected. Land was available for sale in the irrigated area, owned by an outsider, but no money could be found to buy it. The twenty-two land-owners were challenged about sharing their land, but the committee (ten of whom were land-owners) were not keen. After they were asked to imagine themselves in the role of those without land in the area, they agreed to lease a portion of their land on a 'Bathya' system. This traditional arrangement allows the farmer and the land owner to share the crop on a 50:50 basis. An agreement was drawn up and all parties signed it.

The biogas plant and engine shed were built in Madhubasa in 1983 and were running by early 1984. The rota system for putting cattle dung into the plant was slow to get going. The engine (purchased from JADP and adapted for dual-fuel use) runs well on biogas and is being used to pump water to the drinking water tank and for irrigating a winter wheat crop. The initial income from the sale of wheat proved disappointing: the crop yields were much lower than expected, mainly because the villagers were not used to growing wheat. However, the village has become involved in another development project: growing tree seedlings for a joint HMG/aid agency reafforestation project. Part of the water pumped for the drinking water supply is being used to irrigate these seedlings, which earn a good income for the village. There is enough money from the sale of these seedlings to repay the loan and interest as well as improving the living standard of everyone living there. Few people in the village now have to cut firewood to sell to gain extra income.

10.6 Conclusions about community biogas

While a larger biogas plant does give some economy of scale, it is insufficient to reduce the price per m^3 of biogas to that which a poor farmer can afford. Even with a 50 per cent subsidy the villagers of Tikuligarh were concerned about repaying their loan while they were only using biogas for domestic purposes. The real value of a community biogas plant comes when it is used to earn an income for the group or the village. Biogas used to fuel a dual-fuel engine offers real financial benefits, an important new dimension in the concept of community biogas.

People's commitment to a cooperative project depends on the benefit they receive from it. If the project is earning a cash income in which all the members of the community can share, they will work to keep the project going. The benefits from a domestic biogas plant are not valuable enough to offer a high incentive.

Once people discover the benefits they can gain from working together they are more likely to try other projects. Madhubasa was chosen as the village in which to set up a tree nursery because of the way in which they had worked together on the biogas scheme. Both Madhubasa and Tikuligarh are places to which other groups are brought to demonstrate the idea of community biogas. The King of Nepal visited Madhubasa in 1985, (although he only had time to look at the project from a helicopter). All these things lead to a growth in people's status and confidence in themselves.

The second factor which encouraged success in the Nepal community biogas programme was the close cooperation of SFDP and JADP. Technical expertise was readily available to train villagers in the use and maintenance of engines, the most effective use of irrigation water and the best way to grow wheat. Mechanisms were also available for giving low-interest loans and subsidies for cooperative projects, and the villagers were used to using them. They had learnt to trust the officials of ADB/N and were prepared to take the risk of a much larger debt to pay for the biogas projects. This trust had been built up over several preceding years by the GO/ARFs, who had been trained and motivated through the FAO scheme.

The experience from Nepal demonstrates that community biogas can work if the right approaches are used within the biogas programme. An effective community programme demands involvement from people with many skills. A sociologist or anthropologist is needed to choose the area and communities within which to work, to make initial contacts with people and to train and motivate them in their working together. The selection of suitable technologies with which to use biogas will involve both engineers with suitable experience and economists to consider the economic feasibility. If biogas is used for irrigation, water engineers and agronomists are needed to advise on the best ways to find, supply and use the water. The staff of the biogas extension programme will be involved in the building of the plants and their on-going follow-up. Training and follow-up are also required for the engines used in the projects. A biogas programme should have its own technicians trained in the repair and maintenance of the engines used in these projects. Help can also be sought from local agents for the engine suppliers.

In Nepal most of these skills were already available in DCS, ADB/N, SFDP and JADP. In India KVIC, PRAD and IIM neglected some of these areas, especially those of sociology, management and economics, and discovered many problems. In other biogas extension programmes arrangements need to be made to ensure that people with these skills are employed by the project or are available as consultants from other cooperating agencies.

CHAPTER 11
Biogas Research and Development

Research and development is an important aspect of a biogas programme. Biogas plant and equipment designs need to be adapted to local conditions and resources. Biogas plants are generally considered expensive, so ideas for reducing costs without reducing reliability or effectiveness need to be tested. The digestibility of different feedstocks needs to be tested, so local people can be advised as to the best ones to use. Experts need to be available who can assist the extension programme to find out the reasons for any plant failures.

11.1 Biogas research and development in India, Nepal and China

The Indian biogas programme has always had a research and development dimension. The work at IARI, Delhi,[1] inspired the setting up of the KVIC Biogas Research Centre on the outskirts of Bombay,[2] and the PRAD test centre in Ajitmal (near Etawah, U.P.) in the 1950s.[3] After 1975 several other organisations were encouraged to get involved in biogas R & D, including ASTRA,[4] part of the Indian Institute of Science in Bangalore, the TATA Energy Research Institute in Bombay,[5] the Indian Institute of Management in Ahmedabad[6] and many others.[7,8]. There are a wide range of different problems identified within the Indian biogas programme and there appears to be a growing interest in them.[9]

In Nepal, too, there has always been a close connection between biogas R & D and extension. The original HMG/N programme was planned and organised by staff of the Soil Science and Agricultural Chemistry Laboratory (part of the Department of Agriculture) at Kumaltar, near Patan.[10] The Gobar Gas Company was formed around the staff of the Biogas Project in DCS, Butwal, in 1977. DCS continued the R & D part of this project for anover seven years, offering technical back-up to the staff of the company as well as testing improved designs of biogas plants and equipment. An R & D laboratory was set up within the Gobar Gas Company in 1983, with staff trained by DCS to continue this work.

In China the Cultural Revolution in the early 1970s inspired a reaction against academics, so there was little formal R & D work on biogas until after 1978. There are now over 1,000 scientific and technical personnel involved in biogas research as the leaders of the programme attempt to catch up for lost time.[11] Before 1978, though, many peasants themselves were engaged in informal R & D, testing new ideas, especially better and cheaper designs of biogas plants. While this informal approach was inefficient and wasteful, with members of many different communes facing the same problems and making the same mistakes, it did work. Peasant farmers were able to make cheap biogas plants that produced sufficient gas to provide cooking fuel for a Chinese family.

11.2 Biogas plant development

The early Indian and Chinese approaches to biogas R & D were very different. The Indian approach started with institutions and moved via semi-government organisations to local labourers building plants for farmers. The Chinese approach started with the farmers, with research and extension organisations being formed to meet the needs of the farmers. Now, both programmes seem to be moving towards middle ways that are very similar.[12]

The Indian emphasis on institutions, meant that extension organisations took the results of the institutional R & D work without a clear understanding of their implications for the designs they were making. When local labourers started to build these designs for farmers in villages, they, in turn, did not understand what they were building or how the plants were supposed to work. A lack of effective communication between researchers, designers, builders and farmers meant that when problems occurred with new plants there was no-one available who could put them right. Also farmers were not trained in the correct use of their plants or in basic maintenance.

For example, an early Indian design used a counter-balanced gas drum,[9] to reduce the gas pressure to below atmospheric, as the R & D results suggested that reduced pressure increased gas production. A more careful examination of this result shows the extra 'biogas' was carbon dioxide coming out of solution from the slurry. This design was also very dangerous, as air could be drawn into the low pressure in the drum, making an explosive mixture. Poor communication also led to a single design (the KVIC floating drum design) being used for a wide range of different applications. There was very little flexibility in the system.

Once more research and extension organisations became involved in the biogas programme the approach became more flexible. The 'Janata' (fixed dome) plant was introduced into the extension programme (originally by PRAD) and taken up by these other organisations. Floating ferrocement drums (introduced by SERC) also became available.[13]

Poor communications with builders and owners leads to high failure rates for plants. Many biogas technicians are only taught to follow a set procedure, without being given an explanation of why the different tasks need to be done. Where conditions exist that are not normal, such as poor soil or a high water table, the technician cannot adapt his approach to suit these conditions. If farmers do not have an understanding of the biogas process they are likely to make mistakes in operating the plant, such as introducing toxic substances (antibiotics, detergents, etc.) into the digester.

Again, since voluntary organisations, such as AFPRO (Action For Food Production, New Delhi) and Gandhian groups have been involved in biogas extension,[8] much more emphasis has been placed on training local biogas technicians and farmers in basic biogas technology.

The two main 'popular' thrusts in the Chinese biogas programme, in the 1950s and 1970s, were based firmly in Chinese village communes, with peasant farmers building (and often designing) their own biogas plants. Combined with strong government propaganda, this approach meant that a large number of people gained a basic understanding of biogas technology and could attempt innovations at a local level. However, this understanding was limited and many of the early designs had basic flaws. The design used extensively in the 1950s had a rectangular gas storage volume.[14] Attempts to duplicate this design in Nepal showed that the corners of the flat roof were sites of high stress.[15] When movement of the roof occurred (as the internal gas pressure varied) the plaster seal in these corners cracked and leaked gas.

The dome-shaped gas storage volume seems to be an idea that occurred to several different people in different communes, as there are now a number of different versions of it.[16] The shapes range from a completely spherical plant to a cylindrical digester pit with shallow domes top and bottom. Theoretical analysis suggests that the best shape for the gas storage volume is a spherical segment with an internal included angle of less than 100°.[15] If the spherical segment includes an angle larger than this parts of the shell are under tension. Unreinforced concrete only shows high strength when compressed.

The materials used in the Chinese biogas plants of the 1970s were often of poor quality. During this time emphasis had been placed on rural cement plants, using local supplies of coal and limestone, but the quality of the product was very variable. A cement made from lime (calcium hydroxide) and pozzolana (such as crushed brick or burnt rice husk) was also used. This is very dense, so reduces gas leakage, but makes concretes and mortars that are much weaker than those based on conventional cement.

Once the idea of formal R & D had again become acceptable to the Chinese authorities and central biogas organisations had been established, national standards were defined for biogas plants and equipment.[11] These are issued by the National Bureau of Standards and the Ministry of Agriculture, Animal Husbandry and Fishery and are based on scientific criteria.[16] The effective implementation of these standards is ensured by training biogas technicians, incorporating them into biogas building teams and making it illegal for non-certified people to build biogas plants.[11]

The close link between R & D and extension enabled the Nepal biogas programme to avoid most of the expensive mistakes of others. DCS started their research and development work by doing detailed follow-up surveys on the first ninety-five plants built to the KVIC-style floating drum design. These surveys revealed several design weaknesses that only became obvious after the plants had been run by a farmer more than a year. For example, the flexible plastic pipe used to withdraw gas from the top of the drum had a short life-time (six to nine months) and many farmers had problems in replacing it. A different arrangement for removing the gas was designed. The high water table in the Terai of Nepal meant that much shallower pits had to be used, so the 'taper' design was made. The other major fault was that the gas drums rusted badly.

When alternative designs to the KVIC one were investigated DCS decided to use the same approach. Several innovative designs were built for farmers, such as plants with hemi-spherical ferrocement floating gas drums and a flat-roofed displacement digester.[15] An interesting design used a trapezoidal gas holder, hinged at one end to allow the other end to float up and down in the slurry. The customers were told of the experimental nature of the design and usually paid a reduced price for the plant. Unfortunately, most of these designs failed and the customers became upset. Eventually, most of the plants were replaced with conventional designs by DCS at their expense, although one owner insisted on receiving his money back.

This approach was not helpful to the reputation of biogas technology in Nepal. It is interesting, however, that one or two farmers, having seen these prototypes made of cement, wanted similar plants for themselves, despite knowing that the prototypes were not working. They instinctively trusted concrete rather than steel and were convinced that the biogas research group could make them work eventually. A test site was set up where new prototype designs could be built and thoroughly tested before field tests were undertaken. The Nepali version of the fixed dome design was first built on the test site and various systems tested for making a gas-tight seal over the gas dome, before the acrylic plastic emulsion approach was found.

Once the prototype fixed dome design had been proved on the test site field tests were undertaken. Twenty plants were built for customers of the Gobar Gas Company in one geographical area (around Pokhara). While the customers paid a market price for these plants, a guarantee fund was set up by the research group that would allow all of these plants to be replaced if they had failed. Detailed follow-up surveys were made of these plants and all problems were noted.[17] The main difficulties appeared to be leakage of gas from the main gas valves, blockages caused by slurry entering the gas outlet pipe and faults with the scum breaker mechanism.

A scum breaker is probably unnecessary for a fixed dome plant, as owners did not experience a loss in gas production after the mechanism broke. Minor design changes and a better design of gas valve were the answers to the other problems.

An effective approach to the development of biogas plant designs involves both a central research team and also the farmers using biogas systems. The central team must include people with good scientific and technical training and experience, who can analyse the problems and know how to look for solutions. Their work, however, must be done in the context in which the results are to be applied. They must seek to solve the real problems faced by the farmers using biogas technology. The answers devised by these scientists must be tested by normal biogas users in the field, to ensure they work well and do not introduce further problems.

11.3 Biogas equipment development

Biogas equipment, such as valves, stoves, lights and engines, is easier to test than biogas plants as it is small enough to be run in a laboratory. The approach to the development of biogas equipment has been very similar to that of biogas plants.

KVIC produced standard designs for biogas stoves, lights and valves, based on good town gas equipment, and licensed Patel Gas Crafters in Bombay to make them. Other companies also made their own, cheaper versions, which were used by other extension agencies, such as PRAD. Kirloskar Oil Engine Company,[18] Pune, produced a design of dual-fuel engine, based on their standard diesel engines with a mixing-chamber-type gas carburettor fitted to the air-inlet manifold. This engine was extensively tested in Kirloskar's own laboratories.[10]

In China the peasant farmers made their own gas stoves and lights, from tins packed with stones or using simple fired-clay designs.[14] The gas piping was made from soft PVC tube, closed off with simple clips that pinched the tube.[19] These designs were not very efficient, but they worked satisfactorily. Again, official standards have been issued for the design of stoves and lights, using the best of the peasant designs with improvements based on scientific principles.[11]

DCS was concerned about biogas equipment development from early in the biogas programme. Supplies could be obtained from India, but the designs were either expensive or unreliable. The standard plug cock, made in Calcutta, was adapted by fitting a tensioning spring to hold the plug tightly in the body even when it was worn down. Even this design leaked at the higher gas pressure from displacement digesters. Attempts were made to find better designs.[20] A cheaper, but reliable gas stove was developed by DCS and was made in workshops in Nepal. Attempts were also made to develop a cheap, reliable gas light.

111

The development of effective, low-cost biogas equipment is as important as the work on biogas plants. The research and development facilities of a biogas programme should include testing areas and equipment for valves, stoves, lights and engines.

11.4 Laboratory testing of biogas technology

The main job of a biogas laboratory is to check the digestibility of different feedstocks and to analyse samples brought in from the field. The feedstocks may be different farm residues or plants available to the local farmers. Digestibility testing is also important to check the reasons for failure of plants belonging to customers of the extension programme.

Laboratory biogas reactors are usually glass flasks of between 1 and 5*l* in volume. Plastic flasks could be used, but they are very difficult to make gastight. The reactors need to be kept at a constant temperature, either in a temperature-controlled room or in water baths. Water baths are usually cheaper and easier to set up as well as being more flexible, in that several small systems can be run at different temperatures at the same time (Appendix III).

Laboratory reactors can be either batch or semi-continuous, continuously or intermittently mixed. The biogas given off needs to be collected and measured and samples of slurry need to be removed so that parameters such as pH and volatile solids and COD content can be measured. Gas is usually collected in a bottle containing water that is displaced into a second bottle by the gas. The second bottle is usually placed higher than the first, allowing the gas to be collected under a positive pressure (Appendix III). The end of the sampling pipe, used to remove and add slurry, should dip well below the surface of the slurry to prevent air entering the gas space. The positive pressure also makes mixing difficult (Appendix III). If the reactors are used to simulate low-rate rural digesters, then an occasional shake by hand is sufficient.[23]

11.5 Test site and field tests

The monitoring of the performance of full-scale digesters, whether on a test site or using plants owned by customers, involves different problems to those met in the laboratory. While the temperature of the plant may not be controlled, it should always be monitored (Appendix III). Samples of slurry can be removed from the inside of the digester pit using a dipper bucket (Appendix III) passed through the slurry inlet or outlet.

Most rural plants are not heated if they are used in tropical or sub-tropical climates, so most plants, including test-site plants, do not have a temperature-control system. Heat losses in these plants can be reduced by placing straw or compost over the top in cold weather. The few test-site

112

plants that may be heated would be those which have been designed for cold-climate use and are being tested in a cold region.

There are two aspects to the measurement of the gas production from a full-scale biogas plant: the gas used and the gas remaining in the plant. When plants are run on a test site the gas is usually retained in the plant and released through a gas meter (Appendix III) twice a day. The gas is either lost or collected in a secondary store. The testing of plants on a customer's site means that the gas used each 24 hours, as measured by a meter, needs to be corrected according to the volume left in the plant at the beginning and end of each measuring period (Appendix III). Despite the greater difficulty of field tests the results are very valuable as a sample of different plants to the same design can be tested. The effects of peculiarities in individual plants and the ways different owners run them can be statistically removed. Operating mistakes by different owners can also be identified and the effects measured, so that advice on the best way to run plants can be given to all customers.

11.6 Gas and slurry analysis

An accurate assessment of the performance of a biogas system should include the volume of methane produced, so samples of biogas need to be analysed for content. Various devices are available to do this (Appendix III), some of which can be used in the field. The pH of the slurry is a measurement that is often made, because it offers a guide as to the health of a biogas plant. Measurements are most easily done in the field (Appendix III).

Slurry analysis must be done in the laboratory (Appendix III), although slurry samples collected in the field can be placed in sealed pots for later analysis. If the samples are to be kept for more than a few hours, they should be kept cool (eg. in a refrigerator). The measurement of total solids and volatile solids require a furnace that can be run at 100°C and 500°C.

COD and alkalinity measurements require the use of chemicals and glassware (Appendix III), so the facilities of a simple chemical laboratory and trained technicians are required. Gas burners are useful as the chemicals need to be boiled for COD measurement and biogas from a test site plant can be used to run them.

BOD, total phosphorous, potassium and nitrogen and C:N ratio measurements require more specialised apparatus and training. They are best done by university or government research laboratories specialising in soil science or waste disposal work.

11.7 Biogas plant modelling

The results of all the measurements on laboratory-scale, test-site and field digesters need to be analysed and interpreted. Although a detailed investigation may result in thousands of different data points, these must be resolved into two or three figures that allow the performance of a plant design or the digestibility of a feedstock to be assessed and compared with others. Mathematical models—a simplified mathematical description of how a biogas plant works—provide a way of doing this.

The actual mechanism inside the plant, with many different types of bacteria all contributing to the production of biogas, is very complex and impossible to define, so any model must be a gross simplification of reality. The most effective models seem to be the simplest, mainly because they define clearly two or three parameters by which a plant design or a feed-stock can be assessed. A good model should roughly predict how much gas a customer can get each day from his plant, given that it is a particular design and uses a particular feedstock under defined conditions.

Several different models have been suggested for biogas plants, many based on simpler biological systems.[23,24] The most effective seems to be the first order kinetic model in which it is suggested that the rate of substrate (feedstock) digestion is directly proportional to the substrate concentration (Appendix IV). The substrate concentration can be expressed as total solids, volatile solids, COD or BOD. This model was used by Pfeffer to analyse his data from continuous cattle dung digesters in USA.[21] It has been applied to both batch and semi-continuous systems by Lau-Wong in Nepal.[22]

The derived models for both batch and semi-continuous digesters attempt also to define a rate of gas production in terms of other parameters, particularly time (see Appendix IV). A yield constant is also defined: the gas production per unit mass of substrate. There are many ways of express-ing this constant, which have been used by different workers. The substrate can be defined in terms of total solids, volatile solids, COD or BOD; the gas production can be defined in terms of the substrate added to the digester or that destroyed within the digester (input less output). The value of this constant is related to another constant used by some workers: the ultimate biodegradability of the substrate.[23] This is the theoretical gas production that could be achieved if the substrate could be left in the digester for a very long time.

11.8 Results of biogas modelling

There have been few studies of the kinetics of batch digesters using the first order model. Maramba noticed two regions in his cumulative gas produc-tion curves from the digestion of pig manure in the Philippines. They indicated a higher rate of gas production at short retention times (22 days at 31°C) than at longer times (32 days).[25]

Chowdhury, using a more analytical approach on her results from cattle dung, based on the first order model, also found two digestion rates.[23] She

114

suggested that the high rate was due to the break-down of easily digested material, and the low (background) rate from the digestion of materials, such as cellulose, for which the rate-limiting process is hydrolysis.[26]

Both Chowdhury and Maramba found that the lag time appeared to be very short (about one day), probably because they were both using a starter, so the bacteria were able to start biogas production immediately on encountering a new source of feedstock. Chowdhury also noticed sharp oscillations in the daily gas-production curve (Fig. 11.1).

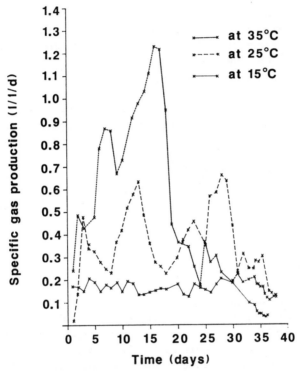

Figure 11.1 *Daily gas production curves at different temperatures*

More workers have looked at the kinetics of continuous biogas systems, although they have used a variety of models. Pfeffer used the first order model with his results from cattle dung reactors in USA, although he assumed that the yield constant was a constant (547l/kg.VS. digestible, based on the theoretical maximum).[21] Lau-Wong, using results from full-scale biogas plants fed mainly with cattle-dung in Nepal, found that both the yield constant and the rate constant varied with temperature.[22] The variation of the rate constant with temperature fitted an Arrhenius equation (Appendix IV).

115

Chowdhury found similar results to those of Pfeffer and Lau-Wong and demonstrated that the yield constant and the rate constant at three temperatures differed from those derived from the analysis of the results from batch reactors run in the same water baths.[23] Pfeffer found a second, lower-rate reaction at longer retention times and Chowdury's results indicated a possible similar conclusion.

Biogas modelling does offer a means of analysing and interpreting the results from measurements of solids degradation and gas production from biogas plants, both laboratory and full-scale. The results from such modelling can be used to predict the overall performance of a biogas plant, although it will not give a detailed description of the way the daily gas production may vary. A simple model, such as the first order model, will not predict phenomena such as 'wash-out', the failure of a continuous digester at very high loading rates.

The results from batch reactors cannot be used to predict the behaviour of continuous biogas plants. If laboratory trials of the digestibility of suitable feedstocks for use in semi-continuous digesters are to be undertaken, then semi-continuous laboratory-scale reactors should be used.

11.9   Staff for research and development

The collection of sufficient data from biogas reactors to give statistically meaningful results is very labour-intensive. Ideally, at least ten reactors should be run under the same conditions and the results averaged to remove the effects of random variations in feed composition and bacterial population. The collection of this data from laboratory reactors is a full-time job for at least one person. If results are required from field reactors, then two or more people may be required, depending on how far apart the chosen reactors are sited. Since reactors must be run for at least sixty days to give meaningful results (or two retention times for semi-continuous reactors), data collection is also very time-consuming. Semi-continuous laboratory and test-site reactors need to be fed daily, so rotas are required that ensure staff are available at week-ends and during holiday periods.

Planners for biogas programmes must therefore ensure that the research programme is given sufficient staff. As well as scientists and laboratory assistants, the research programme needs people to collect fresh feedstocks (daily if possible) and to visit field plants for taking measurements and doing follow-up surveys. This type of work is excellent training for extension staff, as it provides a basic understanding of how a biogas digester works. Trainee field supervisors should be given a chance to spend time on this type of work and staff can be rotated between the research and extension programmes as necessary.

CHAPTER 12
The Politics of Biogas

The sharp rise in the price of oil in the early 1970s brought energy suddenly into the realm of politics. Many of the less-developed countries had committed themselves to a process of development based on an increasing use of imported energy. They were faced with the choice of scrapping their plans and the investment they had already made or taking large loans to pay for the oil to run their new industries. Alternative fuels, such as biogas and alcohol technology, became politically important as leaders of many countries tried to discover if they could offer a way out of this dilemma. The United Nations and its specialist groups, such as ESCAP, FAO, UNDP and the World Bank, also became interested in alternative energy, as it appeared to offer the possibility of help towards the solution of these economic problems.[1]

Biogas technology was unable to provide an immediate answer as it was poorly developed and more related to the needs of rural families than to those of the new industrial areas that were demanding more energy. However, despite the fall in the oil price in the mid-1980s, biogas technology has remained, along with other alternative energies, on the agenda of government and United Nations' planners and in the political arena.

Planners and administrators in a biogas programme need to recognise the political influences on their programme, not only at the international and government levels, but also among the customers with whom the programme is working and the staff of the programme. The arguments for emphasising biogas technology over other demands need to be clearly defined, ready for use in applying for financial grants, subsidies and government help

12.1 National views of biogas technology

Biogas is a resource for rural areas, so does not have the immediate priority for government ministers demanded by other energy sources such as liquid fuels. Politically, the needs of the urban elite for fuel for transport and industry tend to gain precedence, as they have a powerful voice. Civil servants and journalists, especially, belong to this group and can make their needs known to politicians with a much greater urgency than the poor majority in their distant villages. Biogas cannot easily be used in urban areas as it requires space, which is expensive, and the transport of waste products, such as night soil and animal dung, which are bulky and obnoxious to many urban people.

Biogas has found a place where governments have deliberately placed emphasis on the needs of the rural population. The large biogas programmes in both China and India came from the commitment to rural developments of leading political figures, notably Mao Tse-Tung and those in the Indian government who were concerned to respect the aims of Mahatma Gandhi.

In other developing countries, while biogas technology has been given an important place in national energy policy, it has never had a real priority. In Nepal, for example, biogas is seen by HMG/N to have an important part in their energy programme and planners have recognised the need for subsidies to allow more people to build plants. However, each year other needs seem to displace biogas plant subsidies in the national budget and they either do not appear in the list of priorities or are allocated at an inadequate level.

12.2 Biogas and the fuel crisis

The most important argument for the value of biogas technology is that of the crisis in domestic fuel supply. The world is facing an energy crisis that has nothing to do with the supply or price of oil. The drop in oil prices in the mid-1980s has not helped this second energy crisis at all, because it is to do with the supply and demand for firewood. As populations grow in most parts of the world, people need more wood to build houses and to cook food. They also need more land on which to grow food, so they clear forests and reduce the wood supply even further. As less wood is available, people begin to burn agriculural wastes, such as dried animal dung and crop residues, which could otherwise have been composted to make fertiliser. These fuels are also inefficient, giving smokey flames.

As forest cover is removed and land is impoverished by the growth of more food crops, with less and less fertiliser to replace the plant nutrients, soil erosion occurs. This problem is worst in mountainous areas, such as Nepal, where the monsoon rains quickly wash away unprotected top soil. As the soil cover is lost, the sides of the mountains become unstable and landslides can happen, destroying land, crops and homes. Increased water run-off on deforested slopes means floods downstream in the monsoon and less water absorbed by the mountain rock strata. Thus less water is stored underground in the mountains for the dry season, so springs and streams dry up earlier in the year. A natural cycle of flood and drought is therefore intensified and people are not only short of fuel, food and fertiliser, but water also.[1]

The attraction of biogas technology is that it offers a way of cutting across this vicious circle. A biogas plant can produce both fuel and a good

118

fertiliser from the same animal dung and crop residues. Because biogas is a high grade fuel and can be used in stoves of high efficiency, a fixed mass of residues will produce more usable energy if digested, than if it were dried and burnt on an open fire. The value of the fertiliser from a biogas plant is also higher than that produced if the same wastes were composted in traditional ways.

Biogas-fuelled irrigation schemes, where underground water is available, mean that crops can be grown in the dry season, without having to cut down forest to create more agricultural land. Cottage industries, powered by biogas, could also mean that fewer people would have to cut firewood to sell, as they could earn extra cash in other ways through village cooperatives. This would cause the price of firewood to rise, making domestic biogas plants look more economic.

Theoretically, biogas technology does have the potential for making an impact on these problems in a country such as Nepal. It has been calculated that three-quarters of the fuel wood used in Nepal could be replaced, if all the available cattle dung were digested to biogas.[2] However, such calculations ignore the cost of all these biogas plants and the resources, in manpower and materials, such as cement, that they would require. At the present rate of construction, it would take centuries before the biogas programme begins to make an impact on these problems. The problems themselves are likely to reach crisis dimensions within decades!

12.3 Local concepts of biogas technology

Biogas technology has an inbuilt advantage in the nations in which it has spread most rapidly, in that it has been culturally acceptable. The Chinese people seem to have always seen the benefits of composting residues to make fertiliser. The idea of a composting system that not only produces a good fertiliser, but also a fuel gas, is very attractive.

For Hindus in India and Nepal the cow is a holy animal and cattle dung is considered a ritually clean substance. Most village houses, and especially kitchens, have floors made from dried cattle dung and mud, which are replastered several times a week. Therefore the idea of cooking on 'gobar' (cow dung) gas is culturally attractive. Biogas has not had the same impact in Pakistan and Bangladesh, where Moslems do not have the same beliefs.

Socio-economic surveys suggest that people's motives for purchasing biogas plants are varied.[3,4] The economic argument for domestic plants is weak, the financial benefits are marginal (Chapter 9). Some of the more enlightened and better educated farmers recognise the problems of deforestation, so are motivated by a social conscience to build biogas plants. Others see biogas as a status symbol, wanting a plant because it is new and different. In some areas of India and Nepal, a biogas plant offers advantages in marriage negotiations, as a new wife will not have to work so hard in her husband's home.

Once rural women get used to biogas and overcome their fear of a new technology, they usually like it very much. It saves them the hard work and time required to collect and prepare other fuels, such as cutting firewood or moulding cattle dung and crop wastes into lumps for drying. Biogas is also much cleaner to use: cooking utensils, clothes and the whole kitchen are free from soot and smoke and the smell of burning. A few people complain that some foods lack the characteristic flavour that is imparted when they are cooked over burning cattle dung,[3] but, in general, biogas technology is seen by rural women as a real benefit to them in their hard lives.

The main reason for many farmers wanting to build a biogas plant is persuasion by extension workers. In China, especially, many people had become so used to following the lead of the revolutionary cadres that they agreed to build biogas plants, too. In India, the biogas extension workers are often involved in other extension work. Many farmers wanting help in other areas, such as getting supplies of fertiliser or high-quality seed, agree to build a biogas plant to help the extension agent fulfil his quota for plant sales.

12.4 Staff motivation

One of the problems faced by extension agencies with staff working mainly in the field is the management of these people. Unsupervised young field agents can spend time sitting in tea shops rather than making the effort to go out to inaccessible villages to meet farmers, who are probably away working in their fields. Even highly motivated agents can achieve very little if they have to travel long distances to meet the relatively few people who are able to afford loans for domestic plants.

Many agencies have incentive schemes, such as the offer of a bonus for each biogas plant sold. These need to be carefully administered, especially to avoid jealousy between different groups of staff. Construction staff can also be offered incentives to sell plants to people coming to visit new plants out of curiosity. In Nepal, these bonuses were even extended to bank staff, as they often had to visit farmers in connection with loans for other projects.

Money should not be the only bonus for staff. Effective training in biogas should include all the arguments for the use of biogas technology, so that people are inspired by a concern for the environment and a conviction that their work could have a beneficial effect. The organisational structure should allow staff to see different aspects of the work and include prospects for advancement for those who work hard and effectively.

12.5 Political aspects of community biogas

The cooperative aspect of community plants should not be heavily emphasised in the publicity of a biogas programme. The idea of cooperatives has
a political flavour: right-wing governments are suspicious of the concept
and left-wing governments often have a fixed idea of how they should be
organised. In Nepal, cooperative concept had a poor image because previous
attempts had not been very successful, including the Farmers' Cooperative
Bank, the forerunner of the ADB/N. The reasons for the failures were
usually based on preconceived ideas of the way cooperatives should be
organised. These ideas were applied to rural groups without adapting
organisational structures to the cultural situations of the people involved.

When a community project is set up it is important to involve local
politicians. As far as possible local decision-making structures should be
used when making plans for the project. Community leaders can be given a
place on planning committees, even though these positions may only be
honorary, with little real influence. While the winning-over of local leaders
may be a time-consuming task at the beginning of the project, their support
may save time later. Other local people will be much less suspicious of
requests made by staff involved in the project and many potential problems
may be averted by local political support.

Successful projects attract a lot of interest and many people, especially
the local politicians, try to take some of the credit for the success. The
opposite is true for unsuccessful projects, where politicians try to
find someone else to take the blame. The Madhubasa project in Nepal
(Chapter 10) gained a great deal of interest, especially from the Department of Agriculture. The Minister of Agriculture became involved, resulting in visits by many high officials to the village. Articles about the project
appeared in national newspapers and even the King of Nepal made a visit,
hovering over the village in his helicopter. This type of interest and publicity
can be used to encourage similar projects elsewhere.

The key person in a community project is the extension worker, who
needs to be highly motivated to work with villagers and motivate them.
Financial incentives are seldom enough to motivate these people; they
need a philosophical or religious drive to make them leave the benefits that
their education has given them to go and spend time in villages. The SFDP
approach, inspired by FAO, of using community projects as the basis for
the motivator to gain material towards a higher degree (eg. a Ph.D. in
sociology) proved effective. Other rural workers have been inspired by the
philosophies of Mahatma Gandhi or Mao Tse-Tung. People inspired by a
Christian commitment to community and the sharing of resources have
also proved good motivators. The right selection and training of these
motivators is one of the most important factors in the success of a community projects.

APPENDIX 1
Basic Building Techniques

It is important to select a suitable site for a biogas plant (Chapter 5). Sufficient building materials should be available close to the site before work is started. The site is first cleared and levelled before the positions of the digester and slurry inlet and outlet are marked out with pegs in the ground. A datum level should be marked with pegs and string, in a way that allows measurements to be made from it during excavation and construction.

Excavating digester pits

Most biogas plants are built in a hole in the ground. If the soil is strong the digester pit can be dug and lined with masonry or cement plaster. Building gauges and templates are helpful to define the shape accurately. A simple building gauge to check the diameter of a circular hole is a length of rope looped around a pipe held in the centre of the hole with rope and pegs (Fig. I.1). Masonry walls need to be supported by packing the space between each course and the sides of the hole with earth and ramming it firm, dampening the soil with water if necessary.

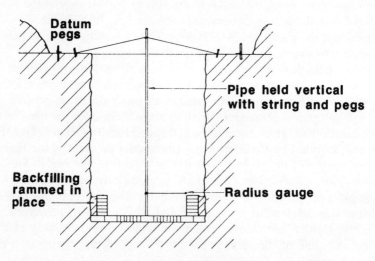

Figure I.1. *Building gauge used for cylindrical pit*

122

If the soil is weak and liable to fall into the hole the sides need to be supported as it is dug. A technique used in building wells can be adopted for floating drum and fixed dome plants. The lining of the pit is made close to where the pit is to be dug, usually of reinforced concrete or ferrocement rings. Alternatively spun concrete pipes can be purchased. These rings are placed, one by one, above the hole, which is excavated from within the lining. As earth is removed, the lining sinks into the hole, supporting the walls. Long troughs, for extended dome, bag and tent digesters could be made in a similar way, using precast concrete sections sunk into the ground to form walls. Internal struts of steel or reinforced concrete would be required to support these walls, when the earth is removed from inside the digester pit.

Building materials

The main building materials for a biogas plant are brick or stone masonry and concrete. Sheets of plastic or rubber are also used in bag and tent plants. Materials affected by moisture, such as unburnt brick and wood, are not suitable.

Bricks should be fired and of good quality. Porous bricks may leak slurry, so a wall built of them may need to be coated with cement plaster. Stone walls need more cement mortar, but can be used where bricks are not available. The stones should be free from soil.

Sand used in mortar and concrete must be free from vegetable matter and mud. Dirty sand can be washed before it is used. Each batch of sand is placed in a container (eg. a wheelbarrow) and water flushed through it. If the sand is fine, or has mica in it, more cement may have to be used to ensure a strong mortar. A 'bag' of sand (usually an empty cement bag) contains about 35l and weighs 50kg to 60kg.

The broken stones and gravel used as aggregate in concrete should be between 5mm and 25mm in size. They can be screened by passing them through wire netting with the appropriate sized holes. The stones should be free of soil and other matter.

The Portland cement used for mortar and concrete should be as fresh as possible. Cement that has become wet and lumpy is useless, so bags should always be stored in a dry place.

Cement mortar should be of the same strength as the bricks or stones it binds together. A ratio of 1:6 cement:sand is average, but the ratios can vary between 1:4 and 1:9. Ideally material quantities should be measured by weighing, using a bucket and a spring balance. In practice, measurement by volume is easier and is usually adequate. The density of cement is 1.44kg/l and that of sand, between 1.44 and 1.76kg/l.

Concrete used in these designs is normally a 1:2:4 mix of cement, sand and aggregate, although a 1:3:3 mix gives a more compact concrete for

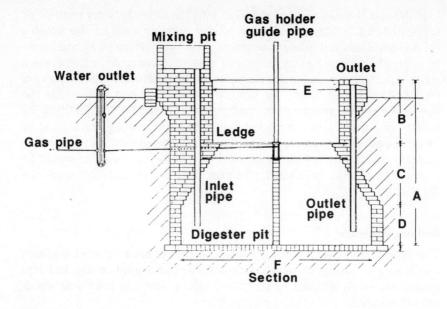

Water outlet

Mixing pit

Gas holder
guide pipe

Outlet

Gas pipe

Ledge

Inlet
pipe

Outlet
pipe

Digester pit

Section

E

B

C

A

D

F

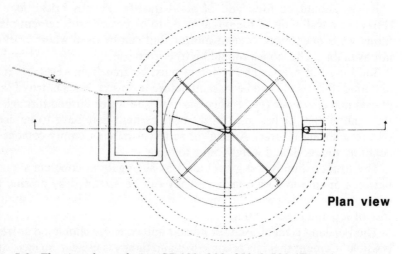

Plan view

Figure I.2. *Floating drum design SD100, 200, 350 & 500 (Taper)*

cement dome plants. As the concrete is laid or put in a mould, it must be carefully compacted to avoid air pockets (6 per cent air voids in concrete means a 20 per cent loss in strength).[1] The concrete must be well mixed, with just enough water to give a good consistency. Once it is put in place the concrete should be cured in a damp atmosphere for seven days before any load is placed on it, by covering it with wet sacks or water. Small sections can be cured under water in a pond or stream.

124

Flat concrete pieces, such as reservoir covers, need reinforcement. 6mm steel rods, spaced at 120mm in 50mm-thick concrete are adequate. Transverse rods may be spaced at wider intervals (200mm to 300mm).

The plaster used to line digester pits is 25 to 30mm thick. It is usually applied in three layers, of 1:6, 1:4 and 1:3 cement to sand mixes, respectively.[2] If the soil is poor the first coat can be reinforced with wire mesh (as ferrocement). The mesh is held to the soil surface with wire staples, while the plaster is applied.

Details of the floating drum design

The floor of the floating drum design can be made of brick or concrete (Fig. 1.2). The inlet and outlet pipes (100mm diameter) are usually made from spun cement, reinforced with fibre, such as asbestos. A central dividing wall is often built between the inlet and outlet pipes to stop slurry passing directly between them. A ledge (300mm wide) is made below the gas drum to support it when it is empty and to deflect gas into the drum. Sizes and typical material quantities used in Nepali designs are given in Tables I.1 and I.2.[3]

The gas drum is made from steel sheet welded to a frame made from angle iron. The roof should slope outwards so rainwater does not collect. Handles around the drum make it easier to carry and to rotate when in place on the plant. The welds can be checked by filling the inverted drum with water and inspecting it for leaks. The completed drum should be carefully cleaned and painted to avoid rust. The black mill-scale on the steel sheets can be removed with rotary wire brushes or sand blasting. A coat of metallic anti-saline primer should be put on as soon as possible after cleaning, followed by two coats of bituminous paint. The top coat of paint

Table I.1 Dimensions of taper type drum plants

Dimension (mm)		Let.	SD100	SD200	SD350	SD500
Digester Volume	(m³)		7.1	13.0	24.0	34.0
Drum Volume	(m³)		1.7	3.4	6.0	8.5
Mixing Pit Volume	(m³)		0.12	0.22	0.47	*
Depth of Digester		A	2 520	3 090	3 300	3 770
Depth Deflect. Ledge		B	1 030	1 270	1 270	1 500
Depth Taper Section		C	910	910	1 220	1 220
Depth Lower Section		D	580	910	810	1 050
Diam. Upper Section		E	1 600	2 000	2 600	2 900
Diam. Lower Section		F	2 500	2 900	3 900	4 230

Notes: * The SD500 plant usually uses a mixing machine.

125

can be applied after the drum has been transported to the site for the biogas plant, to cover any scratches.

Details of the fixed dome design

A pilot hole is usually first dug in the ground and covered with boards before the mud mould for the dome is made (Fig. I.3). A template made

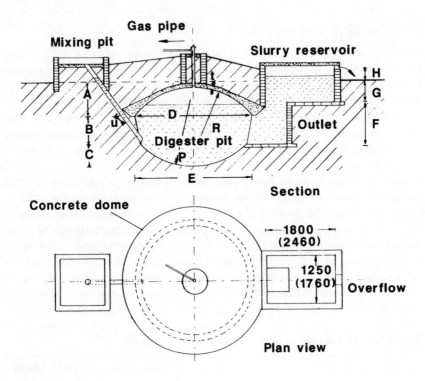

Figure I.3 *Details of fixed dome design*

from welded steel rod is used to shape the mould. If the soil is weak the foundations for the collar of the dome should be increased in area to spread the load. Sizes and typical material quantities used in Nepali designs are given in Tables I.3 and I.4.[3]

The radii of the dome and floor are chosen so that they can each be checked with a gauge made from a length of string attached at the centre of the other. The gas outlet pipe can have holes drilled in the bottom edge to allow this string gauge to be fastened to it.

The sizes and typical material quantities for extended dome plants are given in Tables I.5 and I.6 (Fig. I.4).

126

Table I.2   Material quantities for drum plants

Plant Type		SD100	SD200	SD350	SD500
Cement kg (bags)		630 (14)	990 (22)	1,530 (34)	2,025 (45)
Sand *l* (bags)		2,450 (70)	3,850 (110)	5,950 (170)	7,875 (225)
Bricks		3,000	5,000	7,500	10,000
Drum Weight	(kg)	132	246	392	454
Cement Pipe	(m)	4.8	7.1	5.4	7.4

Notes: If stone masonry is used, the quantities of cement and sand should be doubled.
The inlet pit should be 300 mm above the slurry outlet.
Space should be left at the bottom of the inlet and outlet pipes to allow debris (soil, stones) to collect.
The top of the plant should not normally protrude more than 500 mm above the ground level. It is possible to make the walls higher out of the ground, if the bricks are reinforced with bands of galvanised wire tightened around each course.

Table I.3   Dimensions of concrete dome plants

Dimension (mm)	Let.	CP10	CP15	CP20
Dome Volume (m^3)		3.3	5.6	5.6
Digester Volume (m^3)		7.3	9.7	14.1
Working Volume (m^3)		9.0	12.5	16.9
Reservoir Volume (m^3)		1.3	2.1	2.9
Mixing Pit (m^3)		0.22	0.34	0.43
Dome Outside Depth	A	800	920	920
Dome Inside Diameter	D	3,100	4,000	4,000
Dome Radius of Sphere	R	2,000	2,800	2,800
Dome Shell Thickness	t	60	80	80
Collar Thickness	u	250	300	300
Depth Conial Section	B	780	270	785
Depth Digester Floor	C	580	1,090	875
Radius Spherical Section	P	2,100	1,200	2,500
Inside Diameter	E	2,900	3,800	3,800
Res. Overflow to datum	H	240	160	120
Res. Datum to Floor	G	560	680	630
Res. Floor to Outlet	F	1,060	630	1,195

Note: The turret should be at least 750mm high to ensure enough earth is placed on the dome to hold it down against the gas pressure inside.

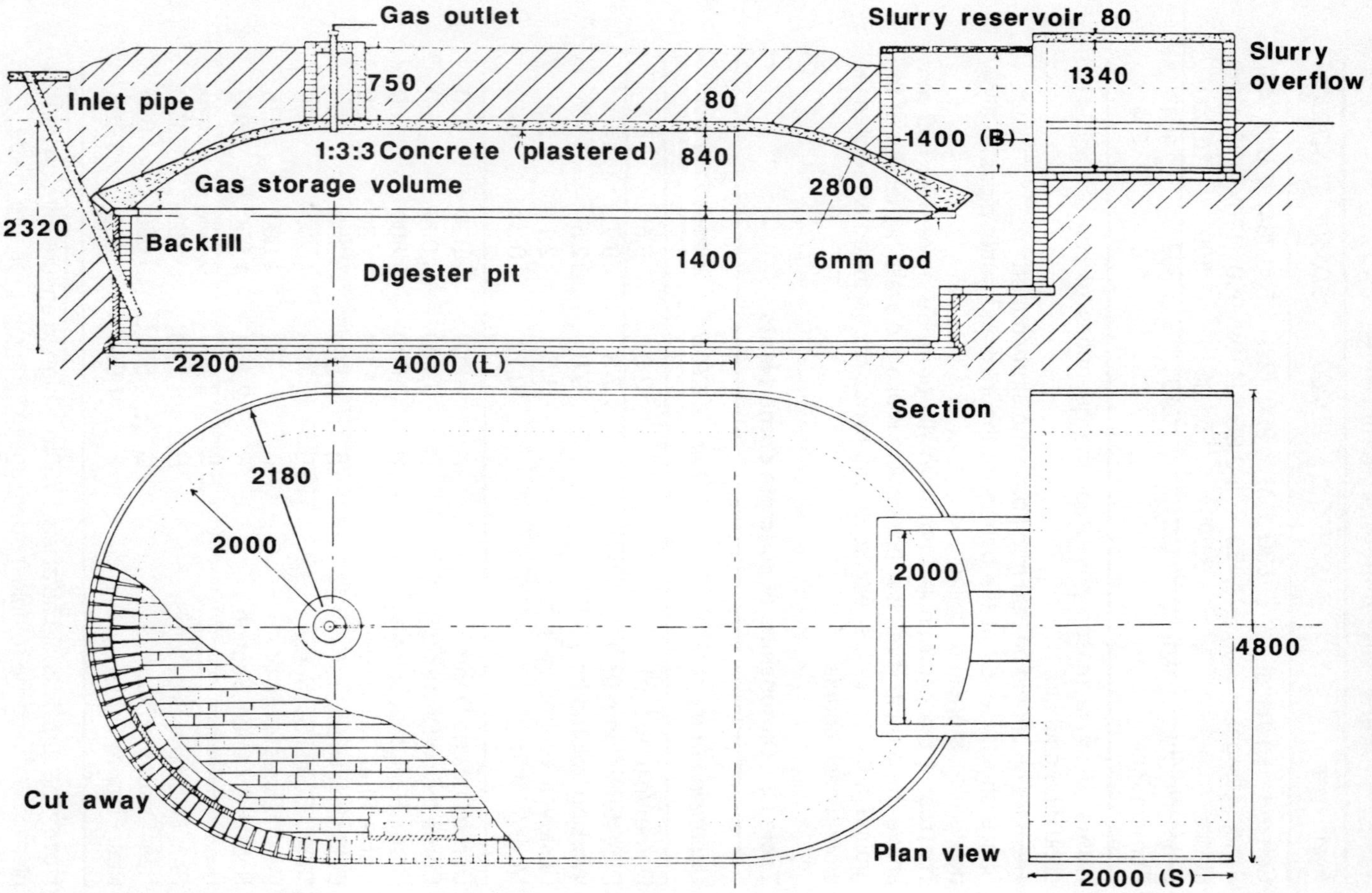

Figure I.4 *Extended dome biogas plant (EP50)*

Slurry overflow

Slurry reservoir 80

1340

1400 (B)

2800

6mm rod

80

840

1400

Gas outlet

750

1:3:3 Concrete (plastered)

Gas storage volume

Digester pit

Backfill

Inlet pipe

4000 (L)

2200

2320

Section

4800

2000 (S)

2000

2180

2000

Plan view

Cut away

Table I.4 Material quantities for concrete dome plants

Type of Plant		CP10	CP15	CP20
Cement	kg (bags)	690 (14.5)	1,130 (23.5)	1,180 (26)
Sand	l (bags)	1,630 (49)	2,490 (73)	1,830 (82)
Aggregate	l (bags)	640 (19)	1,300 (38)	1,380 (40)
Bricks		1,300	1,500	1,900
Cement Pipe	(m)	2.5	3.0	3.0
Steel Rod	(6mm)	40m	50m	75m
Acrylic Paint	(l)	2	3	3

Table I.5 Dimensions for extended dome plants

Plant Type	L (m)	S (m)	B (m)	Dome Vol. (m^3)	Digester Vol. (m^3)
EP20	0	0	2,320	5.4	17.5
EP35	2,000	1,000	1,800	10.0	28.7
EP50	4,000	2,000	1,400	14.6	39.9
EP65	6,000	3,000	1,400	19.3	51.1
EP80	8,000	4,000	1,400	23.9	62.3
EP95	10,000	5,000	1,400	28.5	73.5

The reservoir pit is large and deep enough for an animal or a child to drown in so it must be covered. Reinforced concrete pieces or wooden boards or slats can be used. These covers also prevent water evaporating from the slurry, which may otherwise become too dry.

Table I.6 Material quantities for extended dome plants

Materials		EP20 Plant	2 m Tunnel (T)	EP50 (EP20 + 2T)	EP95 (EP20 + 5T)
Bricks		3,000	1,100	5,200	8,500
Cement	kg	950 (22)	700 (16)	2,350 (54)	4,450 (100)
Sand	l	2,400 (70)	1,500 (44)	5,400 (156)	9,900 (285)
Aggreg	l	1,400 (41)	1,200 (35)	3,800 (110)	7,400 (212)
Steel Rod	m	130	0	100	100
Cement Pipe	m	2.7	0	2.7	2.7

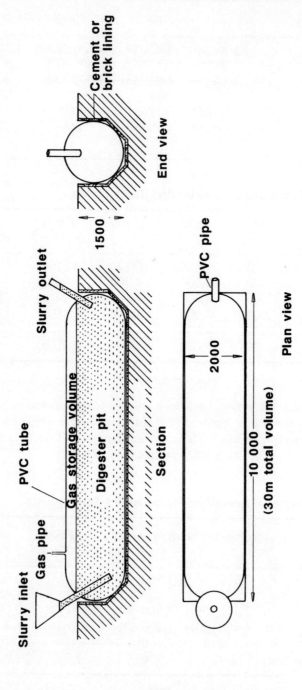

Figure I.5 *Bag digester details*

Details of bag and tent digesters

A bag digester needs a smooth trench in which to lie, that will support the sides of the bag and the weight of slurry within it (Fig. I.5). The walls of the trench should be free from stones or any sharp objects that may puncture the bag. A smooth cement-plaster-walled trench is suitable, although wire mesh reinforcement would be required if the soil were weak. The shape of the trench can be checked using a template made to the shape that the bag will form when full of slurry.

A tent digester needs a similar trench, although it must be made to a higher standard to ensure the slurry does not leak out. The edges of the trench need to be carefully shaped to suit the system adopted for attaching the edges of the plastic tent. There are many different ways in which the tent can be fixed down. One effective way is to fold the tent edges around metal or plastic pipes which are set into grooves in the digester wall and clamped in place (Fig. I.6). More details, such as typical material quantities and costs may be obtained from the manufacturers of the plastic sheeting.[4,5]

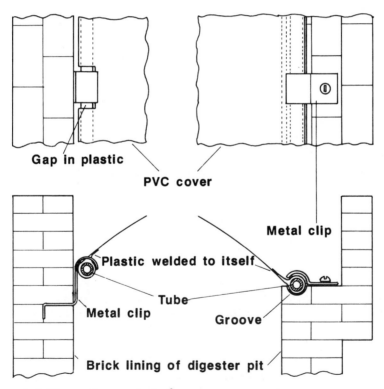

Figure I.6 *Clamps for tent design*[6]

Gas Appliance Design

The design of systems to distribute and use biogas has received much less attention than the design of biogas plants in many biogas programmes. The layout and installation of pipework and the design and manufacture of effective and efficient stoves, lights and engines is important. An efficient stove, for example, allows a limited supply of biogas to be used to the best advantage.

Gas pipes

Gas lines need to be fitted with water drains at appropriate points (see Chapter 5). Two designs were used in Nepal, the 'T' trap (Fig. II.1) for shallow gas lines and the 'U' trap for pipes laid deeper in the soil (Fig. II.2)

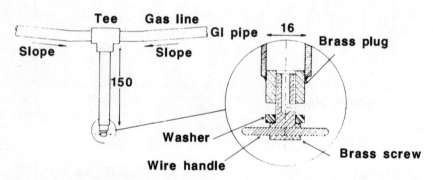

Figure II.1 *'T' Type water trap.*

The pressure drop along a gas line can be calculated using the following equations.[1] If a pipe of diameter: D (metres) has a gas flowing down it at a rate: Q (m³/sec = *l*/min/60,000), the velocity of the gas (u, m/sec) is:

$$u = \frac{4.Q}{\pi.D^2} \text{ m/sec.} \tag{II.1}$$

If the gas pressures at two points along the pipe (L metres apart) are: p_i and: p_z (mm WG), the pressure difference ($\triangle p = p_i - p_z$) is given by:

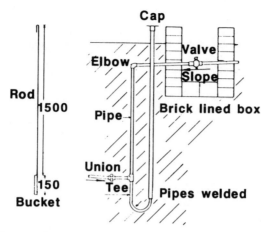

Figure II.2 *'U' type of water trap.*

$$\Delta p = \frac{f.L}{D.g.} .u^2.\rho \qquad (II.2)$$

where: f = the friction factor.

The friction factor (f) depends on the Reynolds number: Re:

$$Re = \rho.D. \frac{u}{\mu} \qquad (II.3)$$

where: ρ = the density of biogas (1.0994 kg/m^3 at 30°C)
   μ = the viscosity of biogas (1.297 × 10^{-5} kg/m/sec)

If the Reynolds number is less than 2,000, the flow is laminar:

$$f = \frac{64}{Re} \qquad \text{(Hagen–Poiseulle formula)}[2] \qquad (II.4)$$

If the Reynolds Number is more than 4,000, the flow is turbulent:

$$f = \frac{0.316}{\sqrt{\sqrt{Re}}} \qquad \text{(Blasius formula)}.[2] \qquad (II.5)$$

In the transition region, with a Reynolds number between 2,000 and 4,000, f has a value between those given above.

Graphs of flow for two values of Δp (10mm WG—for a drum plant— and 50mm WG—for a dome plant) are shown in Figures II.3 and II.4.

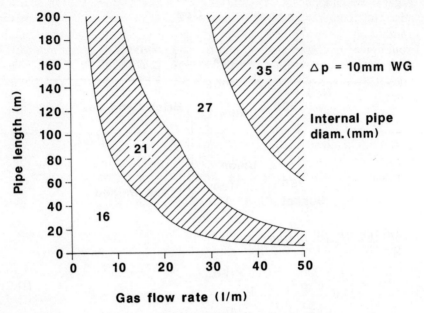

Figure II.3 *Gas flow rate verses pipe length for drum plants*

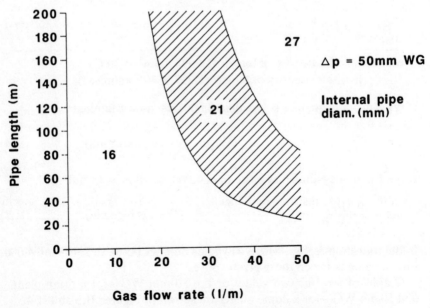

Figure II.4 *Gas flow rate verses pipe length for dome plants*

Biogas burner design

A gas burner supplies heat by burning a fuel gas in air, 4.184kJ of heat will raise the temperature of $1l$ of water 1°C. $1l$ of biogas, burnt with the optimum of air, will give 21.5kJ of heat, so a biogas burner using $7.5l$/min would give 161kJ/min. This should heat 1 litre of water in 2 minutes from 20°C to 100°C. In practice, it takes 4 minutes, as some of the heat is lost. The DCS stove is about 55 per cent efficient, which means 45% of the heat is not used.

A medium-sized gas burner ($7.5l$/min) and two gas lamps ($2 \times 2.4l$/min) are to be used in a house 38m away from a gas plant. The maximum flow rate is then $12.3l$/min. Choosing a 16mm pipe:

$$u = \frac{4 \times 12.3 \times 10^{-3}}{n \times 0.016^2 \times 60} = 1.02 \text{ m/sec.}$$

Taking a drum plant, with pressure 70 mm WG, the maximum pressure loss (Δp) is 10 mm WG.

$$Re = \frac{1.099 \times 0.016 \times 1.02}{1.297 \times 10^{-5}} = 1412$$

$$Re < 2000, \text{ so } f = 64/Re = 0.045$$

$$L = \frac{2 \times 10 \times .016 \times 9.81}{.045 \times 1.02^2 \times 1.0994} = 61.0 \text{ metres}$$

Since 61m is longer than 38m, a 16mm pipe can be used for the pipeline.

Example II.1 Use of gas pipe formulae.

The rate at which gas is delivered to the stove (Q, l/min) depends on the size of the gas jet (Diameter: d_o, Area: A_o, m^2) and the gas pressure (p, mm WG) (Figure II.5):

$$Q = 3.90.C_d.A_o. \sqrt{\frac{p}{s}} \times 60,000 \tag{II.6}$$

Where C_d is the discharge coefficient of the jet (0.73) and s is the specific gravity of the gas (0.94)

The rate at which heat is supplied to the burner (H, kJ/sec or kW) is:

$$H = 3900. C_d.A_o.W.\sqrt{p} \tag{II.7}$$

where W is the Wobbe number for the gas ($22.2kJ/l$).[3]

135

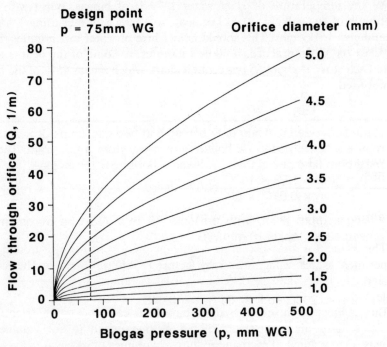

Figure II.5 *Gas flow vs gas pressure for various jets*

Table II.1   Properties of biogas.[3,4,5]

Biogas: assumed 58% CH_4 and 42% CO_2 saturated with water vapour at 30°C and standard pressure. (Range of values)

Calorific value	21.5kJ/*l*	(20.1 to 25.9)
Effective molecular weight	27.35*l*	(24 to 29)
Density	1.0994 kg/m³	(0.96 to 1.17)
Specific gravity	0.94	(0.82 to 1.00)
Viscosity	1.297 × 10⁻⁵ kg/sec/m	
Optimum air to fuel ratio	5.5:1 (15% biogas)	
Flammability limits	9% to 17% biogas in air	
Wobbe number	22.2 kJ/*l*	
Burning velocity	0.25 m/sec in air	

The Wobbe number is a measure of the heating effectiveness of the gas. Biogas (22.2) is less effective than natural gas (50.7) and bottled gas (80) The heat available is the heat supplied times the efficiency of the stove. If a

136

stove designed for natural gas is to be used for biogas, the area of the jet must be almost doubled (50.7/22.2). A stove designed for bottled gas must have a jet area about 3.6 times (80/22.2) larger.

The DCS ring burner has a jet size (d_o) of 2.5mm.

$A_o = \dfrac{\pi}{4} \times 0.0025^2 = 4.91 \times 10^{-6} \text{ m}^2$

$Q = 3.9 \times 0.73 \times 4.91 \times 10^{-6} \times \sqrt{\dfrac{75}{0.94}} \times 6 \times 10^4$

$\quad = 7.46$ l/min at 75mm WG pressure.

$H = 3900 \times 4.91 \times 10^{-6} \times 22.2 \times \sqrt{75}$

$\quad = 2.69$ kW $= 161$ kJ/min.

which is: $161 \times 0.55 = 88.6$ kJ/min available heat, since the stove is 55% efficient.

Example II.2 Gas and heat flow from DCS stove

The value for the discharge coefficient ($C_d = 0.73$) was found by experiment. This value may vary between different jets of the same design, if burrs and surface irregularities affect the shape of the hole.

Biogas must be mixed with air to burn. For complete combustion, the 'stoichiometric air requirement' is 5.5 volumes of air to one volume of biogas. One volume of methane requires 2 volumes of oxygen:

$$CH_4 + O_2 = CO_2 + 2\,H_2O,$$

and there is 58 per cent (approx) methane in biogas and 21 per cent oxygen in air.

The gas stream, as it comes from the jet, enters a 'throat', where it entrains primary air through the air holes. The 'entrainment ratio' (r), the number of volumes of air entrained by one volume of gas, is:

$$r = \sqrt{s}.\left(\sqrt{\dfrac{A_t}{A_o}} - 1\right) = \sqrt{s}.\left(\dfrac{d_t}{d_o} - 1\right) \qquad \text{(Priggs formula) (II.8)}$$

where A_t and d_t are the Area and diameter of the throat.[3]

Prigg's formula holds if the total flame port area (A_p) is between 1.5 and 2.2 times the area of the throat. This ratio is approximately independent of the gas pressure and the flow rate. The primary air supply is rarely enough to give a stoichiometric mixture.

The primary aeration (r) can be varied by altering the area of the jet orifice, the area of the throat or the area of the air inlet holes. The first option is used in lamp burners. The closing of the air holes means that the

The DCS burner has a throat diameter of 16mm, giving an area of 201 mm². There are 20 flame port holes of diameter 5mm giving a total area of: 393 mm², 1.95 times the throat area.

$$r = \sqrt{0.94} \times (\frac{16}{2.5} - 1) = 5.2,$$

which is almost a stoichiometric mixture.

Example II.3 Entrainment ratio in DCS Burner.

entrainment ratio is not constant with gas pressure and flow. A better burner design uses a tapered throat (Fig. II.6), into which the jet can be moved to give a good flame.[6]

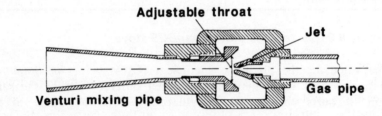

Figure II.6 *Tapered throat design of gas burner*

The mixing tube between the throat and the flame ports should be long enough to allow the gas and air to mix thoroughly (at least 10 times d_t). The mixing tube can taper outwards towards the flame ports, making a 'venturi', which can be shorter than a straight tube ($6 \times d_t$).

A gas flame consists of several regions (Fig. II.7). The preheat region,

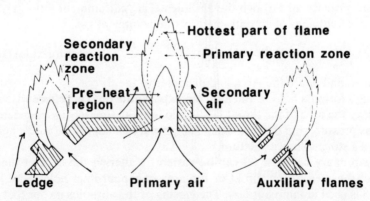

Figure II.7 *Details of gas flame and means of stabilisation*

where the gas and air are heated, is seen as a paler cone in the centre of the flame. The primary reaction zone is where gas burns with the primary air and the secondary reaction zone is where secondary air takes part in the reaction. Secondary air must have free access to the flame ports. The hottest part of the flame lies at the tip of the primary reaction zone, so the stove should be designed so the pots to be heated touch this point of the flames. If the cold surface of a pot touches the preheat region, the flame will be quenched and burn inefficiently.

Biogas has a low burning velocity (less than 0.25m/sec in air), so 'light back', the burning of the gas in the mixture tube, is almost impossible. Flame traps are therefore not needed. 'Blow off', the lifting of the flame from the ports, is a problem. The flame ports need to be close together (about 5mm apart) and be of a suitable size (5mm), so that the velocity of the mixture through the holes (v_g) is much less than the burning velocity:

$$v_g = Q_m/A_p << 0.25\text{m/sec},\tag{II.9}$$

where Q_m (m^3/sec) is the mixture flow rate (r.Q), and: A_p (flame port area) is in m^2.

The flame can be stabilised by surrounding the main flame port with a series of smaller holes, such as in a lamp nozzle. A second way is to provide a ledge that controls the flow of secondary air to the flame (Fig. II.7).

Gas lamp and stove parts can be made of ceramic materials such as fire-clay, fired in a kiln. One design of lamp made in China, uses a ceramic mixing tube and nozzle (Fig. II.8). Ceramic stoves have been designed and made in India. Another design was made and tested at Reading

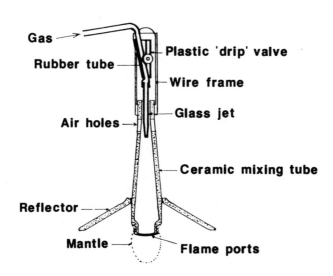

Figure II.8 *Ceramic gas lamp—made in China*

139

University (Figure II.9). It works well, although improvements could be made.

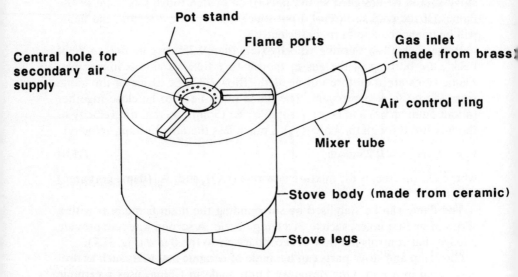

Figure II.9 *Ceramic gas stove*

Carburettors for mixing biogas and air

When a diesel engine is adapted to be a dual-fuel engine, the main alteration is the addition of a carburettor to mix the biogas and air in the correct proportions. The simplest type of gas carburettor is a mixing chamber (Fig. II.10). The pressure drop across a paper air filter sucks biogas through the gas valve during the intake stroke of the engine. This type of carburettor has been used with several types of Indian-made diesel engines and works well. Improvements could be made: for example, the engine performance could be adjusted by making the air orifice adjustable.[7]

This carburettor did not work with a Japanese engine that had a higher compression ratio than the Indian models (23:1 instead of 17:1). A paper air filter constricted the air supply to the engine; if this was replaced by an oil-soaked wire-mesh filter to improve the air supply, the pressure drop across it was too low to suck in sufficient biogas. A venturi type of gas carburettor was designed (Fig. II.11), which fitted between the air intake pipe and the air manifold in the cylinder head. As air is drawn through the ventury, the pressure at the centre is reduced, sucking biogas into the air stream.

140

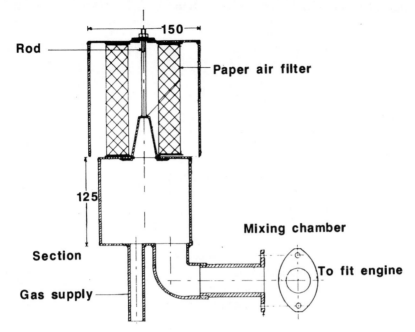

Figure II.10 *Mixing chamber type of carburettor*

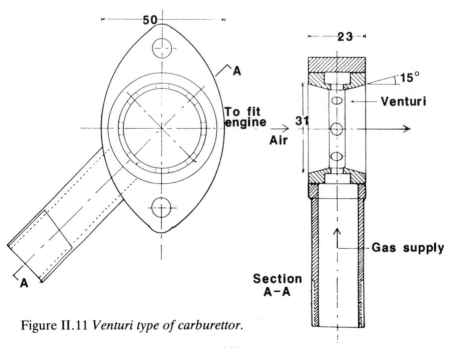

Figure II.11 *Venturi type of carburettor.*

141

Table II.2 Variables used in Appendix II.

A_o	—Area of gas jet	(m^2)
A_t	—Area of throat	$(m^2$
A_p	—Area of flame ports	(m^2)
a	—Atmospheric pressure	(10332 mm WG)
C_d	—Discharge coefficient for jet	$(-)$
D	—Pipe diameter	(m)
d_o	—Diameter of gas jet	(m)
d_t	—Diameter of throat	(m)
f	—Friction factor	$(-)$
g	—acceleration due to gravity (9.81)	(m/sec^2)
H	—Heat delivery rate for burner	(kW)
L	—Length of pipe	(m)
p	—Gas pressure at a point in the pipe	(mm WG)
Q	—Gas flow rate down pipe	(m^3/sec)
Q_m	—Flow rate of gas/air mixture	(m^3/sec)
Re	—Reynolds number	$(-)$
r	—Entrainment ratio for burner	$(-)$
s	—Specific gravity of biogas (wrt. air)	$(-)$
u	—Gas flow velocity	(m/sec)
v_g	—Velocity of mixture through flame ports	(m/sec)
W	—Wobbe number of gas	$(-)$
p	—Density of biogas	(kg/m^3)
μ	—Viscosity of biogas	(kg/m.sec)

APPENDIX III
Research Techniques

Apparatus for laboratory and full-scale tests on biogas reactors will often need to be purchased, although some can be made in local workshops. Some less-developed countries (such as India) do have their own scientific equipment suppliers, from which much of the apparatus is available. Other, more specialised, equipment must be obtained from a developed country, such as Britain or the USA.

Water baths

Suitable water baths for laboratory reactors are available from many scientific suppliers, but simple versions can be made in a local workshop.[1] Suitable containers are required in which to place the reactors: washing-up bowls are cheap and convenient. Pumps are required to circulate the water and heaters to raise the temperature (Fig. III.1). The heaters are switched on and off by thermostats, usually obtained from a developed country. A mercury-in-glass thermometer that has an adjustable wire that makes contact with the mercury to complete an electrical circuit is an effective and accurate device. An electronic amplifier and relay is required to allow the small current that can flow in the mercury to switch the power to the heater (usually around 1kW).

Most water-bath controllers (purchased or home-made) need a temperature difference of about 5°C between the water in the bath and the ambient temperature to work effectively. If the ambient temperature is high or tests are required at low temperatures, a water cooler is also needed. An old refrigerator is the best solution; the water can be circulated through the ice box, or the compressor and heat exchanges can be removed from the cabinet and used to cool the bath directly.

Laboratory-scale reactors

Laboratory biogas reactors are usually glass flasks of between 1 and 5l capacity. Plastic flasks can be used, but they are difficult to make gas-tight. Special digestion bottles are available from specialist suppliers, but these are expensive. Suitable conical flasks can be obtained from suppliers in many countries. The neck of the flask must be wide enough to allow at least two or three access pipes to pass through the bung closing it. A gas outlet is

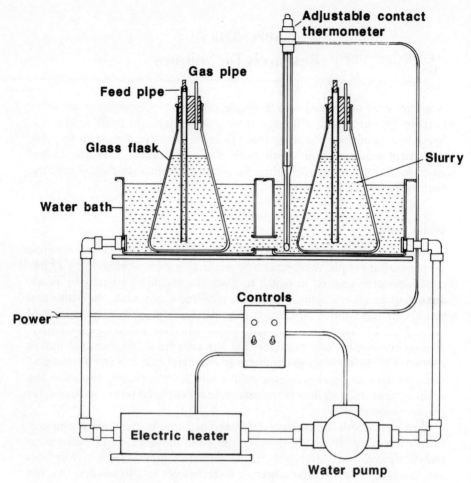

Figure III.1 *Schematic diagram of a temperature-controlled system*

required as well as a sampling tube through which to add and remove slurry samples. A third pipe is required if a mechanical mixer is to be used.

Gas is usually collected into a bottle over water that is displaced into a second bottle (Fig. III.2). The water should have added salt (sodium chloride) and acid (hydrochloric or sulphuric) to stop carbon dioxide dissolving. The gas-collecting bottles can each be graduated, but the usual practice is to connect the bottles from several reactors through a valved manifold to a single graduated cylinder (Fig. III.2). This is filled with acidulated brine via a pipe in the bottom connected to a reservoir bottle. The pressure of the gas in the cylinder can be adjusted by raising or

144

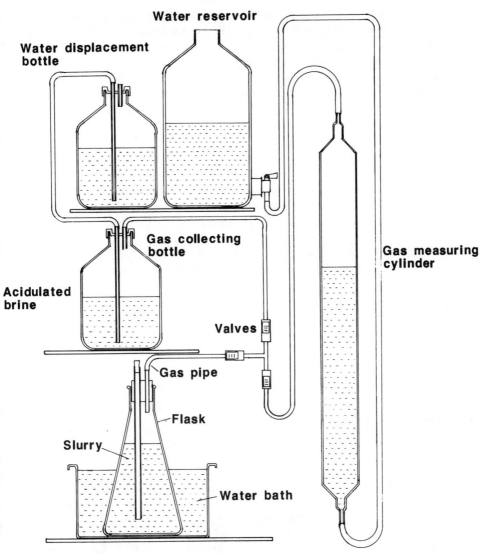

Figure III.2 *Schematic diagram of a digesting system.*

lowering this bottle. Volume readings should always be taken at zero gauge pressure, ie. with the level of water in the reservoir being held at the same level as the water in the cylinder.

Since the water-receiving bottle from each reactor is usually placed above its gas-collecting bottle, the gas is collected under a positive pressure

(200mm to 500mm water gauge). The pipe through which slurry samples are removed, and added in the case of semi-continuous reactors, should therefore be sealed against this pressure. Samples are taken or added when the pressure is removed, such as when gas measurements are taken. The end of this sampling pipe should dip well below the surface of the slurry to prevent air entering the gas space. For semi-continuous reactors it is usual to remove a fixed volume of slurry before replacing it with the same amount of fresh, the exact volume being related to the feeding rate and retention time defined for the reactor. If slurry samples are being regularly removed from a batch reactor the total volume of slurry in the reactor will obviously decrease and allowance for must be made for this in the calculations.

The positive pressure also makes mixing difficult. A stirrer driven by a rotating magnet is not very effective, especially if the slurry is thick and viscous. The shaft of a mechanical stirrer needs to be sealed against gas or slurry leakage. If the reactors are used to simulate low-rate rural digesters, then an occasional shake by hand is sufficient (2 to 3 minutes one to four times a day.[1]

At higher reactor temperatures (30°C and above) water vapour may be carried over with the gas. To ensure accuracy, this water may be absorbed (eg. in a tube of drying agent) and the same weight of fresh water added each day.

Temperature measurement in full-scale reactors

The most obvious way to measure the slurry temperature is to place a thermometer in a sample of slurry dipped from the digester pit. Samples of slurry can be removed from the inside of the digester pit usng a dipper bucket (Fig. III.3) passed through the slurry inlet or outlet. Unless a digester is being heated, the slurry temperature is very uniform and changes

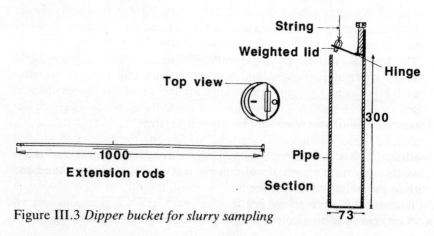

Figure III.3 *Dipper bucket for slurry sampling*

146

very slowly,[2] so a single daily reading is sufficient. An easier approach is to use a soil thermometer with a long temperature probe. The read-out can be a dial for single readings, although a recording thermograph will give a continuous plot of temperature for a week at a time. These machines can be powered by clockwork or batteries for operation in places remote from a power supply.

Gas production measurements

There are two aspects to the measurement of the gas production from a full-scale biogas plant: the gas used and the gas remaining in the plant. Cumulative wet-type gas meters are very accurate and can be made of materials that are unaffected by biogas (obtainable from suppliers in India and the developed world). Normal domestic gas meters usually contain parts made of plated steel, which are quickly corroded by the hydrogen sulphide in biogas. Most wet-type gas meters are not designed to cope with the higher pressures from a displacement digester. The gas may be passed through a pressure regulator before its volume is measured. DCS, in Nepal, designed their own gas meter, made from acrylic plastic (perspex or plexiglass) and capable of withstanding these pressures (Fig. III.4).[3]

The gas remaining in a drum plant is easy to measure: it is the height at which the drum is floating in the slurry times the cross-sectional area of the drum. The gas remaining in a dome plant can be estimated from its pressure and the position of the slurry surface in the reservoir (Figure III.5).[4] The determination of the gas in a bag plant is very difficult, unless the bag is full.

Gas analysis

Instruments for gas analysis are used extensively by the oil industry, so are available in many parts of the world. More sophisticated apparatus must be obtained from a supplier in a developed country.

The best way to analyse biogas samples is to use a gas chromatograph, although these are expensive and delicate instruments, accurate to better than 0.1 per cent. A column designed for the separation of permanent gases should be used with a thermal conductivity detecter. The supplier should be approached for advice about the correct column to use. A molecular sieve column will separate hydrogen, oxygen, nitrogen and methane, but is permanently contaminated if carbon dioxide and water pass through it. A 'Carbosieve' column will separate air, methane and carbon dioxide and even oxygen and nitrogen, if used carefully. Hydrogen or helium gas is used as a carrier.

A much less expensive device for gas analysis is the Orsat Apparatus,

147

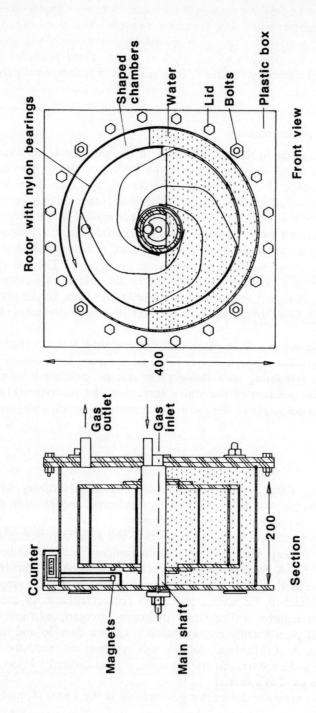

Figure III.4 *Plastic gas meter design*

148

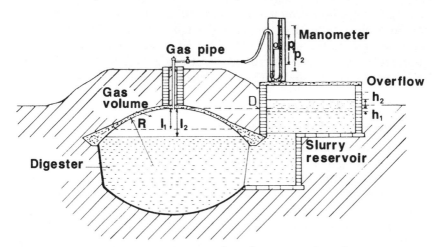

Change of volume of gas in dome = $\pi.(l_1^2 - l_2^2) R - \frac{1}{3}.(l_1^3 - l_2^2)$ where l_1 and l_2 are levels of slurry at two different times.

Slurry level: $l = p - h$

　　Where p = pressure of gas (measured in mm.H_2O by a manometer)

　　　　　h = height of slurry in reservoir from datum point: D.

Figure III.5 *Measurement of gas left in a dome plant*

which consists of a series of bulbs, full of suitable solutions to absorb different gases. The volume of a sample of biogas is measured before and after it is passed into a bulb to absorb a constituent, such as potassium hydroxide to absorb carbon dioxide. Methane cannot be absorbed directly, so it is usually combusted over a catalyst (such as platinum) and the carbon dioxide produced measured. It is a laborious piece of equipment to operate,[5] but it can produce accurate results (around 1 per cent) if used carefully. This instrument can be obtained from manufacturers in India.

A simpler version of this apparatus is the carbon dioxide analyser, which only uses one bulb filled with potassium hydroxide solution. As the carbon dioxide is absorbed, a rubber diaphragm allows the liquid to rise up the bulb, giving a measure of the original proportion of carbon dioxide in the biogas. While being much less accurate (2 to 3 per cent), it is robust and could be used for field tests.

A fourth alternative is an electronic methane detector. This draws a sample of gas through a cell in which the thermal conductivity of the gas is measured. While these instruments are usually calibrated for a mixture of methane in air, they can be used for rough checks in the field. The instrument can be recalibrated with different known biogas mixtures, although an accuracy of better than 5 per cent cannot be expected.

pH measurement

The simplest way to measure pH is using indicator papers, which can be dipped into a sample of slurry removed from a digester. A set of papers for the region around neutral is very cheap and easy to use. However, slurry can cause discolouration of the paper and make the result difficult to see. A more accurate instrument is a pH meter, an electronic device that uses a glass probe dipped into the slurry. Most models are battery driven and robust enough to be used, with care, in the field.

Total solids and volatile solids analysis

The measurement of total solids involves placing a weighed sample in an oven and drying it for several hours at 105°C. The sample should be kept in a high-temperature glass or glazed ceramic container and care should be taken that the dried sample does not reabsorb moisture from the atmosphere before it is weighed. The proportion of total solids in the sample is given by the weight of the dried sample divided by the weight of the wet original.

Volatile solids content is measured by heating the dried sample at 500 or 600°C for several hours in a furnace and weighing the residue. The heating of animal dung to such high temperatures causes it to burn, so the furnace should be sited where the obnoxious smoke given off does not give offence. The volatile solids proportion is the difference between the weight of the dried sample before and after combustion, divided by its weight before.

COD and alkalinity measurements

Theoretically 1 gram of COD destroyed gives 0.35 litres of biogas, so COD is a useful measure of the concentration of the substrate available for digestion. A homogenised sample of slurry is diluted with water and boiled under reflux with known concentrations of mercuric sulphate, sulphuric acid and potassium dichromate for about 2 hours. After the solution has cooled, it is titrated against a reducing agent, ferrous ammonium sulphate, using a ferrion indicator to measure the concentration of unused oxidising agent.[6] A sample containing no slurry is treated in the same way to give a standard. The quantity of potassium dichromate required to oxidise the slurry sample is a measure of the COD.

Alkalinity is measured by titrating a sample of slurry against dilute sulphuric acid using either an indicator or a pH meter to show when the pH reaches 4.5. The alkalinity is a measure of the stability of the reactor and is measured in milligrammes of calcium carbonate per litre of slurry.

APPENDIX IV
Model for Biogas Digestion

The first order model for biogas digestion is based on two assumptions.[1,2]
1. The rate of substrate conversion to biogas is directly proportional to the substrate concentration:

$$\frac{dS}{dt} = -k.S \qquad \text{(IV.1)}$$

where t is time and k is the first order rate constant (measured in l/days). The substrate concentration (S) can be expressed as total solids, volatile solids, COD or BOD.
2. The volume of gas given off by the digester is proportional to the mass of substrate destroyed:

$$G = C.V.(S_o - S) \qquad \text{(IV.2a)}$$

$$g = C.v.(S_o - S) \qquad \text{(IV.2b)}$$

where G is the cumulative gas production from a batch plant and V is the volume of the reactor, while g is the daily gas production from a continuous plant and v is the daily feed rate. C is the yield constant for the substrate, S_o is the initial and S is the final substrate concentration.

For batch reactors, the substrate remaining in the reactor (S) is given by integrating expression (IV.1):

$$S = S_o.\exp\{-k.(t - t_o)\}, \qquad \text{(IV.3)}$$

where S_o is the initial substrate concentration (in kg.VS/l) and t_o is the 'lag time', the time for the gas production to reach its peak value. The model is obviously inadequate, as it suggests that the substrate concentration can be greater than the initial value when $t < t_o$, but it does offer a useful description of average reactor behaviour at longer times. For analysis, the results are best plotted on a straight line, by taking natural logarithms:

$$\ln(\frac{S}{S_o}) = -k.t + k.t_o. \qquad \text{(IV.4)}$$

151

A regression analysis on the data should give a slope of: $-k$ and an intercept on the 'y' axis of: $k.t_o$.

This equation can be extended (using equation 2a) to predict cumulative gas production:

$$G = C.V.(S_o - S)$$
$$= C.V.S_o.[1 - \exp\{-k.(t - t_o)\}], \tag{IV.5}$$

Taking natural logarithms:

$$\ln\left(1 - \frac{G}{C.V.S_o}\right) = -k.t + k.t_o. \tag{IV.6}$$

If the yield constant: C is known (see equation IV.15), a regression analysis g ves the kinetic constant: k and the lag time: t_o. In principle, the values for these constants should be the same as those found from the results for the substrate concentration data.

For continuous reactors, the rate at which the substrate is consumed by the bacteria depends on the volume feeding rate (v, l slurry per day). This is related to the retention time (R, days) and the loading rate (r, kg.VS./m³/day):

$$R = \frac{V}{v} \quad \text{and} \quad r = \frac{v.TS.VS.1000}{V} = \frac{TS.VS.1000}{R} \tag{IV.7}$$

where V is the reactor volume and TS and VS are the total and volatile solid contents of the feed

$$v.(S_o - S) = k.S.V \quad \text{or} \quad S_o - S = k.S.R,$$

so: $S = \dfrac{S_o}{1 + k.R}$ (IV.8)

and: $g = C.V.S_o. \dfrac{k}{1 + k.R}$ (from IV.2b), (IV.9)

where S is the effluent substrate concentration (eg. in kg.VS).

Rewriting these equations in a linear form:

$$\frac{S_o}{S} = k.R. + 1 \tag{IV.10}$$

and: $R = C.\dfrac{V.S_o}{g} - \dfrac{1}{k}.$ (IV.11)

Plotting substrate reduction data at various retention times as a straight line should give a slope of: k and an intercept of: 1. Similarly, a regression

152

analysis of retention time (R) plotted against $(V.S_o/g)$ should give a slope of: C and an intercept of: $-1/k/$.

The values of k in the above equations should vary with temperature according to an Arrhenius equation:

$$k = A.\exp - \left(\frac{E}{RT}\right) \qquad (IV.12)$$

where A is a constant, E is the activation energy, R is the universal gas constant (= 8314 J/kg. K) and T is the temperature in K.

This equation, too, can be written in a linear form, by taking natural logarithms:

$$\ln(k) = -\frac{E}{RT} + \ln(A). \qquad (IV.13)$$

By plotting $\ln(k)$ against $1/T$, the constants $\ln(A)$ and E/R can be found.

The yield constant: C also appears to vary with temperature, but in a less predictable way.

In order to use the batch model, the gas production of a batch plant should be measured daily and the feedstock concentration at least once a week. The feedstock concentration can be measured in kg. TS, VS, COD or BOD, but the volatile solids measurement is easiest to use.

For batch reactors:

$$C = \frac{G}{(S_o - S).V} \qquad ...(IV.14)$$

so a graph of cumulative specific gas production (G/V) against the concentration of feedstock digested $(S_o - S)$ should give a straight line of slope: C. If this value for: C is used in equation IV.6, then values for rate constant: k and lag time can be found. In practice, there seem to be two values for rate constant depending on the length of time for which the reactor has been run. At short digestion times the rate appears to be defined by how fast simple molecules of feedstock can be turned into methane (methanogenisis is rate limiting). At longer digestion times, once the simple molecules in the feed are used up, the rate is limited by how fast more complex molecules can be hydrolised to compounds that can be utilised by acid-forming bacteria (hydrolysis is rate limiting). Typical values for yield constants and initial and final rate constants for cattle and pig dung are given in Table IV.1.

The cumulative gas production and the volatile solids and COD degradation curves with time are shown in Fig. IV.1 for data from the digestion of cattle dung at 33.5°C in the UK.[2] Fig. IV.2 shows the gas production against VS and COD digested, giving values of C_v of 828 l/kg.VS digested and C_c of 578 l/kg.COD digested (compared to the theoretical value of 583 l/kg.COD digested, assuming 60 per cent methane in the gas). Fig. IV.3 gives the logarithmic plot of the gas production equation, showing the two rate constants at different times. The initial rate constant (k_i) is 0.00961 l/day using the VS data between 0 and 34 days and the final rate constant (k_f) is 0.00239 l/day between 35 and 90 days.

Example IV.1 Analysis of batch reactor results:

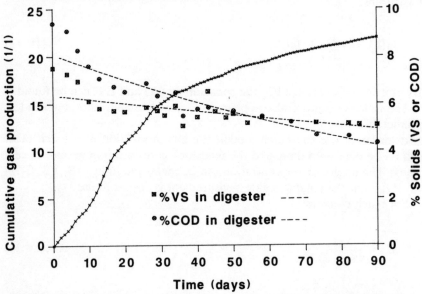

Figure IV.1 *Cumulative gas production, VS and COD degradation with time*

To use the semi-continuous model for biogas digestion a series of reactors must be set up, each with a different retention time. The reactors may have the same volume, but are fed at different rates with slurry from the same source. The daily gas production (g) and the substrate concentration in the influent (S_o) and effluent (S) are measured. After the reactor has become stable, ie. when the daily readings remain roughly the same for at least 5 days running, a series of readings is recorded.[2] This will take at least two retention times (2 × R) and may take longer (up to 4 × R) from the time the digester is started or a new set of running conditions have been established. Using equation IV.11, values for the yield (C) and rate (k) constants can be found for this series of reactors. Again,[3] there is evidence

154

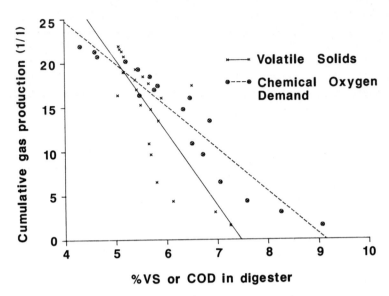

Figure IV.2 *Gas produced against substrate concentration*

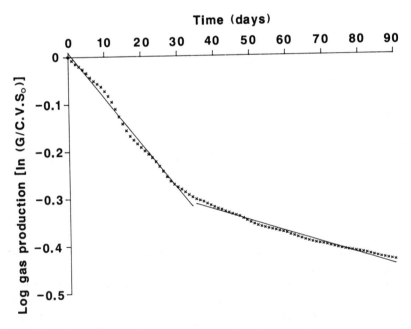

Figure IV.3 *Logrithmic plot of the gas production equation*

that lower-rate constants at longer retention times can be identified. Typical values for yield and rate constants for cattle dung in semi-continuous digesters are given in Table IV.2.

A plot of the data from a series of semi-continuous reactors using cattle dung at $33.5°C^2$ is given in Fig. IV.4. The retention time (R) is plotted against the inverse specific gas production $(V.S_o/g)$ for feedstock concentrations measured in terms of VS and COD. The slope of these lines gives a value for the yield constant (C = 402 l/kg/VS or 347 l/kg/COD) and the intercept gives the rate constant (k = 0.083 l/day in terms of VS data and k = 0.083 l/day based on COD data)

Example IV.2 Analysis of semi-continuous results.

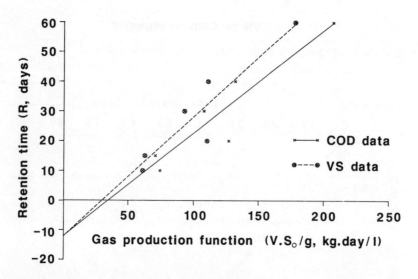

Figure IV.4 *Plot of semi-continuous digester data*

These equations and data can be used to predict the performance of full-size biogas digesters using the similar feedstocks to the experiments. A CD10 plant, run as a semi-continuous digester, is fed daily with 60 l of water mixed with 60 kg of cattle dung from the same source as the experiments in Example IV.2. If the slurry temperature is maintained at 33.5°C, the gas production can be calculated:

$$g = C.V.S_o \cdot \frac{k}{1 + k.R}$$

The working volume (V) of a CP10 plant is 9 m^3 (Table I.3) so the retention time (R = V/v) is 9 m^3/.12 m^3/day = 75 days. The total solids content of cattle dung mixed 1:1 with water is usually around 9 per cent and the volatile solids content is 80 per cent of this, say 72 kg/m^3 (assuming the density of slurry is 1000 kg/m^3).
From Example IV.2: C = 402 l/kg.VS and k = 0.083, so:

$g = 2.99$ m^3/day.

At 16°C: C = 178 l/kg.VS and k = 0.033, so:

$g = 1.10$ m^3/day.

Example IV.3 Use of semi-continuous equation.

Table IV.1   Kinetic constants for batch digesters

Temp. (°C)	Yield (l/kg)		Rate Constant (1.d)				Ref.
	V.S.	COD	VS:Init	Final	Cod:Init	Final	
35	578	–	0.018	0.0022	–	–	4
33.5	895	513	0.0129	0.0033	0.0188	0.0054	1
25	829	525	0.0068	0.0023	0.0090	0.0031	1
16	–	514	–	–	0.0038	–	1

Notes: The yield constants are in terms of V.S. or COD destroyed.
The constants deprived from Maramba[4] are for pig dung, while those for Lau-Wong[1] are for cattle dung, from animals fed in the UK with maize silage and protein concentrates.

The values for these constants derived from semi-continuous results are not the same as those from batch results, even when fed from the same source used for both. The detailed mechanisms of digestion, especially the bacterial poulation balances, are likely to be different between the two modes of anaerobic digestion. Therefore results from laboratory tests on batch digesters should not be used for predicting performance of semi-continuous digesters and vice-versa.

Table IV.2   Kinetic constants for cattle dung in S-C digesters

Temp (°C)	Yield Constant (l/kg)		Rate Constant (l/d)		Ref.
	Vol.Sol.	COD	Vol.Sol.	COD	
33.5	402	347	0.083	0.081	2
30.1	450	–	0.052	–	1
27.5	310	–	0.044	–	1
25	289	237	0.069	0.078	2
24.4	250	–	0.036	–	1
20.3	310	–	0.022	–	1
16	178	164	0.033	0.026	2

Notes: The yield constants are in terms of V.S. or COD destroyed.
The feedstock for Lau-Wong[1] was dung from buffalo in Nepal, fed on straw and dried grass, while that for Chowdhury[2] was dung from cattle in UK, fed on maize silage and protein concentrates.

Table IV.3   Constants used in Arrhenius Equation (IV.12)

Feed-stock	Type	Frequ.Fact.(A)	Energy (E/R)	Ref.
Cattle Dung (Nepal)	S-Cont	7.5×10^9	7780	1
Cattle Dung (UK)	S-Cont	3.6×10^5	4610	2
Cattle Dung (UK) V.S.	Batch	1.6×10^7	6430	2
Cattle Dung (UK) COD	Batch	1.8×10^{10}	8460	2

Table IV.4 Variables used in Appendix IV

A	– Frequency factor in Arrhenius equation	(–)
C	– Gas yield constant	(m^3/kg)
E	– Activation energy in Arrhenius equation	(J/kg)
g	– Daily gas production	(m^3/day)
G	– Cummulative gas production (over time)	(m^3)
k	– Rate of digestion	(l/day)
r	– Loading rate	$(kg.VS/day)$
R	– Gas constant (= 8314)	$(J/kg. K)$
S	– Substrate concentration	(kg/m^3)
S_o	– Initial substrate concentration	(kg/m^3)
t	– Time	(days)
t_o	– Lag time – time to peak gas production	(days)
T	– Absolute temperature (°C + 273)	(K)
v	– Volume feed rate to digester	(m^3/day)
V	– Volume of slurry in digester	(m^3)

Notes: S, S_o and C can be expressed in terms of kilograms of TS, VS, COD, or BOD, as long as one unit is used in all the equations consistently.

Economic Assumptions

Basic equations

The amortization factor (A) is used to calculate the yearly cost of a loan.[1] The total bill includes the repayments of capital plus interest. This is divided into equal yearly portions.

$$A = \frac{I \times (1 + I)^N}{(1 + I)^N - 1}$$

where: I = Annual interest rate (%/100)
$\qquad$ N = Lifetime of loan (years)
If: $\qquad$ C = Capital borrowed: the yearly repayment:
$\qquad$ $R_y = A \times C$, and the total repayment:
$\qquad$ $R_t = A \times C \times N$.

For a loan of Rs.10,000 at 11% annual interest over 7 years:
$\qquad$ $A = 0.212$, R_y = Rs.2,120 and: R_t = Rs.14,840.

The discount factor (D) is used to calculate the 'worth' of benefits or costs,[1] accrued or paid over the lifetime of the project, assuming these are the same each year[1]:

$$D = \sum_{k=0}^{M} \frac{1}{(1 + J)^k}$$

where: J = Discount rate (%/100)
$\qquad$ M = Project lifetime (years).
If: $\qquad$ B = the Benefit or Cost per year, the Nett Present Worth (NPW)
$\qquad$ = $B \times D$.

For a discount rate of 15% and a project lifetime of 10 years:

$\qquad$ $D = 5.019$. If B = Rs.1,000,
$\qquad$ NPW = Rs.5,019 over 10 years.

If the benefits or costs change from year to year:

$$NPW = \sum_{k=0}^{M} \frac{B_k}{(1 + J)^k}$$

where: B_k is the Benefit or Cost for the Kth year.

Assumptions for domestic biogas

The biogas used from a plant is valued in terms of how much fuel wood and kerosene it replaces (Table V.1), using figures for cost and usage for a typical family living near Butwal, on the plains of Nepal, supplied by N.B. Pradhan. These show that 2,578kg of wood (120 bundles at 21.5kg/bundle) are used per year at a cost of Rs.1 per kg. (Rs.21.50 per bundle) plus 146 litres of kerosene at Rs.6 per litre, mainly for lighting.

The value of the fertilizer saved assumes that 44 per cent of the nitrogen available in raw dung is lost if the dung is stored in a pile (normal practice in Nepal). A second assumption is made that only 11 per cent of this nitrogen is lost if the dung is digested in a biogas plant (Table V.2).

Table V.1   Heating values of various fuels used by a family.

Fuel	Heat Val. MJ	Burner Effic.	Fuel/ Year	Heat MJ/yr	Biogas Equiv.	Value £/yr.
Biogas	$19.4/m^3$	55%	$911m^3$	9705	$911m^3$	144
Firewood	18.0/kg	15%	2,578kg	6956	$653m^3$	107
Kerosene	37.7/l	50%	146l	2749	$258m^3$	37

Running a biogas plant is assumed to take about an hour a day. This job is done either by a member of the household (unpaid) or by a domestic servant or a farm worker. A typical unskilled labourer's wage of Rs.10 per day is assumed. The maintenance cost of Rs.100 per year is arbitrary.

Table V.2   Value of fertiliser saved by using a biogas plant

Total dung fed to CP15 plant per year	(wet)	=	32,850kg
	(dry)	=	6,570kg
Nitrogen content of raw dung (1.8%)		=	118kg
Nitrogen content of stored dung (1.0%, 44% loss)		=	66kg
Nitrogen content of slurry (1.6%, 11% loss)		=	105kg
Saving of nitrogen by use of biogas		=	39kg
Equivalent quantity of Urea saved (47% N_2)		=	84kg
Value of Urea saved (at Rs.4/kg)		=	Rs.332
			£14

Assumptions for milling systems

The milling year in Nepal is split into three main seasons: the rice hulling season (November to March), after the main rice crop is harvested, the wheat milling season (April to July), and the slack season (August to October). During the last season, most people mill only enough stored grain to satisfy their domestic needs, although some early rice and maize is also milled. The income for these three seasons is given in Table V.3, which is based on the limited survey of two biogas mills near Butwal.

The amount and value of diesel used in both a 5kW diesel-only mill and a dual-fuel mill is given in Table V.4 for the same three seasons. It is assumed that only 20% of diesel is used in a dual-fuel engine, the rest of the fuel being biogas. In practice, mill drivers seem to often use less than the optimum of 80% biogas. Possibly the engine runs more smoothly with more diesel, or else the wives of the mill owners want enough biogas left to cook the evening meal. The analysis also assumes that, using the heat exchanger, the slurry can be kept at 30°C all the year round, so the maximum gas production (14.5m^3/day) is available from the feed of 300kg of cattle dung or equivalent per day. The spare gas (valued at Rs.3.8/m^3) is assumed to be used for domestic purposes.

Table V.3   Typical income for a 5kW mill

Months	Days/ Season	Hrs/ Day	Quantity/day (kg)		Income	
			Rice	Wheat	Rs(NC)	£
Nov/Mar	151	4	750	26	13,200	550
Apr/Jul	122	4	600	32	9,200	383
Aug/Oct	92	1	50	26	1,600	67
Total					24,000	1,000

Notes: Rice is hulled at 300kg/hr, at Rs5 per 50kg
       Wheat is ground at 38kg/hr, at Rs1.5 per 3kg

Table V.4   Biogas and diesel usage in mills

Months of Seasons	Diesel Used (lit)				Gas used m^3		Gas left m^3	
	DO/day	DF	DO/seas.	DF	/day	/se.	/day	/se.
Nov/Mar	5.6	1.2	840	180	11.2	1,680	3.3	498
Apr/Jul	5.6	1.2	680	140	11.2	1,360	3.3	402
Aug/Oct	1.4	0.3	120	25	2.8	250	11.7	1,076
Totals			1,640	345		3,290		1,976
Values	Rs.(NC)		9,840	2,070		7,770		7,500
	£(UK)		410	86		324		313

Note: Do = Diesel Only, DF = Dual-Fuel Mill.

162

Costs for a diesel-only mill, 1986 prices in Butwal:

	RS.(NC)	£
5kW diesel fuel engine (from India)	18,000	750
Milling machinery	8,000	334
	26,000	1,084

The yearly costs for running the mill are:

Labour to run the milling machinery	4,600	193
Maintenance for all equipment (assumed)	3,000	125
Diesel used	9,840	410
Lubricating oil (assumed)	800	32
	18,240	760

The yearly benefits are:

Income from milling operations (App. V)	24,000	1,000

Cost:Benefit Analysis	Rs.(NC)	£
Capital cost of project	26,000	1,084
Discounted running costs (15%, 10yrs)	91,542	3,814
Present Worth Costs (PWC)	117,542	4,898
Present Worth Benefits (PWB, 15%, 10yrs)	120,450	5,019
Nett Present Worth (PWB–PWC)	2,908	121
Benefit:Cost Ratio (PWB/PWC)	1.02	
Internal Rate of Return	16%	

Example V.1 Economic analysis of a diesel milling system.

Assumptions for irrigation systems.

The key to the analysis is the amount of water available.[2] Assuming a 4.5kW pump and a 5-metre-deep well, the water flow can be calculated:

$$P = \frac{H.Q.g.\rho}{\eta}$$

where
P	=	the engine power	(watts)
H	=	the pumping head	(metres)
Q	=	the water flow	(litres/sec)
g	=	the acceleration due to gravity	(9.81 m/s^2)
ρ	=	the density of water	(1kg/l)
η	=	the pump efficiency.	

Assuming a pump efficiency of 50 per cent, this formula suggests that 45.9 l per second is available, or 165m^3 per hour. The biogas usage per hour is 2.52m^3, plus 0.3 litres of diesel fuel. It is assumed that the limit to the area to be irrigated is defined by the water available, which, in turn, depends on the biogas available. In Madhubasa, the biogas plant is sited about 500 metres away from the engine, so engine-cooling water cannot be used to heat the plant. This means the biogas production is limited during the winter months (Table V.5). The water requirement of the two crops is very variable during the growing seasons and is also influenced by the water available from rain (Table V.5). These water requirement figures are based on a study of crops on the Ganges plain in India,[3] assuming a normal year for rainfall. The critical month for rice is November, when the monsoons have finished, but water is needed to help the grains to fill. If all the available biogas is used to pump water in this month, then 5.2 hectares can be planted with paddy. For wheat, the critical month is February, allowing 8.3 hectares to be planted. The figures for water requirement are corrected for losses, such as water leaching out of the soil and through canal banks and evaporation (using a factor of 0.32 for rice and 0.55 for wheat).[3]

Table V.5a   Water, biogas and diesel requirements

	Rice season (5.2ha)					
Months of the year	June	July	Aug.	Sep.	Oct.	Nov.*
Water requ. (mm/day)	0	25.2	18.9	17.7	16.0	11.6
Rain average (mm/d)	9.3	21.6	24.2	16.5	6.0	1.0
Irrig. requ. (mm/d)	0	3.6	0	1.2	10.0	10.6
Water pump. (m^3/d)	0	18.7	0	62.4	520	550
Hours/day pumped	0	0.1	0	0.4	3.2	3.4
Biogas (m^3.day)	14.5	14.5	14.5	11.5	11.5	8.5
Biogas used (m^3/d)	0	0.3	0	1.0	8.1	8.5
Biogas left (m^3.d)	14.5	14.2	14.5	10.5	3.4	0
Diesel used (1/mon)	0	0.9	0	3.6	29.8	30.6
Diesel value (Rs/m)	0	5.4	0	21.6	179	184
Biogas value (Rs/m)	1,650	1,674	1,705	40	13	0

The crop production and value figures (Table V.6) are based on data[4] from the Janakpur Agricultural Development Project (JADP), a Japanese-funded programme, about 10km away from Madhubasa. An analysis can also be made for a drought year, when rainfall is much less (Table V.7). The area sown to crops is much reduced, but it can be assumed that the crop prices will rise. An analysis can also be made for a diesel-only system, providing irrigation for the same areas of land.

Table V.5b Requirements for irrigation scheme

Months of the year	Wheat season (8.3ha)					
	Dec.	Jan.	Feb.*	Mar.	Apr.	May
Water requ. (mm/day)	3.0	4.8	8.0	3.0	0	0
Rain average (mm/d)	0.2	1.5	1.4	0.7	0.2	0.7
Irrig. requ. (mm/d)	2.8	3.3	6.6	2.3	0	0
Water pump. (m^3/d)	232	274	550	191	0	0
Hours/day pumped	1.3	1.7	3.4	1.2	0	0
Biogas (m^3/day)	8.5	8.5	8.5	11.5	11.5	14.5
Biogas used (m^3/d)	3.3	4.3	8.5	3.0	0	0
Biogas left (m^3/d)	5.2	4.2	0	8.5	11.5	14.5
Diesel used (1/mon)	12.1	15.8	28.6	11.2	0	0
Diesel value (Rs/m)	73	94.8	171.6	67.2	0	0
Biogas value (Rs/m)	613	495	0	1,001	1,311	1,705

Notes: Total value of diesel used: Rs.785 (£33)
Total value of biogas saved: Rs.10265 (£428)
*Critical month for crop.

Table V.6   Costs and income from use of irrigation system

Costs (in 1983 Rs(NC))	Paddy (2.4ha)	Wheat (9.6ha)	Total
Cost of seed (50kg/ha)	780	1,980	2,760
Cost of extra fertiliser	4,460	9,510	13,970
Cost of extra labour	780	8,450	9,230
Benefit (in 1983 Rs(NC))	3.0–2.0t/ha	2.5t/ha	
Income—sale of crop	11,700	56,000	67,700

Notes: The costs and profits for paddy are the extra ones resulting from
an irrigated crop instead of a rain-fed one.

Table V.7a   Water, biogas and diesel requirements in drought

			Rice season (4.4ha)			
Months of the year	June	July*	Aug.	Sep.	Oct.	Nov.
Water requ. (mm/day)	0	25.2	18.9	17.7	16.0	11.6
Rain average (mm/d)	9.3	3.6	9.9	0.5	0	0
Irrig. requ. (mm/d)	0	21.6	9.0	17.2	16.0	11.6
Water pump (m^3/d)	0	950	396	757	704	510
Hours/day pumped	0	5.8	2.4	4.6	4.3	3.1
Biogas (m^3/day)	14.5	14.5	14.5	11.5	11.5	8.5
Biogas used (m^3/d)	0	14.5	6.0	11.5	10.8	7.8
Biogas left (m^3/d)	14.5	0	8.5	0	0.7	0.7
Diesel used (1/mon)	0	53.9	22.3	41.4	40.0	27.9
Diesel value (Rs/m)	0	324	134	248	240	167
Biogas value (Rs/m)	1,650	0	1,001	0	82	82

Table V.7b   Requirements for irrigation scheme in drought

			Wheat season (7.0ha)			
Months of the year	Dec.	Jan.	Feb.*	Mar.	Apr.	May
Water requ. (mm/day)	3.0	4.8	8.0	3.0	0	0
Rain average (mm/d)	0	0	0	0	0	0
Irrig. requ. (mm/d)	3.0	4.8	8.0	3.0	0	0
Water pump (m^3/d)	210	336	560	210	0	0
Hours/day pumped	1.3	2.0	3.4	1.3	0	0
Biogas (m^3/day)	8.5	8.5	8.5	11.5	11.5	14.5
Biogas used (m^3/d)	3.3	5.0	8.5	3.3	0	0
Biogas left (m^3/d)	5.2	3.5	0	8.2	11.5	14.5
Diesel used (1/mon)	12	19	29	12	0	0
Diesel value (Rs/m)	72	114	174	72	0	0
Biogas value (Rs/m)	613	412	0	966	1,311	1,705

Notes: Total value of diesel used: Rs.1,321 (£55)
Total value of biogas saved: Rs.7,822 (£926)

Glossary

Abbreviations

ADB Asian Development Bank, Head Office, Manilla, Philippines.

ADB/N Agricultural Development Bank of Nepal, Head Office, Ram Shah Path, Kathmandu, Nepal.

AFPRO Action for Food Production, C17 Community Centre, Safdarjang Development Area, New Delhi 110 017, India.

AICB All India Committee on Biogas, Dept. of Science and Technology, Delhi, India.

BORDA Bremen Overseas Research and Development Association, Hoffnungstrasse 30, D2800 Bremen 1, West Germany.

BTI Butwal Technical Institute, Butwal, Lumbini Zone, Nepal.

DCS Development and Consulting Services, PO Box 8, Butwal, Lumbini Zone, Nepal.

FAO Food and Agricultural Organisation of the United Nations, Head Office, Rome, Italy.

GO/ARF Group Organiser/Action Research Fellow—people employed by the SFDP as community motivators.

GOBAR GAS CO. Gobar Gas tatha Krishi Yantr Bikash (P) Ltd., Head Office, Kupondol, Kathmandu, Nepal.

HMG/N His Majesty's Government of Nepal (Nepal is a constitutional monarchy).

IIM India Institute of Management, Vastrapur, Ahmedabad 380 015, India.

JADP Janakpur Agricultural Development Project, Janakpur, Nepal.

JTA Junior Technical Assistant: extension workers for the Department of Agriculture in Nepal.

KVIC Khadi and Village Industries Commission, Head Office, Gramodaya Ida Road, Vile Parle (West), Bombay 400 056, India (and Gobar Gas Research and Development Centre, Kora Gramodyog Kendra, Borivli (West), Bombay 400 092, India).

KIRLOSKAR Kirloskar Oil Engines Ltd., Head Office, 13, Laxmanrao Kirloskar Road, Pune 411 003, India.

NBEO National Biogas Extension Office, Beijing, China.

NGO Non-Governmental Organisation.

NSPRC The National Standard of the People's Republic of China, San Li He, Fu Wai, Beijing, China.

PRAD Planning, Research and Action Division, State Planning Institute of Uttah Pradesh, Kalakankar, Lucknow (and Biogas Office, Ajitmal, near Etawah, U.P., India).

PEACE CORPS An organisation, based in USA, which sends short-term volunteers (usually for two years) to work in developing countries.

R & D Research and Development.

RCUP Resource Conservation and Utilization Project, run under the direction of USAID in Nepal.

RMP Red Mud Plastic, a PVC (Poly-Vinyl Chloride) plastic that uses a waste product from aluminium smelting as a filler.

SERC Structural Engineering Research Centre, Roorkee, U.P., India.

SFDP Small Farmers' Development Project, a programme set up by FAO, in co-operation with ADB/N in Nepal.

UMN United Mission to Nepal, PO Box 126, Kathmandu, Nepal.

UNDP United Nations Development Programme, Head Office, New York, USA.

USAID United States Agency for International Development, Washington, USA.

Specialist Terms

ACIDOGENESIS Production of acids by bacteria.

AEROBIC With oxygen.

ANAEROBIC Without oxygen.

AQUIFER Underground rock strata (layers) that carry water.

B:C Benefit:Cost ratio, the ratio of the financial benefits to costs of a project (PWB/PWC).

BACKFILLING Replacing soil behind a wall and ramming it firm.

BOD Biological Oxygen Demand, a measure of the polluting potential of a waste.

BUFFER To control the pH of a solution.

C:N Carbon:Nitrogen ratio—as measured in a feedstock.

COD Chemical Oxygen Demand, a measure of the polluting potential of a waste.

CP— Concrete Dome—the design of biogas plant that uses a fixed, partly spherical gas storage volume (the number refers to the total internal volume in m^3).

CARBURETTOR A device for mixing fuel and air in the correct proportions for combustion in an engine.

CRORE Indian rupees are expressed in lakhs and crores, a Hindi word meaning 'Ten Million' (and written 1,00,00,000). *See* lakh.

CRYOPHYLES Bacteria that operate best at low temperatures.

DATUM A fixed line from which measurements are taken.

DIGESTION Breakdown of foodstuffs to simpler chemicals by living organisms for their own use.

EP— Extended Dome—the design of biogas plant that uses a fixed gas storage volume made as a tunnel with domed ends (the number refers to the total internal volume in m^3).

EFFLUENT That which comes out—slurry that has given up its biogas.

ENTRAINMENT The drawing in of one fluid (air) by another (fuel gas), as it flows from a jet.

ENZYMES Organic catalysts that enable processes, such as digestion, to proceed.

FACULTATIVE Able to live with or without oxygen.

FERROCEMENT A building material made from cement plaster reinforced with wire mesh.

FIBRE-CEMENT A building material made from cement plaster reinforced with plastic or natural fibres.

FLUME A channel made for irrigation water, usually lined with concrete.

GAUGE A rod (or rope) of a fixed length, used to check the main dimensions of a construction.

GI Galvanised Iron—steel or cast iron coated with zinc as protection against corrosion.

GOBAR Hindi word meaning 'cattle dung'.

HDPE High Density Poly-Ethylene—a high-quality form of polythene plastic.

HYDROLYSIS The process of adding oxygen from water to a chemical.

IRR Internal rate of return—an economic assessment of the earning potential of a project.

JANATA Hindi word meaning 'of the people'.

KINETIC CONSTANT A measure of how fast a reaction (such as biogas digestion) proceeds.

LAKH Hindi word meaning 'One Hundred Thousand' (and written 1,00,000).

MESOPHYLES Bacteria that operate best at medium temperatures.

METHANO-GENESIS Production of methane and carbon dioxide by bacteria.

NPW Nett present worth—Difference between the economic benefits and costs of a project (PWB–PWC).

NIGHT-SOIL Human wastes, especially faeces.

OBLIGATE ANAEROBES Bacteria that cannot function in the presence of oxygen.

PH A measure of the acidity of a solution.

PWB Present Worth of Benefits, an economic valuation, in financial terms, of the benefits from a project.

PWC Present Worth of Costs, an economic valuation in financial terms of the costs of a project.

POZZOLANA A volcanic ash used as a mortar or hydraulic cement.

REACTOR A container in which a reaction (eg. biogas digestion) occurs.

REGRESSION ANALYSIS A mathematical technique used to find how closely data would fit a straight line when plotted on a graph.

RETENTION TIME Length of time a feedstock effectively remains in a digester.

SD—— Steel Drum—the design of biogas plant that uses a floating gas holder (the number refers to the nominal daily gas production in ft^3).

SLURRY A liquid with finely divided solids dispersed in it.

STOCHIOMETRIC Optimum ratio of fuel gas to air for complete combustion to occur.

SUBSTRATE Feedstock for bacteria to use.

TS Total Solids—a measure of the dry matter in a slurry.

TEMPLATE A pattern or shape which can be used to check the dimensions and shape of a construction.

TERAI The plains area of Nepal, which used to be covered in thick forest. Many of the trees have been removed to make fertile fields to grow rice and wheat.

THERMOPHYLES Bacteria that operate best at high temperature.

THERMOSTAT A switch that operates at a pre-set temperature.

THROAT The region in the mixing tube of a gas burner with the smallest cross-sectional area.

TOXIC Poisonous to living things, such as bacteria.

VS Volatile Solids—an approximate measure of the organic content of a feedstock.

VENTURI A tube that tapers from both ends to a narrower region between them.

WORKING VOLUME The volume of slurry in a biogas digester that effectively contributes to gas production.

Notes and References

Chapter 1

1. Moulik (1985)
2. Cui (1985)
3. Eggling (1979)
4. Hollingdale (1979)
5. Stuckey (1984)
6. da Silva (1985)
7. Moulik (1982)
8. Roy (1981)
9. Tam (1982)
10. Fry (1974)
11. Bell (1973)
12. Nyns (1984)
13. van den Berg (1983)
14. Hruska (1983)
15. Poland (1985)
16. Nyns (1985)
17. Fulford (1978a and 1978b)
18. Zeikus (1985)
19. Zhao, Y.H. (1985)
20. Wolfe (1983)
21. Mah (1983)
22. Konisky (1985)
23. de Marcario (1985)
24. FAO 40 (1977)
25. van Buren (1979)
26. Pang (1978)
27. Barnett (1978)
28. Prasad (1974)
29. Makhijani (1976)
30. Maramba (1978)
31. Pyle (1979)

Chapter 2

1. Cui (1985)
2. Moulik (1985)
3. McGarry (1978)
4. Huang (1985)
5. Stuckey (1982)

6. NSPRC (1984)
7. Idnani (1974)
8. Moulik (1982)
9. Sathianathan (1975)
10. Singh (1973, 1974)
11. Patankar (1977)
12. Kijne (1984)
13. Lichtman (1987)
14. Raman (1979)
15. Fulford (1978c)
16. Moulik (1975)
17. Saubolle (1976)
18. ERDG (1976)
19. Fulford (1978b)
20. Pyakural (1978)
21. Gorkhali (1984)
22. Fulford (1978a)
23. Barnett (1978)
24. da Silva (1985)

Chapter 3

1. For example: Beenhakker (1980), Chambers (1973), McGrath (1978), Oxfam (1975)
2. Kijne (1984)
3. For example: Beenhakker (1980), IHC (1986), Harper (1984), Oxfam (1985)
4. For example: Beenhakker (1980), Oxfam (1985), Little (1974), ACVAFS (1978)
5. Moulik (1982)
6. Moulik (1984)
7. For example: Harper (1984), Dickson (1986), McGrath (1978)

Chapter 4
1. Gunnerson (1986)
2. Mah (1983)
3. Zhao, Y.H. (1985)
4. Speece (1985)
5. Speece (1983)
6. Yawalker (4th ed. 1977)
7. Murphy (1986)
8. McFarlane (1981)
9. Maramba (1978)
10. NAS (1981)
11. Makhijani (1976)
12. Jewell (1980, 1981)
13. Stuckey (1984)
14. Meynell (1976)
15. House (1978)
16. Gopal (1981)
17. van Soest (–)
18. El-Halwagi (1980)
19. Shen (1985)
20. Lau-Wong (1985)
21. FAO 40 (1977)
22. Cui (1985)
23. McGarry (1978)
24. Hobson (1979)
25. FAO 41 (1978)
26. Idnani (2nd ed. 1974)
27. Fulford (1981)
28. Sathianathan (1975)
29. Cott (1984)

Chapter 5
1. Maramba (1978)
2. Pyle (1979)
3. Gunnerson (1986)
4. Sathianathan (1975)
5. KVIC (1975)
6. Reddy (1980)
7. Finlay (1978)
8. Moulik (1982)
9. Srinivasan (1978)
10. Raman (1979)
11. Finlay (1980)
12. Stafford (1980)
13. NSPRC (1984)
14. van Buren (1979)
15. Ghate (–)
16. Huang (1985)

17. Peng (1985)
18. Tang (1985)
19. Fulford (1985a)
20. Fang (1985)
21. Zhao, C.Y. (1985)
22. Jewell (1980)
23. Tentscher (1986)
24. da Silva (1985)
25. Fry (1974)
26. Bansal (1984)
27. ESCAP (1980)

Chapter 6
1. Cui (1985)
2. Finlay (1978)
3. Lichtman (1983)
4. Bulmer (1985)
5. Abdullahi (1986)
6. House (1978)

Chapter 7
1. Maramba (1978)
2. Mosey (1979)
3. Picken (–)
4. Fry (1974)
5. Kirloskar (–)
6. Hollingdale (1979)
7. Chen (1982)
8. Meier (1978)
9. Garg (–)
10. Gunnerson (1986)

Chapter 8
1. Finlay (1978)
2. Maramba (1978)
3. Lau-Wong (1985)
4. Reddy (1980)
5. Picken (–)
6. Jewell (1980)
7. Speece (1985)
8. Chen (1982)

Chapter 9
1. Bulmer (1979)
2. Moulik (1982)
3. Barnett (1978)
4. Little (1974)
5. Lau-Wong (1984)

172

6. Lichtman (1983)
7. Makhijani (1976)
8. Gunnerson (1986)
9. Pang (1978)
10. McGarry (1978)
11. Chen (1982)
12. Bajracharya (1983)
13. Bhatia (1985)

Chapter 10
1. Chen (1982)
2. Cui (1985)
3. Bulmer (1980)
4. Moulik (1984)
5. Roy (1981)
6. RAFE (1978)
7. Clark (1977)
8. Bajracharya (1983)
9. Fulford (1984)

Chapter 11
1. Idnani (1974)
2. Patankar (1977)
3. Singh (1973, 1974)
4. Reddy (1980)
5. Mazumdar (1982a and b)
6. Moulik (1984)
7. Lichtman (1983)
8. Kijne (1984)
9. Sathianathan (1975)
10. Fulford (1978b)
11. Cui (1985)
12. Moulik (1985)
13. Raman (1979)
14. McGarry (1978)
15. Fulford (1984)
16. NSPRC (1984)
17. Fulford (1985a)
18. Kirloskar (a and b)
19. FAO 41 (1978)
20. Bulmer (1985)
21. Pfeffer (1974a and b)
22. Lau-Wong (1985)
23. Chowdhury (1987)
24. Gunnerson (1986)

25. Maramba (1978)
26. McFarlane (1981)

Chapter 12
1. UNESCO (1983)
2. ERDG (1976)
3. Bulmer (1979)
4. Moulik (1985)

Appendix I
1. Merrit (1978)
2. CAI (1969, 1972)
3. Bulmer (1985)
4. Jiao
5. Lee
6. Tentscher (1986)

Appendix II
1. Bird (1960)
2. Streeter (1971)
3. Pritchard (1977)
4. Perry (1973)
5. Weast (1979)
6. Amal (1972)
7. Lichtman (1983)

Appendix III
1. Chowdhury (1987)
2. Reddy (1980)
3. Bulmer (1985)
4. Lau-Wong (1985)
5. Rogers (1980)
6. HMSO (1977)

Appendix IV
1. Lau-Wong (1984)
2. Chowdhury (1987)
3. Pfeffer (1974)
4. Maramba (1978)

Appendix V
1. Little (1974)
2. Rice (1986)
3. Bhatia (1985)
4. Lau-Wong (1984)

Bibliography

ACVAFS *Approaches to appropriate evaluation* (1978).

ADB *Nepal Agricultural Sector Strategy Study*; Asian Development Bank, HMG, Kathmandu: Vol. I and Vol. II (Dec. 1982).

APHA *Standard Methods for the Examination of Water, Sewage and Industrial Wastes*; American Public Health Assoc., New York (10th ed. 1955).

Abdullahi, *Biogas Stoves and their Designs in Nigeria*; A dissertation submitted in partial fulfilment for Post-Graduate Diploma, Dept. Engineering, University of Reading, UK (1986).

Amal, *Natural Draft Injectors for Burning Sludge Gas*; Amal Ltd., Birmingham, B6 7ES, UK: List 403/3 (1972).

Bajracharya, D., 'Organising for Energy Need Assessment and Innovation' (in *Energy for Rural Development*); Resource Systems Inst., East-West Center, Honolulu, Hawaii (1983).

Bansal, A., Ram, S., Bandal, N.K., 'Performance of a Greenhouse Coupled Biogas Plant in the Winter Months of Northern India' (in *Enneus*); Indian Inst. Technology, New Delhi, India (1984).

Barnett, A., Pyle, L., Subramanian S.K., *Biogas Technology in the Third World*; International Development Research Center, Ottawa, Canada: IDRC–103e (1978).

Beenhakker, A., *A System for Development Planning and Budgeting*; Gower (1980).

Bell, Boulter, Dunlop, Keiller, *Methane, Fuel of the Future*; Andrew Singer, Bottisham, UK (1973).

Bente, P.F., *The International Bio-Directory*; Bio-Energy Council, Washington, USA (1981).

Bhasin, K., *A South Asian Experience of Training for Participatory Development*; Freedom From Hunger Campaign: FAO, Bangkok and Rome (Jan. 1979).

Bhasin, K., Palshikar, V., Rao, L., *The Role and Training of Development Activists*; FAO, New Delhi and Rome or CDRA, Madras (1980).

Bhatia, et al, *Choice of Technology for Lifting Irrigation Water*; Council of Scientific and Industrial Research (CSIR), New Delhi, India (also SATA) (1985).

Bhatia, R., Niamir, M., *Renewable Energy Sources: the Community Biogas Plant*; Seminar at the Dept. of Applied Sciences, Harvard Univ., USA (1979).

Bird, R.B., Stewart, W.E., Lightfoot E.N., *Transport Phenomena*; John Wiley, New York (1960).

Bulmer, A., 'A Survey of Three Community Biogas Plants in Nepal' (from *NTIS*: PB83-166-991); DCS, Nepal (1980).

Bulmer, A., Finlay, J.H., Fulford, D.J., Lau-Wong, M., *Biogas, Challenges and Experience from Nepal*; United Mission to Nepal, PO Box 126, Kathmandu (1985).

Bulmer A., Schlorholtz, A., 'Gobar Gas Survey in Nepal' (from *NTIS*: PB83-166-991); DCS, Nepal (Jan. 1979).

Caceres, R., Chiliquinga, B., 'Experience with Rural Biodigesters in Latin America' (in *CSBA*); Latin American Energy Organisation, Quito, Ecuador (1985).

CAI, *Concrete Handbook*; Concrete Assoc. of India, Bombay (1969).

CAI, *Cement Plastering*; Concrete Assoc. of India, Bombay (1972).

Cambell, J.B., *People and Forests in Hill Nepal*; Community Forestry, Ministry of Forestry, HMG/N, Kathmandu (1983).

CBS/HMG, *Foreign Trade Statistics of Nepal* (1967–1971); Central Bureau of Statistics, HMG/N, Kathmandu (1972).

CEDA, *The Status of Women in Nepal*; Centre for Economic Development and Administration, Tribhuvan Univ., Kathmandu (1981).

Chambers, R., *Managing Rural Development* (1973).

Chantavarapap, S., 'Biogas Programme of Thailand'; (in El-Halwagi b) Energy R & D Division, National Energy Admin., Thailand (1984).

Chen, R.C., *Up-to-date Status of Anaerobic Digestion Technology in China* (unpublished); Macau Water Supply Co., China (1982).

Chowdhury, R., *Kinetic Studies of Anaerobic Digestion, comparing the Performances of Batch and Semi-Continuous Systems*; M.Phil. thesis, University of Reading (Jan. 1987).

Chung Po, *Animal Waste Treatment and Utilization*; Council for Agricultural Planning and Development, Taipei, Taiwan (1980).

Clark, G.C., Crowley, M.M., de los Reyes, B.N., *Annual Report on Nepal's Experimental Field Action-cum-Research Project*; Small Farmers' Development Unit, FAO, Bangkok (May 1977).

Clyde, *'O' Ring Specialists*; Clyde Rye Bearings Ltd., London SW6 1DW, UK.

Coburn, B.A., *Study of the Energy Needs of the Food System in Nepal*; Progress Report, American Peace Corps, Kathmandu, Nepal (1977).

Cott, A., 'Anaerobically Digested Pig Slurry as a Resource for Crop Production' (in *Enneus*); Univ. College, Cardiff, UK (1984).

CSBA, *Proceedings of the Fourth International Symposium on Anaerobic Digestion*; China State Biogas Assoc., Guangzhua, China (1985).

Cui, X., Xie, Z.H., 'An Outline of Biogas Development in China' (in *CSBA*); China State Biogas Assoc., China (1985).

da Silva, N.A., 'Biogas in South America' (in *CSBA*); SAIN, Brazil (1985).

de Macario, E.C., 'Immunologic Probes for Identification of Methnogenic Bacteria in Anaerobic Digesters' (in *CSBA*); New York State Dept., Health, USA (1985).

Devkota, G.P., 'Plastic Bag Digester'; *Biogas Newsletter*, Shakti Pubs., PO Box 1309, Kathmandu, Nepal: N.23 (Nov. 1986).

Devkota, G.P., *Biogas Research and Development in Nepal*; International Workshop on Renewable Energy Resources, Lahore, Pakistan (Gobar Gas Co.) (1983).

Devkota, G.P., *Efficiency of Gobar Gas Stoves*; Gobar Gas tatha Krishi Yantra Bikash Ltd., Butwal, Nepal (1982).

Devkota, G.P., *Report on Second Inspection Visit to Dome Design of Gobar Gas Plants*; Gobar Gas tatha Krishi Yantra Bikash Ltd., Butwal, Nepal (1982).

Devkota, G.P., *Utilisation of Eupatorium Species as an Alternative Feedstock for Producing Biogas*; Gobar Gas tatha Krishi Yantra Bikash Ltd., Butwal, Nepal (1983).

Dickson, D.E.N. (ed), *Improve Your Business*; I.L.O., Geneva, Switzerland (I.T. Publications) (1986).

Dunn, P.D., *Appropriate Technology, Technology with a Human Face*; Macmillan, London, UK (1978).

ECDC-TCDC, 'Renewable Sources of Energy' Vol II, *Biogas*: ESCAP, United Nations, Bangkok, Thailand: ST/ESCAP/96 (1981).

Eggling, G., Guldager, R. and H., Hilliges, G., Sasse, L., Tietjan, C., Werner, U., *Biogas, Manual for the Realisation of Biogas Programmes*; BORDA, Bremen, West Germany (1979).

El-Halwagi, M.M., *The Development and Application of Biogas Technology in Rural Areas of Egypt*; National Research Centre, Egypt: Applied Science and Technology Project No. 263–0016 (1980).

El-Halwagi, M.M., 'Force-field Analysis of Biogas Systems and Proposed Means for Optimising their Prospects'; (in *El-Halwagi* b) National Research Centre, Cairo, Egypt (1984a).

El-Halwagi, M.M., *Biogas Technology, Transfer and Diffusion*; Elsevier Applied Science Pubs., London, UK (1984b).

Ellegard, A., Jonsson, A., Zellergrist, A., *Biogas – Not Just a Technology*; SIDA, Gothenburg, Sweden (1983).

Enneus, H., *Bioenergy '84*; University of Göteborg, Sweden (1984).

ERDG, *Nepal, The Energy Sector*; Energy Research and Development Group, Tribhuvan University, Kathmandu (Nov. 1976).

ESCAP, *Guidebook on Biogas Development*; United Nations Energy Resources Series: 21, ST/ESCAP/96 (1980).

Fang, G.Y., 'The Utilisation of Red Mud Plastics in Biogas Technique'; (in *CSBA*) Sichuan, China (1985).

FAO 40, *China, Recycling of Organic Wastes in Agriculture*; Food and Agricultural Organisation. Rome: (1977).

FAO 41, *Azolla Propogation and Small Scale Biogas Technology*; FAO, Rome (1978).

FFHC, *People's Participation in Development*; Indian Freedom From Hunger Campaign Society, Calcutta (also FAO, New Delhi and Rome) (1973).

Finlay, J.H., 'Operation and Maintenance of Gobar Gas Plants'; (from *NTIS*: PB83-162-107) DCS, Nepal (1978).

Finlay, J.H., Shrestha, P.C., 'First, Second & Third Inspection Visits to 95 Nepali Biogas Plants'; (from *NTIS*: PB83-166-694) DCS, Nepal (1976–1980).

Freemen, C., Pyle, L., *Methane Generation by Anaerobic Fermentation, Annotated Bibliography*; Intermediate Technology Pubs., London, UK (1977).

Fry, L.J., *Practical Building of Methane Power Plants*; Fry, Santa Barbara, USA (1974).

Fulford, D.J., 'A Commercial Approach to Biogas Extension in Nepal'; *Appropriate Technology*, I.T. Pubs., London: V.8 N.2 p.14 (1978a).

Fulford, D.J., 'Appropriate Biogas Development in Nepal'; (in *Enneus*) DCS, Butwal, Nepal (1984).

Fulford, D.J., 'Biogas Research and Development in Nepal'; *Appropriate Technology*, I.T. Pubs., London V.13, N.2 (1985a).

Fulford, D.J., 'Biogas in Nepal, State of the Art'; (from *NTIS*: PB83-166-702) DCS, Nepal (1978b).

Fulford, D.J., 'Gobar Gas Irrigation in Nepal'; *Biogas Newsletter*, Shakti Pubs., PO 1309, Kathmandu: N.13 p.6 (1981).

Fulford, D.J., 'Community Biogas in Nepal'; (in *Enneus*) DCS, Butwal, Nepal (1985b).

Fulford, D.J., Peters, N. 'Survey of Present Gobar Gas Work in India'; (from *NTIS*: PB83-166-991) DCS, Nepal (1978c).

Gardiner, M., 'Running a 'Fridge on Cowdung Gas'; *Biogas Newsletter*, Shakti Pubs., PO 1309, Kathmandu: N.5 p.3 (1979).

Garg, M.K., *The Development of an Appropriate Technology for Decentralised Pottery Industry in Rural India*; Appropriate Technology Development Assoc., Lucknow, India.

Ghate, P.B., *A Pilot Project to Investigate a Decentralised Energy System*; Planning, Research & Action Div., Lucknow, India.

Gittenger, J.P., *Compounding, and Discounting Tables for Project Evaluation*; Economic Development Inst. of the International Bank for Reconstruction and Development, Washington, USA.

Gopal, Sharma, 'Water Hyacinth Composition'; *Typographus*, New Delhi (1981).

177

Gorkhali, H.G., 'Summary of Nepal Biogas Programme' (in *El-Halwagi* b) Biogas and Agricultural Equipment Development (P) Ltd., Kathmandu, Nepal (1984).

Gunnerson, C.G., Stuckey, D.A., *Principles and Practice for Biogas Systems*; UNDP Integrated Resource Recovery Report No.5; World Bank Technical Paper 49, New York (1986).

HMSO *Chemical Oxygen Demand (Dichromate Value) of Polluted and Waste Waters*; H.M. Stationery Office, London, UK (1977).

Hackett, W.F., Conners, W.J., Kirk, T.K., Zeikus, J.G., 'Microbial Decomposition of Synthetic 14C-labelled Lignin in Nature'; *App. Environ, Microbiology*: V.33 N.43 (1977).

Halsall, J.J.H., *How to Read a Balance Sheet*; I.L.O., Geneva, Switzerland (also I.T. Pubs.) (1985).

Harper, M., *Small Business in the Third World: Guidelines for Practical Assistance*; Wiley & Sons (also I.T. Pubs.), London, UK (1984).

Hawkes, D.L., Rosser, B.L., 'Computer-Aided Design of Anaerobic Digesters'; (in *SAD 3*, 1983) Polytechnic of Wales, Pontypridd, Wales, UK (1983).

Hobson, P.N., Summers, R., Bousfield, S., 'Uses and Analysis of Digested Sludge'; (in *UCC*, 1979) Rowett Inst., Aberdeen, UK (1979).

Hollingdale, A.C., Coward, L.D.G., *Biogas Technology in Cold Climatic Conditions in Korea*; Tropical Products Inst., ODA, London WC1X 8LU, UK (1979).

Horton, H.L., Schubert, P.B., Garratt, G. *Machinery's Handbook*; Industrial Press, New York (9th ed. 1971).

House, D., *The Compleat Biogas Handbook*; VAHID, Aurora, CR7002, USA (1978).

Hruska, R.L., Hashimoto, A.G., 'Commercialisation of Anaerobic Digestion in USA'; (in *Enneus*) Agricultural Research Centre, Nebraska, USA (1983).

Huang, Z.J., 'Analysis of Economic Feasibility for Biogas Construction in China'; (in *CSBA*) Energy Research Inst., China (1985).

Idnani, M.A., Varadarajan, S., *Fuel Gas and Manure by Anaerobic Fermentation of Organic Materials*; Indian Council of Agricultural Research, New Delhi: ICAR-TB/46 (2nd ed. 1974).

IHC, *Organisational Techniques*; Indonesian Handbook Committee; (trans. Smith K.H.) English version, Overseas Education Fund, Washington, USA (1986).

Israelson, O.W., Hansen, V.E., *Irrigation Principles and Practices*; John Wiley, New York (1962).

Jewell, W.J., Chandler, J.A., Dell'Orto S., Fanfoni, K.J., Fast, S., Jackson, D., Kabrick, R.M., *Dry Fermentation of Agricultural Residues*; Solar Energy Research Inst., Golden, 80401, USA; SERI/TR-09038-7 (from NTIS) (Sept. 1981).

178

Jewell, W.J., Dell'Orto, S., Fanfoni, K.J., Hayes, T.D., Leuschner, A.P., Sherman, D.F., *Anaerobic Fermentation of Agricultural Residues*; Cornell Univ., New York 148 53, USA (from NTIS) (April 1980).

Jiao Qing-Yu, Director, *Liaoning Province Research*, Institute of Energy Research, Yinkou, Liaoning Province, China.

Khan, A.W., Trotter, T.M., 'Effect of Sulphur Containing Compounds on Anaerobic Degradation of Cellulose to Methane by Mixed Cultures Obtained from Sewage and Sludge'; *App & Environ. Microbiology*: V.35 N.6 (1978).

Khanna, P.N., *Indian Practical Civil Engineers Handbook*; Engineers Pubs., PO 725, New Delhi, India (1979).

Kijne, E., *Biogas in Asia*; Consultants for Management of Development Programmes bv (CDP), Utrecht, Holland (1984).

Kirloskar, *Dual Fuel Biogas Engine*; Kirloskar Oil Engines Ltd., Pune, India (a).

Kirloskar, *Operation and Performance of Engines Running on Biogas*; Kirloskar Oil Engines Ltd., Pune, India (b).

Konisky, J., 'Genetic Engineering of Methanogens: Current Status' (in *CSBA*, 1985) University of Illinois, USA (1985).

KVIC *Gobar Gas, How and Why*; Khadi and Village Industries Commission, Bombay 400056, India (1975).

Kwon, I., Kim, H., 'Studies on Biogas Production from Several Animal Faeces'; *ESCAP*, Expert Group Meeting on Biogas, Bangkok (Seoul National Univ., Suwon, Rep. of Korea) (1978).

Lau-Wong, M.M., *Evaluation and Analysis of Chemically Treated Straw and a Stochastic Simulation Model of the Ruminant's Digestive System*; Cornell Univ., New York, USA: Ph.D. Thesis (1979).

Lau-Wong, M.M., 'Enhancement of Biogas Production in Cold Climate'; UNESCO/COSTED Conference, Kathmandu, (from *NTIS*: PB85–123305) DCS, Nepal (May 1982).

Lau-Wong, M.M., 'The Economics of Biogas Systems'; (in *El-Halwagi* b) DCS, Butwal, Nepal (1984).

Lau-Wong, M.M., 'The Effect of Operational Parameters on Biogas Production and a Comparison of Three Reactor Designs'; (in *CSBA*) DCS, Nepal (also in Bulmer) (1985).

Lee, Daniel F., President, Lupton Engineering Corporation, 3F, 24, Ching Hsin Road, Ching Mei, Tapei, Taiwan.

Lichtman, R., 'Toward the Diffusion of Rural Energy Technologies: Some Lessons from the Indian Biogas Programme'; *World Development*, V.15, N.3 pp.347–374 (1987).

Lichtman, R.J., *Biogas Systems in India*; Volunteers in Technical Assistance, Arlington 22209-2079, USA (1983).

Little, I.M.D., Mirrlees, J.A., *Project Appraisal and Planning for Developing Countries*; Heinemann, London (1974).

McFarlane, P.N., Pfeffer, J.T., 'Biological Conversion of Biomass to Methane'; Solar Energy Research Inst., Golden, 80401, USA: SERI/TR-98357-1 (from *NTIS*) (1981).

McGarry, M.G., Stainforth, J., *Compost, Fertilizer and Biogas Production from Human and Farm Wastes in the People's Republic of China*; IRDC, Ottawa, Canada: IRDC-TS8e (1978).

McGrath, E.H., *Basic Managerial Skills for All* (1978).

Mah, R.A., 'Interactions of Methanogens and Non-Methanogens in Microbial Ecosystems'; (in *SAD3* Univ. California, USA (1983).

Mahato, K., *Case Study of Group No.7; Small Farmers' Development Project*, Freedom From Hunger Campaign, FAO, Bangkok, Thailand: SFDP N-35 (April 1979).

Makhijani, A., Poole, A., *Energy and Agriculture in the Third World*; Ballinger, Cambridge, USA (1976).

Maramba, F.D., *Biogas and Waste Recycling, The Philippines Experience*; Liberty Flour Mills Inc., Metro Manilla, Philippines (1978).

Mazumdar, A., *Biogas Handbook*; TATA Energy Research Inst., Bombay 400023, India (1982a).

Mazumdar, A., *Review of the Literature on the Promotion of Biogas Systems*; TATA Energy Research Inst., Bombay 400023, India (1982b).

Meier, U., *The Pauwa Energy System*; SATA, PO 113, Kathmandu, Nepal (1978).

Merrit, F.S., *Standard Handbook for Civil Engineers*; McGraw Hill, New York (2nd ed. 1978).

Meynell, P.J., *Methane: Planning a Digester*; Prism Press, Dorchester, UK (1976).

Mosey, F.E., 'Sewage Treatment using Anaerobic Fermentation'; (in *UCC*) Water Research Centre, Stevenage, UK (1979).

Moulik, T.K., Murthy, N., Subramanian, A., *India's Experiments with Community Biogas Systems*; Indian Institute of Management, Ahmedabad (1984).

Moulik, T.K., *Biogas Energy in India*; Academic Book Centre, Ahmedabad, India (1982).

Moulik, T.K., *The Biogas Programme in India and China: A Comparative Analysis of Experiences*; Indian Institute of Management, Ahmedabad, India: WP No. 555 (1985).

Moulik, T.K., Srinivasta, U.K., *Biogas Plants at the Village Level, Problems and Prospects in Gujurat*; CMA, Indian Institute of Management, Ahmedabad, India: IMM Monograph 59 (1975).

Murphy, J.P., 'Experimental Mbuzi (goat) Gas Generator'; *Biogas Newsletter*, Shakti Pubs., PO Box 1309, Kathmandu, Nepal: N.23 (Nov. 1986).

NAI *Methane Digesters for Fuel and Fertiliser*; New Alchemy Inst., Woods Hole, 02543, USA: No.3 (1973).

NAS *Methane Generation from Human, Animal and Agricultural Wastes*; National Academy of Sciences, Washington, USA: No. 19 (1981).

NSPRC *The Collection of Designs for Household Hydraulic Biogas Digesters in Rural Areas*; National Standard of the People's Republic of China, State Bureau of Standardisation: GB 4750 4752 – 84 (1984).

NTIS National Technical Information Service, Springfield, Virginia, USA.

Nyns, E.-J., 'Biogas Plants in the European Community and Switzerland'; (in *Enneus*) Univ. Louvain, Belgium (1984).

Nyns, E.-J., 'Success or Failure of Biogas Plants in Europe'; (in *CSBA*) Univ. Louvain, Belgium (1985).

Oxfam, *Field Director's Handbook*; Oxford, UK (1985).

Pang, A., 'Economics of Gobar Gas' (from *NTIS*: PB83-166-694); DCS, Nepal (1978).

Patankar G.L. Recent developments in gobar gas technology; Gobar Gas Development Centre, KVIC, Bombay (1977).

Peng, Z.B., 'The Emulsified Polychloroprene Rubber Base Coating as Sealing Paint'; (in *CSBA*) Research Inst., Min. of Agriculture, China (1985).

Perry, R.H., Chilton, C.H., *Chemical Engineers Handbook*; McGraw Hill, New York (5th ed. 1973).

Pfeffer, J.T., 'Temperature Effects on Anaerobic Fermentation of Domestic Refuse'; *Biotech. and Bioeng.*, V.16 pp. 771–787 (1974a).

Pfeffer, J.T., *Reclamation of Energy from Organic Refuse*; Nat. Envir. Research Center, US Envir. Protect. Agency, Cincinnati, USA: EPA–670/2–74/015 (1974b).

Picken, D.J., *Uses of Biogas for Thermal, Mechanical and Electrical Power Generation*; Leicester Polytechnic, UK.

Poland, F.G., Harper, S.R., 'Biogas Developments in North America' (in *CSBA*) Georgia Institute of Technology, USA (1985).

PRAD Community Biogas Plant; Planning, Research and Action Division, Lucknow, India.

Prasad, C.R., Prasad, K.K., Reddy, A.K.N., 'Biogas Plants: Prospects, Problems and Tasks'; *Economic and Political Weekly*: V.IX, pp.32–34, Special Number (1974).

Pritchard, R., Guy, J.J., Connor, N.E., *Industrial Gas Utilisation*; Bowker, Epping, UK (British Gas) (1977).

Pyakural, Karki Axinn, 'Techno-Socio-Economic Study on Biogas'; *Biogas Newsletter*, Shakti Pubs. PO 1309, Kathmandu, Nepal: N.2, p.6 (1978).

Pyle, D.L., 'Anaerobic Digester Designs in the Third World'; (in *UCC*) Imperial College, London, UK (1979).

RAFE 36, *Small Farmers' Development Manual*; Food and Agricultural Organisation, Bangkok (1978).

Raman, N.V., Narayanaswarmy, V.P., Sharma, P.C., Jayaraman, H. B., 'Ferrocement Gas Holder for Biogas Plants'; *Journal of Ferrocement*, AIT, Bangkok: V.9, N.2, p.93 (April 1979).

Reddy, A.K.N., *Rural Technology*; Indian Inst. Sciences, Bangalore, India (1980).

Rice, G., 'Small Engines for Rural Use in Both Developed and Developing Countries'; *2nd Schumacher Conference*, Melbourne, Australia (Nov. 1986).

Ripley, L.E., Boyle, W.C., 'Anaerobic Digestion Models: Implications for the Design Engineer'; (in *SAD3*) Univ. Wisconsin, USA (1983).

Rogers, G.F.C., Mayhew, Y.R., *Engineering Thermodynamics, Work and Heat Transfer*; Longman, Harlow, UK (3rd ed. 1980).

Roy, R., 'Family and Community Biogas Plants in Rural India'; *Appropriate Technology*, I.T. Pubs., London: V.8 N.1 p.17 (June 1981).

Ruchen, C., Nianguo, L. 'The Development of Biogas Utilisation in China' *Biogas Journal*, App. Science Pub., London: V.1, N.1, pp. 39–46 (Sept. 1981).

SAD3 *Proceedings of the Third International Symposium on Anaerobic Digestion*; Cambridge, Mass., USA (1983).

SATA, *Mountain Environment and Development*; Swiss Assoc. for Technical Assistance in Nepal, PO 113, Kathmandu, Nepal (1977).

Sathianathan, M.A., *Biogas Achievements and Challenges*; Assoc. Voluntary Agencies for Rural Development, New Delhi, India (1975).

Saubolle, B.R., *Fuel Gas from Cow Dung*; Sahayogi Press, Kathmandu, Nepal (1976).

Sharma, C.K., *Ground Water Resources of Nepal*; Kathmandu, Nepal (1974).

Sharma, C.K., *River Systems of Nepal*; Kathmandu, Nepal (1977).

Sharma, C.K.H., *Land Slides and Soil Erosion in Nepal*; S. Sharma, Kathmandu, Nepal (1974).

Shen, R.Z., 'The Utilisation of Biogas Digester Residue in China'; (in *CSBA*) Shanghai Academy of Agric. Sciences, China (1985).

Shibatasan, *Irrigation Variety Trial on Early Paddy in 1980, Proposed Cropping Pattern and Expected Production Increase on Model Infrastructure Programme*; Janakpur Agricultural Development Project, Janakpur, Nepal (1980).

Singh, R., Chhabra, N.N., *The Economics of Cow-Dung Gas Plants*; Indian Council of Agricultural Research, New Delhi, India (1976).

Singh, R.B., *Biogas Plant Designs with Specifications*; Gobar Gas Research Station, Ajitmal (Etawah), India (1973).

Singh, R.B., *Biogas Plants*; Gobar Gas Research Station, Ajitmal (Etawah), India (1974).

Speece, R.E., 'Toxicity in Anaerobic Digestion'; (in *CSBA*), Drexel Univ., USA (1985).

182

Speece, R.E., Parkin, G.F., 'The Response of Methane Bacteria to Toxicity'; (in *SAD3*) Drexel Univ., USA, (1983).

SPIIBD, *Constructon of March-Gas-Producing Tanks (Digesters) in Simple Ways*; Sichuan Provincial Inst. of Industrial Building Design, China (copied by SATA, PO 113, Kathmandu).

Srinivasan, H.R., *Gobar Gas, Retrospects and Prospects*; Khadi and Village Industries Commission, Bombay 400056, India (1978).

Stafford, D.A., Hawkes, D.L., Horton, R., *Methane Production from Waste Organic Matter*; CRC Press, USA (1980).

Stern, P.H., *Small Scale Irrigation*; I.T. Publications, London (1976).

Stevens, M.E., *Land Use Patterns for Marginal Land*; APROSC, Kathmandu, Nepal.

Streeter, V.L., *Fluid Mechanics*; Mcgraw Hill, New York (5th ed. 1971).

Stuckey, D.C., 'Biogas: A Global Perspective'; (in *El-Halwagi*) Imperial College, London, UK (1984).

Stuckey, D.C., *Biogas in China*; Report for International Reference Centre for Waste Disposal, Dubendorf, Switzerland (1982).

Stuckey, D.C., 'Biogas in Developing Countries: A Critical Appraisal'; (in *Enneus*) Imperial College, London, UK (1984).

Subba-Rao, *Soil Micro-organisms and Plant Growth*; Oxford and IBH Pub. Co. New Delhi 110001, India (1980).

Subramanian, S.K., *Biogas Systems in Asia*; Management Development Institute, New Delhi 110057, India (1977).

Tam, D.M., Thanh, N.C., 'Biogas Technology in Developing Countries'; *Environmental Sanitation Reviews*, AIT, Bangkok Thailand, 19 (1982).

Tang, Z.G., Xie, X.U., Wu, D.C., 'Study on Polymer Seal Paint of Concrete Biogas Digester'; (in *CSBA*) Chendu Univ., Sichuan, China (1985).

Tentscher, W., *Construction Cost and Performance of Biogas Digesters with Special Reference to the Plug Flow Design*; Division of Energy Technology, Asian Institute of Technology, Bangkok, Thailand (1986).

Thery, D., 'The Biogas Progress in India and China'; *Ecodevelopment News* N.19, UNEP, Paris (1981) (also Resource Management and Optimisation, V.1(4), p. 289 (Oct. 1981).

UCC, *A Symposium on Anaerobic Digestion*; University College, Cardiff, Wales, UK (1979).

UNESCO, *International Directory of New and Renewable Sources of Energy*; United Nations Education, Science and Cultural Organisation, Paris, France (1982).

UNESCO, *The Fragile Mountain*; film, United Nations Education, Science and Cultural Organisation, Paris, France (1983).

Vaclav, S., 'Biogas Production in China'; *Development Digest*, USAID, Washington, USA: V. XVII N.3 pp.25–28 (World Development V.4 N. 10–11 pp. 929–937, Nov. 1976) (1979).

Van Buren, A., Crook, M., *A Chinese Biogas Manual*; I.T. Publications., London (1979).

Van Soest, P.J., Robertson, J.B., *Composition and Nutritive Value of Uncommon Feedstuffs*; Dept. Animal Science, Cornell Univ., New York, USA.

Van den Berg, L., Kennedy, K.J., 'Comparison of Advanced Anaerobic Reactors'; (in *SAD3*) National Research Council of Canada (1983).

Von Brakel, J., *The Ignis Fatus of Biogas*; Delft Univ. Press, Holland (1980).

Weast, R.C., Astle, M.J., *Handbook of Chemistry and Physics*; CRC Press, Boca Raton, USA (60th ed. 1979).

Wolfe, R.S., 'Fermentation and Anaerobic Respiration in Anaerobic Digestion'; (in *SAD3*) Univ. Illinois, USA (1983).

World Bank, *Agricultural Credit, Sectors Policy Paper*; World Bank, Washington, USA (1975).

Wyatt, Smith J., *The Agricultural System in the Hills of Nepal*; Agricultural Projects Research Centre, Kathmandu, Nepal: paper 1 (1982).

Yawalker, K.S., Agarwal, J.P., Bodke, S., *Manures and Fertilisers*; Agri-Horticultural Pub. House, Nagpur, India (4th ed. 1977).

Zeikus, J.G., Chartrain, M., Thiele, J., 'Microbial Physiology in Anaerobic Digestion' (in *CSBA*) Univs. Michigan and Winconsin. USA (1985).

Zhao, C.Y., 'The Using of the Red Mud Plastic in Biogas Project'; (in *CSBA*) Ying Kou, Liaoning, China (1985).

Zhao, Y.H., Zhang, H., Liu, G.Y., Lian, L.W., Yiao, Y. Zhou, W. B., 'Primary Microbial Population in Rural Biogas Digesters in China'; (in *CSBA*) Chengdu Bio-Institute, China (1985).

Index

185

Dung – use in biogas plants: 35, 36, 77, 87, 114–16, 118

Economics of biogas: 4f, 15, 85–95, 98–9, 102, 104, 160–5
Efficiency of biogas burners: 64–5, 135
Effluent slurry: 38–40, 60, 101, 152
Electricity generation by biogas: 73
Engines – use of biogas with: 1, 68–74, 87–95, 140–2
Entrainment of air: 65, 137–9
Equations – biogas burner design: 135–9
Equations – gas flow down pipes: 132–3
Equations – gas production: 151–9
Europe – biogas in: 2
Evaluation: 22–4
Extended dome design: 50–1, 126–8
Extension of biogas technology: 13, 15, 16, 24–6, 67

Facultative bacteria: 30, 56
Feedstocks: 10, 17, 33–6, 76–7, 113–16, 150
Ferro-cement: 11, 46, 49, 108, 110
Fertiliser: 1, 38–40, 87, 118–19, 161
Filling a digester: 76–7
Finance for biogas: 15, 17, 26–7, 85f
Firewood: 1, 27, 86–7, 95, 101, 161
Fixed dome design: 47–51, 53–6, 109, 126–9
Flammability of biogas: 84, 136
Flame stabilization: 138–9
Flexible bag design: 51–3, 56, 131
Flexible gas pipe: 45
Floating drum design: 43–7, 53–6, 76, 77, 110, 125–6
Follow-up of biogas plants: 14, 16
Four-stroke cycle for engines: 68–9
Fuel crisis: 118–19

GI (Galvanised Iron): 46, 61
Gas meters: 147
Gas pipes: 60–2, 132–4
Gas production: 112–13, 144–7, 151–7
Gas valves: 63–4, 83, 111–12
Gate valves: 63
Glass shields for biogas lamps: 67
Glossary: 167–70
Gobar Gas Company: 3, 13–14, 19, 20, 23, 29, 67, 107
Grain mill – run by biogas: 71–3, 87–90, 100–102, 161–3

Group biogas: 100–102
Guarantee fund: 14, 19

Heat exchangers: 71, 79
History of biogas: 1–3, 8–14
Human faeces: 4, 35–26, 58, 83, 97, 118
Hydrogen sulphide: 39
Hydrolysis: 31

India: 1, 10–12, 19, 20–7, 53, 96–8, 107–13, 118
Industrial uses of biogas: 74–5
Insulation: 55, 78–9
Internal Rate of Return: 86, 88–9, 91, 93–4
Irrigation: 73, 90–5, 102–6, 163–6

Joints in Pipes: 61–2

Kerosene: 1, 27, 86–7, 88, 101, 161
Korea: 1

Lag time: 37, 115
Lamps used with biogas: 66–7, 111–12, 139
Latrines with biogas: 58, 83, 97
Leaks of gas: 62, 84
Lignin: 34, 35
Loans: 5, 12, 13, 15, 17, 53, 88, 91, 93, 96, 101, 104, 105

Madhubasa Village: 102–6, 121
Management: 21–9
Mantles used in biogas lamps: 66–7
Material quantities: 127, 129
Mesophylic bacteria: 33
Meters for gas: 147
Methanogenic bacteria: 31, 82
Microbiology of biogas: 3, 30–2, 40, 81–3
Milling with biogas: 1, 71–3, 87–90, 101–2, 161–3
Mixing of slurry: 59–60, 54, 58, 76, 112
Modelling of biogas process: 114–16, 151–9
Motivation: 100, 106, 119–20

Nepal: 3, 12–14, 19, 20–9, 53, 55, 96–8, 100–6, 107–113, 118
Net Present Worth: 81–2, 83–4, 85–6, 88–9
Night soil (human faeces): 4, 35–6, 39, 58, 83, 97, 118

186